DATE DUE

Adolescent Lives 4

A series edited by Jeanne Brooks-Gunn

Out of the Woods

Tales of Resilient Teens

Stuart T. Hauser
Joseph P. Allen
Eve Golden

Harvard University Press
Cambridge, Massachusetts
London, England
2006

Library of Congress Cataloging-in-Publication Data

Hauser, Stuart T.

Out of the woods : tales of resilient teens / Stuart T. Hauser, Joseph P. Allen, Eve Golden.

    p. cm.—(Adolescent lives ; 4)
Includes bibliographical references and index.
ISBN 0-674-02173-8 alk. paper
1. Problem youth.   2. Adjustment (Psychology) in adolescence.
3. Adolescent psychology.   I. Allen, Joseph P. (Joseph Patrick), 1958–
II. Golden, Eve, 1951–   III. Title.   IV. Series.

   HV1421.H38 2006
   155.5—dc22   2005052671

Contents

Preface

THIS BOOK DRAWS UPON MANY YEARS OF CONNECTION with teenagers: our own, and the many we have come to know in our work as psychotherapists, researchers, and administrators in the field of child guidance. The metamorphosis of adolescents into young women and men never fails to amaze and excite us, but it is a transformation that can never be taken for granted. Adolescence is a time of surprises; there is no room for complacency when boys and girls are coming of age. Unexpected turns of fate forge new identities and desires; greater skills open new ambitions and possibilities; and values and beliefs of all kinds build themselves ever more deeply into maturing characters. There is no room for sentimentality, either, because surprises can be bitter as well as sweet. We can't assume that the new identities, skills, and values will necessarily lead kids to such high aspirations as teaching or carpentry or science; they may just as well lead to criminal aspirations, or to no aspirations at all. As one wild sixteen-year-old masters the demons of sex and violence and drugs, another may be angrily succumbing—or dead.

The wish to tilt the odds toward hopeful outcomes burns bright in the hearts of devoted parents—indeed of all who work in the field of child protection. But we don't yet know how to make it come true. "There are plenty of ways to explain psychopathology," a perceptive colleague commented to us once. "But how do you explain how any of us grow up *healthy*, given what we face in our lives?"

This book represents one approach to that challenging question. We hope that it will give the many concerned and responsible people who do not work in our field some new ways to think about the critical importance of adolescence—its promise, its dangers, and the way Western society envisions and encounters this crucial time. Many before us have written about *resilience*, the capacity for successful adaptation in adversity, and research is now providing important clues about what predicts, enhances, and threatens it. But however welcome a development resilience may be, it remains obscure. In these pages we will take a new approach to the subject. We wanted to discover how troubled individuals actually *make* their pivotal changes—how they work within themselves to create environments and relationships that can support healthy growth. In pursuit of a deeper understanding of the processes of resilience, we turned to the personal narratives of teenagers who recovered from serious psychiatric illness and went on to lead fulfilling lives. And we found that they had a lot to tell us.

THE HIGH VALLEY RESILIENCE STUDY was conceived, designed, and carried out by Stuart T. Hauser and Joseph P. Allen over the years 1989 to 1994. The "we" in the text refers to them. In September 2002, Eve Golden joined them as collaborator and chief writer, to guide this volume to completion.

Acknowledgments

SUSTAINING A LONG-TERM STUDY OF ADOLESCENTS and families is an arduous and complicated task. Miles F. Shore and Joseph T. Coyle were exemplary and imaginative department heads, ever available to help solve our funding and space needs. A Career Development Award from the National Institute of Mental Health and a grant from the Spencer Foundation launched the overall longitudinal study out of which the resilience project unexpectedly surfaced. Subsequent funds were provided by the MacArthur Foundation, the Psychoanalytic Research Fund of the American Psychoanalytic Association, the William T. Grant Foundation, and the John Weil Foundation. Major continuing funding came from the National Institutes of Mental Health, through Career Development Awards, and through direct research grants to Stuart Hauser and Joseph Allen. In later phases of the adolescent part of the project, we were assisted by grants from the Maternal and Child Health Research Grants Program and the National Institute of Child and Human Development.

Many colleagues from our project staff are now off on their

own career paths. Those who worked on the young-adult years of the study are recognized within this text. For the past twelve years, Heidi Gralinski-Bakker has played a crucial role as project director, and we are very grateful to her for the many ways in which she has sustained this complex longitudinal study.

Many thanks from all of us to Elizabeth Knoll at Harvard University Press for her persistence, tolerance, and patience, as well as for her clear editorial vision. And to Maria Ascher for her moral support, her eagle eye, and her musical ear.

Stuart Hauser would like to thank Elliot Mishler, who has been an inspiration to him since Stuart's first year of psychiatric training. Elliot introduced Stuart to the study of individuals and families over time, and then to the promise of narrative approaches to experience and development. It was he who first wondered how any of us "grow up healthy."

Since then, David Reiss, William Kates, Bert Cohler, Mary Main, Emily Carlisle, Bob Waldinger, Jim Sabin, Richard Almond, and Hans Bakker have generously helped and encouraged our efforts to bring a narrative approach to the study of resilient development. Peter Fonagy, Linda Mayes, and Bob Emde have discussed many of the ideas in this book during our years of teaching together. They are wonderful models of curiosity and openness. Friends and colleagues from our local psychiatric and psychoanalytic communities helped at many stages of this project, including George Vaillant, Dan Buie, Edward Shapiro, Silvio Onesti, and Lewis Kirshner. Thanks to Arthur Kleinman, John Gilles, Frank Furstenburg, and Carl Morris at the Center for Advanced Studies in the Behavioral Sciences at Stanford, where many of the ideas in this book incubated during Stuart's 1993–1994 sabbatical. Thanks too to Joseph Coyle for facilitating that wonderful year.

Over the past ten years, Stuart Hauser has benefited richly

from his colleagues at Harvard and its Judge Baker Children's Center; Julius Richmond, Martha Minow, Richard Weisbourd, and John Woodall were especially helpful. Robbe Burnstine made a tremendous contribution with her combination of astute questions, organization, and tenacity. The visionary new president of Judge Baker's Children's Center, John Weisz, and its competent and forbearing staff, including Katherine Forsythe, Kevin Hepner, Mariellen Diemand, and Laura Skriner, helped us to survive the final stages of manuscript preparation.

Ethan and Joshua Hauser tolerated their father's psychological and physical absence as he became immersed yet again in an enveloping project. They gave him first-hand glimpses of the complexities of adolescent development, and as adults continue to contribute many insights into that process. Joshua and his wife, Juliet Bromer, have given us a new generation of kids to love and learn from. As ever, Stuart is greatly indebted to his wife, Barbara, for her dedication, loyalty, intelligence, wisdom, and encouragement.

Joseph Allen would like to thank Claudia for her consistent support, thoughtfulness, and sensitive advice. Appreciation is also extended to William Kahn for his steadfast friendship throughout this endeavor, and to Luke, Olivia, and Eve Allen for all they have taught through their own growth and resilience.

Eve Golden thanks Robbe Burnstine for her fierce interest, her capacious memory, and her grasp of the resilience literature, which on several occasions kept the book project from foundering. Thanks also to Jacquie Olds for triangulating memories, to Karen Rockow for her level-headed pragmatism, and to Sarah Wernick for tough love and for the experience and wisdom that she shared so generously. Thanks to Ken Kronenberg, a shining exemplar of resilience and a true mensch. Above all, thanks to Helen and Howard Golden for seeing it all through.

Out of the Woods

1

The Puzzle of Resilience

HAPPY ENDINGS ARE MOST INTRIGUING WHEN they're hard won. Perhaps it's the private knowledge that we, too, could be overtaken by disaster that makes stories of triumph over adversity so fascinating. But when children break out of vicious cycles of violence, abandonment, or abuse and grow up to be productive adults and gifted parents, we can't help wondering: How did they do it?

That is what this book is about. We had an opportunity to study recovery from serious psychiatric illness in the narratives of people who were so disturbed as teenagers that they had to be confined to the locked wards of a residential psychiatric hospital. A dozen years after that crisis, many of the former patients were still leading disturbed and unhappy lives. A few, however—nine out of sixty-seven—felt successful and optimistic. They looked forward to the future with pleasure and excitement, and their subjective confidence was mirrored in their performance on objective appraisals of young-adult development. Their stories are complicated stews of trial and error, hope and discouragement, total disgruntlement and stubborn persistence. They delineate a distinctive inner world, allowing us a new kind of access to the internal resources of highly resilient children and providing some fresh clues about how such resources develop.

Although in their early teens they had suffered periods of dysfunction dangerous enough to require admission to the hospital we call High Valley, a dozen years after that catastrophe nine of the former patients were impressively thriving. We can present in detail here only four of them—a small number, but large enough, we hope, to provoke and engage a much wider interest in how children recover from adversity. To that end, we chose the most diverse bunch of people that our sample afforded. The kids we are calling Pete, Rachel, Sandy, and Billy are no more resilient or special than their five fellows, but in their origins, their personalities, and their adult lives they make a satisfyingly varied group. All came back from the brink to build solid, constructive, and enjoyable lives that they could describe clearly and memorably. Sometimes comical, sometimes harrowing, always distinctive, and ultimately triumphant, their stories are the heart of this book.

THE STUDY OF RESILIENCE—successful adaptation in the face of danger[1]—began quietly about sixty years ago, with an observation. Norman Garmezy, the psychologist widely regarded as the founder of resilience studies, noticed that some patients hospitalized for schizophrenic breakdowns recovered after only brief hospitalizations, while others spent many years in hospitals. He wondered why.[2] Not long afterward, Lois B. Murphy, a child psychologist and another resilience pioneer, warned that it is shortsighted to look only at children's problems and so forfeit insight into their successes: "It is something of a paradox that a nation which has exulted in its rapid expansion and its scientific-technological achievements should have developed in its studies of childhood so vast a 'problem' literature," she said. "Courage and the will to do were crystallized in the mottoes of the nineteenth century; in the twentieth century we became preoccupied with failures. . . . We know that there are devices for correcting, bypassing, or overcoming threats, but for the most part these have not been directly studied."[3] Meanwhile, psychologist Robert W. White was calling attention to the developmental importance of *inner* experience—highlighting, among other things, the differences between what he called the *sense* (the subjective experience) of competence, and competence by more objective (or someone else's subjective) evaluation.[4]

As investigators of child development were inspired by these trailblazers, an almost exclusive concern with the origins and unfolding of psychopathology gradually gave way to questions about how people manage trouble. Scores of studies have addressed the mystery of resilience.[5] Early-childhood determinism (the belief that early-childhood experience is the primary determinant of an individual's life course) still has adherents, but it is now widely recognized that many developmental paths can arise out of adversity, and that their endpoints are very diverse indeed. For example, it is well known that abuse derails children's psychological growth, and that abused children often remain derailed long after the abuse is "over."[6] Many become permanently fearful, withdrawn, or angry, hiding from a threatening world or lashing out at it. They may reproduce abusive situations, or spend lonely lives in safe but superficial relationships, or do to their children what was done to them. Still, some abused children go on to lead satisfying and constructive lives. Resilience studies explore this elusive quality that makes such a difference when life turns hard—the difference between dramatic success and equally dramatic failure, say, or between flourishing and bare survival or even no survival at all.

The Word and Its Definition

Early writings on resilience were striking for their talk of "invulnerability," "invincibility," "supernormal children," "superkids."[7] Such appellations do highlight the marvelous strength of some children, but George Vaillant, a psychiatrist who has studied adaptation over many years, astutely and feelingly points out the need for a more exact terminology. "The concept of resilience is far more accurate and useful than the more popular—but unempathic—concept of invulnerability."[8] For children of adversity *are* wounded, often severely. To imply otherwise is to deny the acuteness of suffering in children, who don't "come" resilient but *become* resilient—*after* they have been hurt. There is no shield that keeps them safe from all harms, no intrinsic toughness such as the older terms imply. It is not the illusory invulnerability of resilient children that should command attention and respect, but their powers of self-healing. And these are powers that vary with circumstance: people's styles of adaptation change and evolve over their lifetimes.

This truth is so important that although the new term first appeared in the literature as *resiliency,* it was later modified to *resilience* in an effort to preserve the useful aspects of the concept while turning away from the earlier implication of a permanent endowment or a protective shield. Because the wish for such a magic charm dies very hard. The glamour of resilience has been applied to everything from skin creams and tyrants and the English language to computer motherboards with Fault Resilient Booting. Resilience is a theme of mythic stature and allure. But the pitfalls of imagining it as a discrete or stable property are real, and precise definitions are important.

Resilience is not a trait of character or constitution like Macbeth's ambition or Ted Williams' eyesight. There is no universal "resilient personality," no peculiar attribute that is recognizable and uniform among all resilient people. No one can be classified as resilient in a static, "forever" way; people may, and often do, show resilient adaptation or functioning at some times in their lives but not at others. Moreover, the experiences that foster the development of resilience may occur at some distance from the original adversity, often well after a period of apparent capitulation. Ann S. Masten studied with Norman Garmezy and now directs the longitudinal resilience study called Project Competence. As she and her colleague Jennifer L. Powell put it, "Resilience is not a trait of an individual, though individuals *manifest* resilience in their behavior or life patterns."[9]

The second principle of resilience is outlined in another statement from Project Competence: "Resilience refers to patterns of positive adaptation *in the context of significant risk or adversity.* Resilience is an inference about a person's life that requires two fundamental judgments: (1) that a person is 'doing okay,' and (2) that there is now or has been significant risk or adversity to overcome."[10]

In other words, without challenge there is no resilience. High competence alone, while a fine thing, is not the same. Neither is the mere fact that someone has survived trauma; to be considered resilient, the survivor has to have survived *competently.* Resilience is defined by the intersection of two conditions: serious risk and good outcome. This means that clear criteria of "success" are crucial to the definition of resilience, and this is a controversial matter. Should competence be defined by capacities that a culture deems necessary, or by the absence of impairment, or by both? Do we use external adaptation criteria (such as academic achievement or an absence of delinquency) or internal criteria (such as psychological well-being or the capacity for self-reflection) or both? (In the High Valley study, we defined competence by both external and internal criteria.) Questions like these remain hotly debated in resilience work.

Risk and Protection

The risk side of the resilience equation has been calculated in many different ways over the years; risks, unfortunately, are many, and they are hard to compare.[11] Socioeconomic, community, and personal *risk factors*—poverty, racism, disorganized early family environments, illness, early parental loss, repeated physical or sexual abuse—have been investigated alone and in combination for their influence on development. Great effort has also been made to define *protective factors*—circumstances and personal attributes associated with recovery from illness or tragedy. Candidates range from fortunate external endowments like wealth and beauty through the psychosocial complexities of good parenting, intelligence, and talent to personal attitudes like optimism and faith.[12] Yet lists of "factors," risk or protective, can't tell us *how* some individuals emerge stronger than they were from experiences that destroy others. There seems to be something deeper than the factors that makes the difference in people who despite real misfortune go on to lead solid and contented lives.

WHAT MIGHT THIS BE? Despite the variety of the risks that threaten children, and despite the multiplicity of putative protective factors, the results of resilience studies have converged rather dramatically upon a small set of conditions that are consistently associated with recovery. As Masten puts it, the best protections against risk, the factors that really can modulate and ameliorate the impact of serious adversity, are "connections to competent and caring adults in the family and community, cognitive and self-regulation skills, positive views of self, and motivation to be effective in the environment."[13]

We know that these regularly appear in concert with resilience, but their workings are as yet poorly understood. They are perhaps the central mystery of resilience.[14] For instance, we know that resilience is not purely, or even primarily, internal. The capacity to surmount misfortune seems to be an interplay among internal strengths, environmental resources, personal endowment, and connections with others. But although the decisive importance of relationships is well known and well documented,[15] and may even appear obvious, in fact we can't explain why this should be so. We don't know how relationships are important, or why they are important, or even what they do. What is it in relationship, what protective potential, that allows a psychologically wounded child to transform past experience and become reasonably whole again? What is it in some children that allows them to mobilize other people even in the most unpropitious circumstances imaginable, thereby keeping themselves on track and sometimes even flourishing? Why and how does one person use a new relationship to reinforce her own overtaxed personal resources, while another thinks other people are just one more drain on flagging strength? Why does a third person choose friends who always manage somehow to make matters worse? The gap between the abstraction—"relationships are important"—and a real understanding of what happens between two people is a compelling question for resilience researchers. In the ongoing acts of sense-making that we call personal narratives, the ways that children actually use relationships are clearly delineated. So are the rich tapestries they weave out of what "happens" to them and what they make of it from their own resources and the resources they derive from others.

Furthermore, children play an active part in the processes

that protect them. Adversity challenges some kids to harvest the barest surroundings with creative determination, while others make no use even of resources that are readily available. Children are more than passive accepters—or rejecters—of helpful relationships with adults; they may recruit and sustain them, treat them with indifference, or resolutely turn them away. This active role in the face of trouble has been observed in the lives of resilient children, but it has not been extensively studied.

What actually happens within children struggling to transcend a life-altering calamity? How do the ones who manage it keep up their morale, maintain their clarity of vision, engage the necessary supports? How do they construct for themselves the psychological and external environments conducive to recovery while their fellows do not? Internal processes of perception, thought, feeling, and interpretation determine how experiences impinge upon us and how we ultimately receive and metabolize them. One possibility, therefore, is that protective factors set in motion internal processes that enable or enhance the capacity to cope—processes that foster sturdy and flexible development instead of fragility and brittleness, such as seeking engagement rather than avoidance when trouble comes.

Another way of thinking about the problem is to recognize that different children make different kinds of sense out of what happens to them. For some, a terrible experience of fear or loss seems to block off the horizon permanently; others manage to look past it. To what extent does people's sense-making—the ways they think and rethink their lives, the stories they tell themselves[16]—contribute to the way they deal with their circumstances? What does the process of sense-making over time have to do with resilience or its absence? This is the question that drove the High Valley Resilience Study.

*   *   *

BETWEEN 1978 AND 1983, as part of a longitudinal study of adolescent development, Stuart T. Hauser and a group of colleagues[17] conducted annual one-on-one interviews over four years[18] with almost 150 teenagers.[19] In the interviews, participants were asked to tell about their histories, their parents, their lives at home and in school, their friends, the futures they imagined. Interviewers asked them how they handled stresses (conflicts, powerful feelings, the vicissitudes of adolescence); encouraged them to talk about their current situations and how they had arrived at them; invited free discussion throughout the interviews. To maintain continuity and encourage trust and openness, interviewer/participant pairs were kept constant. Once a year, a group of reputable standardized tests was administered to provide independent measures of aspects of psychological growth that are not readily visible in interviews.[20] About half of the subjects had been hospitalized in their early teens in the locked Children's Center of High Valley Hospital because they were thought to pose a serious danger to themselves or to others—that is, they were depressed, violent, self-destructive, or otherwise out of control.[21]

The High Valley Resilience Study

In 1989, Stuart T. Hauser and Joseph P. Allen began a follow-up study of the erstwhile teenagers, now young adults. New interviewers who knew nothing of the participants' pasts engaged with them in two more extended interviews, again inviting them to speak about themselves freely, at length and in detail. As in the earlier study, we administered a supplemental battery of very well established assessments of psychological development, this time gearing it to young adults rather than adolescents.[22] Several interviewers mentioned to us at this time how astounded they

9

had been to learn that the young man or woman speaking with them had been hospitalized as a teenager. These people liked their lives and talked about them openly. Their conversation was fluent and lively. They were engaged in satisfying work or training for it; they had lasting relationships; they were trying their wings as parents with enthusiasm and pleasure. They were interested in psychological experience, and their ideas about themselves and other people were discerning and thoughtful in the ways that are characteristic of mature and robust psychological adulthood. They felt adventurous and optimistic about the future. There was no hint in their conversation of the extraordinary derailment that lurked in their pasts.

This was singular indeed. Most of the former patients were still protesting, more than a decade later, the unfairness of their lives, including—especially—their confinements at High Valley. They were guarded and distrustful, preoccupied with the past, dissatisfied with the present, pessimistic or apathetic about the future. It seemed that their dark times, with the immediacy and inevitability characteristic of trauma, were still coloring how they thought about themselves. Their lives and their relationships reflected an ongoing sense of disruption. But the "surprising" group, as we thought of them, seemed to have processed a rough time very differently. They had managed to integrate it, transcending the potential for trauma that had so clearly been realized in their fellows. What was going on?

THE FIRST THING we needed to know in pursuing this mystery was whether objective criteria would support their subjective optimism. We outlined the features that we would expect to see in well-functioning people in their early to mid-twenties: on the positive side, high levels of social and emotional development, close and constructive relationships with friends, realistic and mindful attachments to parents; on the negative side, lack of significant antisocial behavior (such as drug abuse or criminal offenses) or psychiatric symptoms. Then we analyzed the scores of all our participants, whether hospitalized as teenagers or not. We defined as "resilient" any former patient who scored in the top half of the entire group of 143 young adults—that is, the top half *of the entire group of once-hospitalized and never-hospitalized subjects*—on all our measures of positive functioning, and in the bottom half on all our measures of negative functioning. The success of the surprising patients did hold up under that scrutiny, and several other former patients met our criteria as well. In all, four men and five women (13 percent of the former patients) had scores that placed them solidly within the top half of the sample across all of our primary measures. Since most people are above average in some things and below average in others, these nine, who scored above average in *all* categories, were well above average overall and faring far better than the typical former patients.

Upon consideration, we decided not to try to contrast the resilient group with the former patients who were doing most poorly. The latter were isolated, using drugs, losing job after job; some were in prison. We wanted to concentrate on unusual resilience, rather than on unusual failure, so we decided instead to select a contrast group of former patients who were doing about average for the former-patient group. That is, while our resilient group had to be above average on every measure for the study population as a whole (including the people who had never displayed any significant psychiatric problems), we selected for contrast the former patients whose functioning across all of our key measures placed them consistently right in the middle of the once-hospitalized group. Again we did not include people whose scores averaged out in the middle but were high in some areas and low in others. We insisted that *all* scores fall precisely within the middle twenty percentiles for the former-patient group. This gave us a group of seven people who were functioning, to our best determination, as typically as might be imagined for adolescents who had required psychiatric hospitalization in their early teens. They were not startlingly successful, but they were not in desperate social, legal, or psychiatric straits, either—they were hanging in. We called this group of seven the *contrast group*.

We chose that name with great care. Resilience, as we have said, is not a binary quality that a person has or lacks. Masten and Powell go out of their way to emphasize that someone who displays resilience at one juncture may not necessarily do so at another: "One would not expect a resilient person, however defined at one point in time, to be doing well every minute of the day, under all imaginable circumstances, or in perpetuity."[23] So we do not want to imply that the contrast group is "nonresilient," or "less resilient," or in some other way substantively different from the resilient group. Our nomenclature had to take into account that (1) *at the time of testing*, the resilient group scored much higher on tests of adaptation than the contrast group did, but that (2) similar tests several years later might yield very different results. The momentary "averageness" of the other kids is not a judgment, much less a sentence. The differences we eventually found in the narratives of the two groups may likewise be a function of time and circumstance; nothing in our findings precludes the possibility that some members of the contrast group will prove resilient in later years. We were looking for characteristics that support or enable the behavior that gives rise to resilience, and as one member of our contrast group will demonstrate, such characteristics may develop later, in tandem with or in anticipation of other manifestations associated with resilience.

Having established our groups, we examined the hospital records to see whether the different outcomes could be explained by demographic or statistical variations, but we found no support in the data for such suppositions. So we turned at last, with great interest, to the interview texts, a very rich source of information that we had never before fully exploited. They contained our subjects' perceptions, interpretations, and private feelings about their lives. We had heard from these people for years, in their own words and in their own ways, about the ordinary experiences, fulfilling and not, that make up a life. We were wondering what more those stories could tell us.

Narrative and Resilience

It was the great good fortune of our access to this gold mine of interview texts that made the High Valley Resilience Study possible, and in fact the stories proved to be the key. The psychoanalytic therapies are popularly called a "talking cure"; but in the skeptical world of developmental psychology, personal narrative—the stories people tell about themselves—has only recently been recognized as a resource and a tool, and a way of grasping how people create and maintain meaning over time.[24] Yet narrative offers a new window on many of the aspects of resilience that we don't yet understand—how people deal with the internal consequences of disruption over time, for instance, and how their perceptions and styles of coping influence their relationships, their planning, and their intentions.

Individual factors are not the only significant engines of psychological change, as risk and protection studies clearly show.

But one advantage of studying narrative is that narrative reveals people's lives in context. At its best, says Catherine Riessman, a sociologist who uses narrative to investigate complex interpersonal events such as divorce, the study of narrative "illuminates the intersection of biography, history, and society."[25] This is the perfect context for resilience studies, and it was also the context of the High Valley narratives. So we posed three questions: Would the texts of the two groups differ? Would we be able to discern any early manifestations or enablers of protective processes? And could we observe anything about how narrative shapes adaptation?

Narrative has both causal and consequential aspects; we all know that. Things happen to us. We reflect on our experiences, and our reflections alert us to new understandings and new possibilities. We act on these and acquire new experiences that further enlarge our capacity for storytelling. A two-year-old who bumps his head on the kitchen table in a fit of after-supper rambunctiousness may kick the table in retaliation. From an adult point of view, his story—that the table hurt him—hasn't much explanatory power. Yet it is likely to instill in him a new respect for tables, and slow him down a bit so he can attend more carefully to the whereabouts of his sharp-cornered nemesis. This protects him from further knocks, which is adaptive in itself, and it also gives him time, motivation, and opportunity to observe the table and become better acquainted with its nature. In time, a new story will emerge—that it is *he* who moves and bumps, not the furniture—and with it the probability that he will take more responsibility for his locomotion and its consequences. From there he will further develop his narrative about navigating physically in the world, in his own particular way.

Stories help us to bring order out of chaos, but this is a double-edged power. Some new experiences foster growth, while others have potentially disastrous consequences; the same is true of the narratives through which we explore experience. So far, two theories of narrative have received the lion's share of attention from psychologists writing about resilience. One is that narrative *coherence*—the capacity to develop a "good story" in which circumstance and personal experience are meaningfully integrated—in some way *accounts for* successful adaptation.[26] The second maintains that a person's narrative coherence *reflects* a capacity to handle adversity.[27] Yet it is likely that both are right—that narrative both reflects *and* influences adaptation. In the High Valley narratives, we see this reciprocal function very clearly as changes in stories trigger new perspectives—constructive and not—about situations, relationships, goals, and all the other decisive elements in an individual's life, and the new perspectives then influence later choices. The narratives illuminate a very shadowy corner of resilience studies: the question of *how* resilience evolves or doesn't, and how it is informed by experience.

FACED WITH THIS wealth of intimate sense-making, we asked ourselves: Was there anything in these texts that might have hinted at such unexpectedly satisfying lives for the nine resilient young adults *before* we knew who they were (that is, when we first met them as teenagers in the hospital), or even shortly after their discharge? Now that we *did* know who they were, could we find any distinguishing clues in their narratives to the striking changes these people would make over the years? Maybe we would find first hints of strengths we hadn't been able to recognize before—unusual interpretations, perhaps, or special sensitivities or insights or gifts—that could explain, or that might have shaped, such unexpectedly successful young adulthoods. We were looking for *processes* of resilience, a picture of resilience as it is first emerging from adversity. If we could begin to recognize the seeds, we thought, we could learn to cultivate them in other threatened children.

So we analyzed the interviews of our sixteen subjects—the nine resilient ones and the seven in the contrast group—for their content and structure. We watched for recurrent stories and themes, and for variations of coherence and organization in the way the stories were told. We looked at how the narrators talked about change, and about relationships, and about their developing ideas of themselves. Good psychological processing of difficult material is known to be reflected in smoother and richer narratives,[28] so we also noted whether narrators could talk about emotionally laden experience clearly and responsively, or if their stories were marked by interruptions, digressions, or refusals to continue or to disclose.

This was uncharted territory, and we wanted to leave room for the unforeseen. We made note of any themes we hadn't expected, and we made a point of not categorizing stories by their content; we didn't want to identify them as "resilient" or "protective," or as stories of "luck" or "misfortune." It wasn't so much the overt content of a story (say, about hospitalization or a failed relationship) that mattered to us. We were looking for *processes of thought:* Does a speaker stick to generalizations, or can she see nuance within a situation? Is a story flexible and inclusive, or closed and static? Does the speaker welcome opportunities for change, or resist them? Does he see himself in the context of an ongoing plotline, or do things seem to be standing still? How does she deal with important people? Are relationships tolerated, recruited, or rejected as threats? Above all, how do the narrators think about themselves? It seemed likely that in the tellings and retellings of important stories over the years, we would learn something about how the various young people thought about their lives and the ways they changed—or didn't. We were searching for the first small movements of development out of crisis.

EVENTUALLY WE WERE ABLE to establish portraits of these sixteen young people and of the two groups they represented. They had plenty in common. In their early stories, all the kids talk of loneliness, inferiority, despair, helplessness, rage; sometimes there are memories of abuse. But in the years after the resilient former patients leave the hospital, painful experiences become the subject of careful and creative reflection as the young people try to understand them, make sense out of them, and fit them into the context of their new lives. In the contrasting group of former patients, the tortured themes evolve less. They remain frozen, fossils of childhood explanations that never quite grow up.

There are universal themes about relationships, too. The kids all talk at first about terrible feelings of isolation. Relationships are depicted as barren and mean, often dangerous. Yet the resilient kids observe other people very carefully, and think of relationships—even when anxious about them—as if they were greatly important. They pay attention to how they act in relationships, and to the effects of their actions on other people. A less grim picture slowly develops as connections grow from sparse roots into a dense crisscross. The contrast-group kids never accord relationships the scrutiny the resilient kids do. They talk less about other people; they seldom recognize themselves as the common denominator in all of their connections; and the *process* of relationships—the way they work—seems not to interest them at all.

From the outset, all of the kids describe intensely felt visions of themselves and their place in the world. For the members of the contrast group, this initial sense of things remains the dominant one; neither time nor experience alters it. But the viewpoints of the resilient young people change as their lives do, and their descriptions of the process offer a rare look at the way troubled adolescents can perceive and rewrite a perilous history. The resilient patients' ideals and values are just as strongly held as those of their fellows, yet they remain open to elaboration and revision, and develop over the years in ever more complex and inclusive ways. And while the stories of the contrast group tend to be structurally simple, flat, and disorganized, those of the resilient kids are complex, vivid, and clear.

THE HIGH VALLEY RESILIENCE STUDY started out as a happy accident. The discovery of a group of resilient young adults for whom we also possessed extensive interview transcripts offered an opportunity for some psychological natural history that was much too good to pass up. What we saw in the interviews is intriguing and provocative, and will, we hope, give rise to more systematic investigation of these ideas. The differences we found among the groups are tantalizing hints, and they point in important directions.

Early studies of childhood risk and recovery have focused so far on broad dimensions of risk and protection—genetic endowment, parenting, opportunity, and the great social issues of money, education, and status. But this research can't tell us how resilient capacities develop, how they work, or how to nurture them. We have to begin to delineate the small but pervasive psychological processes through which larger forces act upon and make themselves felt within individuals, whether in everyday predicaments or dire and dramatic ones. These processes are the stepping stones by which people negotiate the swamps of adversity—making their way out, holding their own on the surface, or falling deeper in. The High Valley narratives tell us something about how "protective factors" look in operation, and how individuals actually use them.

Resilience and Social Context

Resilience does not come solely from within a child; it depends also on what the child can draw upon from family and community.[29] But what children can elicit from their surroundings depends in part on what their surroundings have to offer them, and this is a very pressing issue.

On the whole, when it comes to mental health, it's better to be rich rather than poor. Higher socioeconomic status is associated with better parenting and cognitive skills and the advantages that seem to come with them.[30] Growing up poor, in a poor community, has a deleterious impact on children's physical health and on their cognitive, intellectual, social, and emotional development, and we know that the greater the cumulative load of risk, the less likely children are to recover.[31] But some people can thrive under conditions of extreme financial duress; conversely, trust funds do not guarantee health or happiness.[32]

So while "short lists" of risk and protective factors taunt us with more questions than they answer, what we learn in resilience studies helps us to look a little further and a little deeper into ills that we don't yet know how to cure. We know that the presence of a caring adult can offer real protection from the ravages of poverty, and although we have not learned to eradicate poverty, we can and do try to make caring adults available to kids who must endure it. But since some children do not make good use of such adults, we will also need to learn how to help them become able to do so. Studies like ours at High Valley are beginning to reveal something about how the strengths and vulnerabilities of individual children protect them, or not, from the risks of their environments. In any group of kids at risk, some do much better than others, and we need to know why. The fact that some are astonishingly resourceful does not relieve us of the responsibility to dismantle pervasive social injustices when we see them. But even once it becomes clear how that might happen, a task of such inconceivable magnitude will not be accomplished quickly. Until we find the means to destroy the evils of socioeconomic disadvantage, we can at least learn to protect children against them.

That *any* children develop significant avoidable psycho-pathology is a matter of vital concern. It is good to know that some manage to rise above adversity; but so long as any do not, the search for resilience remains painfully urgent. The questions raised almost fifty years ago about how children survive threats are only beginning to be answered. We hope that the High Valley Resilience Study will give rise to further work on this key aspect of resilience. We offer as encouragement an intriguing look at the vital and subtle interplay between resilient children and their world—at young people in whom the vital gift of resilience is just germinating and beginning to grow.[33]

2

High Valley

MOST OF THE KIDS AT THE HIGH VALLEY CHILDREN'S Center—"kids" was what they called themselves; "staff" meant everybody else—had been sent there against their will and sometimes without warning by desperate parents when uncontrollable behavior, violent outbursts, or self-destructive preoccupations made it impossible to keep them at home. Psychiatric hospitalization of children is such an extreme measure, and the children's reaction to it such a crucial aspect of their stories, that we have to start by describing High Valley and the kind of place it was.[1]

High Valley Hospital, beautiful, venerable, and prestigious, was a local landmark. It was the crown of the region's mental health establishment, and the High Valley Children's Center was the jewel in that crown. Kids came there from long ways away; it was one of only a very few secure psychiatric facilities for children in an extended area, and its services were in great demand. New drugs and insurance regulations were permanently altering the practice of psychiatry, but a certain mystique still surrounded High Valley. Legend had it that old families sent dotty maiden aunts to drink tea there in genteel confinement, while at the Children's Center the indulged offspring of local intellectuals contemplated their neuroses from an analyst's couch. But it wasn't like that at all. There was little of the indulgent or contemplative about the High Valley Children's Center. It was a strange and often terrifying place.

By the late 1970s a quiet revolution had overtaken private psychiatric hospitals. New healthcare legislation was forcing medical insurers to increase psychiatric coverage, and institutions that had once been fashionable, luxurious, and exclusive now hosted patients from all kinds of backgrounds and with all kinds of problems. High Valley was no exception. Only a handful of the kids at the Children's Center came from moneyed families. The deciding financial factor when we began our work there was no longer affluence, but insurance. Myth notwithstanding, it wasn't the upper-crust parents who wangled extended stays at High Valley for their children, but the ones who worked (often in low-level positions) for huge corporations with generous health benefits. The place was so expensive that even the very wealthy balked at actually paying the daily rate. Ordinary major medical policies covered brief stays of thirty to forty-five days, barely enough for an evaluation; military coverage was sometimes a little more liberal. The state Department of Social Services admitted a few kids in especially unfortunate circumstances, but not usually for long. Only very rarely did a family pay for hospitalization out of its own pocket.

The Children's Center was not reassuring to look at. High Valley had a beautiful old campus of rolling hills on which the kids' building stood out as an intimidating anomaly. An austere ultramodern concrete structure with geometric lines and angular turrets, it would have looked more at home on Star Trek as the fortress of an alien warlord than it did in its sedate surroundings. Most of the walls were straight and squat, studded with rows of square windows that didn't open and somehow seemed always to be bulging from within; the rest were long curving stretches with no windows at all. Inside, the building was divided into halves called "units," each with its own central meeting area, nursing station, and conference room, and a corridor of double bedrooms for the residents. The two units shared a cafeteria that served also as gym and auditorium, for games, movies, parties, and other group activities.

The Center accommodated about two dozen kids. They came from all over and from all kinds of families, and ranged in age from five (very occasionally) to about seventeen. When we were there, the average admission lasted about two months, but that was a misleading statistic—a few very long stays (sometimes of a year or more) balanced out dozens of much shorter ones of three to six weeks. Each unit had a permanent complement of full-time staff, including a supervising child psychiatrist, a consulting psychologist, two or three social workers, and a rich endowment of psychiatric nurses and childcare workers—at least six per shift. Student social workers and psychologists rotated through the service, and every year brought a new contingent of full-time postdoctoral psychologists and psychiatrists (one and three per unit, respectively), who were pursuing advanced training in child and adolescent psychiatry. Residents in adult psychiatry gave time to the Center as well, and the entire children's service was supervised, administered, and advised by a cadre of world-renowned experts in the field. Interdisciplinary teams made and carried out treatment plans for the young patients and their families. The nursing staff played a double role: they participated with their colleagues on the treatment teams, and they were also largely responsible for day-to-day caregiving.

Downhill from the Center was its school. From the outside,

and compared to the main building, it looked ordinary enough. But that was about all it had in common with "regular" schools. It was run by a specialist in education and child psychology who had designed and developed it specifically as a therapeutic learning environment for seriously troubled children. Classes of five or six were the norm, and individual attention was always available. From the kids' point of view, this was not necessarily a good thing; many of them had learned to count heavily on the anonymity and freedom of movement of their large public schools, slipping through whatever cracks they could find in their efforts to avoid people, rules, or homework. They received academic credit for the time they spent at High Valley, but they complained universally and vociferously that the work was "mickey mouse," and when they got back home, the ones who cared about school usually felt that they had fallen behind. Still, the school at the Center (which everyone called the "ed-unit") concentrated on careful analysis of each student's learning style and psychological needs, and tuned the work and the working environment as much to the kids' emotional capabilities as to their intellects. This attention to detail gave many of the Center patients their first experience with academic success.

SOME OF THE CHILDREN at the Center were psychotic and had come there to be evaluated for medication or long-term care. Some were depressed. Some had disruptive neurological problems (such as Tourette syndrome) that made social adaptation difficult. A very few were autistic. Sometimes the juvenile justice system mandated hospitalization for evaluative purposes or as an alternative to incarceration. Occasionally someone was admitted with an "adjustment reaction" to circumstances at home—an ugly divorce, say, or an unexpected death. When a serious medical illness was part of the package and a sick kid was admitted, a special sadness fell over the Center. Self-destructive behavior was common; it ranged from arm-cutting through much more dangerous kinds of self-mutilation to suicide gestures and occasionally a near-successful attempt. Many of the Center kids had one variety or other of conduct disorder. At best this translated into defiance, temper tantrums, and poor self-control; more often it meant serious antisocial behavior such as substance abuse, compulsive or dangerous sexual activity, firesetting, or violence at home or at school. Histories of trouble with the law were very common. But whatever the primary diagnosis, and whatever else was going on, most of the High Valley kids were very, very, very angry. And although its stony concrete mass looked and felt intimidating, the Children's Center was not really a large place—just that bunkerlike building with locked doors and sealed windows, and two dozen wild and furious children pent up inside.

So a primary concern at the Center was containment. Many of the patients were dangerous, either to themselves or to other people, and the first essential of treatment was to ensure for them a safety that they could not achieve on their own. Multiple modes of psychotherapy—individual, parent, family, group— were provided by a carefully selected and very well trained staff. But this was only one aspect of a milieu whose first obligation was the establishment of control. Without that nothing else was possible.

Most of the doors stayed permanently locked, and only staff had keys. The exceptions were the doors to the kids' rooms, and those weren't lockable at all—patients were not allowed to sequester themselves from adult supervision. There were small windows in the bedroom doors for the same reason. Few of the windows opened, and large sections of the building's living areas had no windows at all, so the Center existed night and day in a cold artificial light.

For the times when these protections weren't enough, there were the "quiet rooms," the hated QRs. These had no furniture and smooth blank walls, and an out-of-control kid could be walked over and confined to one for a little while, with a staff member nearby, until he or she calmed down. The QRs were used to remove distraught kids from overstimulation when necessary, and to keep incipient tensions from escalating to the danger point. Restraints were also available, for times when the threat of physical violence could not be contained in any other way. These weren't the canvas-and-leather straitjackets of grade-B movies, but strips of gauze or Velcro by which a child's wrists and ankles could be secured to an ordinary stretcher. Kids in restraints were not left alone, and periods of restraint and seclusion were brief; the younger the kid, the shorter the time. But the patients at High Valley were expected to control their impulses. When tempers got out of control, as they often did, and when gentler measures like talking or time-outs weren't helping, it came down to the QRs, "four points" (as the kids called wrist and ankle restraints), or, rarely, sedating drugs.

RESTRAINT AND SECLUSION were very serious business to both staff and kids. The staff hated to use them, but the assurance of safety was one of their primary responsibilities. Violence that could be stopped in no other way had to be contained for the safety of everyone, including—especially—the violent kid, who would be carefully monitored until he or she had calmed down, and then allowed to decompress with a staff member for company before returning to the unit. And except for the occasional tough guy who solicited restraint as a macho statement to his fellows, the kids hated it too—at least when they were at their wildest, which of course was exactly when it happened. Afterward, once they had settled down, they sometimes felt differently about it—but sometimes they didn't. Even the many kids who were never secluded or restrained at all felt threatened by the existence of the QRs. There was a constant double-edged awareness of the seclusion and restraint potential at the Center; neither the kids nor the staff ever forgot that it was there. To some degree, perhaps, it served as a deterrent. The kids spoke of the QRs with loathing, contempt, and sometimes fear. But when one of their own got out of hand and a restraint became imminent, it was they who began the equivocal chant "*Four* points! *Four* points! *Four* points!" Some of them had borne the brunt of so much sadism that their own was very close to the surface. And most were deeply relieved when order was restored. So it was hard to tell whether the incantation was intended to ward off the dreaded event or to invoke it.

Every effort was made not to hurt the kids or even surprise them, but still these interventions were dramatic and often frightening—for the kids looking on at least as much as for the one in distress, who just might possibly have been feeling a tiny bit of relief. It is shocking to see four big men converge on an angry child, wrestle him to the floor, and carry him off. Staff (as the kids generically called all the adults at the Center) knew, of course, that the more of them there were, the less chance there was of anyone's being hurt, and they were trained to be as gentle and reassuring as possible. They also knew that the kids were terrified of their own rage, and that the promise of restraint reassured them even as it maddened them further. But that was a sophisticated perspective that newcomers didn't start out with, whatever their ages. It took a long time to get used to these episodes, even for the adults who came to the Center as staff.

However often you saw it, the restraining process was chilling to watch.

Discipline was eternal and inexorable, and tolerances were narrow. The Center kids were cauldrons of fearsome energies—at least as fearsome to themselves as to anyone else. But the minute they set foot on the units, all their usual avenues of discharge were gone. No fighting, no pot, no hanging out. Physical expression of emotion was strictly curtailed. There was much less opportunity for exercise than active kids are used to—not on purpose, but because facilities and supervision were in short supply—and even mild horseplay had to be suppressed sometimes, lest it get out of hand. Other familiar opportunities for self-soothing vanished too. Shopping was out of the picture; escapes to books or headphones were limited; overt sexual behavior of any kind ("sexualizing," it was called by kids and staff alike) was strictly prohibited; even sleep time was regulated. The units were funnels for channeling energy into speech. Talking About Feelings was the order of the day. This was a loathsome concept to the Center kids, who mostly didn't know how to do it. But feelings came up all the time—the whole Center was organized to make sure of it—and the only way to avoid them was to keep away from everyone else. Needless to say, that wasn't allowed either.

The kids had little free time, and even less time alone. They got up early. Right after breakfast there were community meetings where patients and staff discussed plans, behavior, anticipated changes or absences, and so on. These "c'unity meetings," as the kids pronounced it, got pretty intense sometimes, since they were the place where staff raised concerns about the emotional climate on the units, and the kids themselves raised (or tried to avoid) personal issues with the staff and with their fellows. The kids said they hated the meetings, but most of the time the process seemed to work pretty well. When something especially upsetting was going on, extra meetings would be called to deal with it.

Long hours at school followed. Late afternoons were filled with evaluations, therapy hours (individual doctor's appointments were known as "DAs," and family therapy sessions were called "family meetings"), and the untold other official rendezvous the kids had to honor on pain of lost privileges and confinement to the unit. Some of the very long-term patients had jobs on or near the grounds. Evenings and free slots in the afternoons were given over to supervised group activities—walks, games, excursions to places where money could be spent, an occasional movie. Kids with a lot of privileges could go by themselves or with friends to the caf, the main hospital cafeteria, for a Coke or a Milky Way, but the rest were limited to monitored pursuits. Weekends meant home visits for the kids who had earned them, and field trips and other group activities for those who had to stay.

The daily schedule alone infuriated the Center kids, many of whom had spent years running their own shows. Their parents didn't know how to handle them, or didn't care to, or were afraid to; some of the kids were masters of intimidation, and others were actively dangerous. But "staff" was a collective organism in a way that parents are not, able to wait out the most stubborn rebellion and disarm the most ominous threats. Self-determination was in very short supply at the Children's Center.

Kids came to the units with no privileges at all. The smallest freedoms had to be earned by strict compliance. Even the right to go to the in-house lunchroom was contingent on good behavior, and it might be weeks before a new patient was allowed outside except for the daily compulsory (and supervised, for the still-unliberated) hike to school. Passes, money, the rare opportunities to spend it, visits with family at the hospital, visits home—all of these were controlled by unit staff and could be withdrawn at any sign of trouble.

These strictures were not intended primarily as punishment, although the kids felt that they were used that way. And sometimes they were. But mostly the Center was trying to establish a delay between impulse and action within which reflection and self-control could have a chance to develop. When the kids began to "lose it," they were quickly pulled back onto the units— the least stimulating environment the Center had to offer—in support of their efforts to keep themselves in hand. The units also offered the highest concentration of personnel, whose job and wish it was to listen with care to what the kids had to say. Even so, feelings could run high. Many of the staff were quite young people, passionately idealistic but with no children of their own. They occasionally fell prey to the belief that they could raise a kid better than the kid's own parents had, and this left them susceptible to disappointment and anger when the kids didn't appear to appreciate their efforts.

Similarly, passes with parents were sometimes denied because the *parents* didn't know how to handle them. Visits home were considered very carefully for the same reason; if things had been good at home, most of the kids wouldn't have been at High Valley at all. But to the kids, being confined on the units meant being confined with themselves, with no distraction and no escape. Since they had few internal resources for handling emotion, this felt to them like the most menacing environment of all, and they tended to meet the overbearing authority that kept them there with clinging or with defiance. The staff marveled privately at the fluency and creativity of the kids' swearing, but officially there was little tolerance for protest. This was the ultimate Catch-22 of the Children's Center, as the kids saw it: protest was considered (and it often was, but not always) yet another triumph of impulse over reflection, behavior that confirmed in itself the need for more enforced time out. Seclusion was a backup measure for the times when close confinement on the unit was not enough, or when even that proved too stimulating. A kid who could not disengage from a struggle with "a staff," for instance, might be escorted to a QR and asked (or required) to stay there until he could refrain from threats, or from physical attacks on himself or anyone else. The nurse or childcare worker with whom he had been fighting would check on him frequently, and go in when the patient showed that he was ready to talk. They'd leave together when things were back under control.

The heat was turned up under these pressure-cooker kids even as their release valves were systematically shut off. Most of them were at the Center because, in one way or another, they didn't get on with other people. They attacked them, lied to them, hid from them, stole from them. The kids of a more directly self-destructive persuasion tried to numb their feelings with drugs, or by cutting their forearms or faces with razor blades. Some tried to kill themselves—with greater or lesser degrees of competence, perhaps, but all with much too much fear and pain. However they handled it, one of the common denominators among them was that they found being with other people insupportable. Other people evoked feelings—fear, rage, envy, shame, longing, sadness—that the kids didn't know what to do with; and when they couldn't avoid feelings, they were accustomed to acting them out.

On the units, however, avoidance was impossible and acting out was not permitted. Private time was generally discouraged, and opportunities were few, because there wasn't enough room for real privacy. New patients were assigned roommates whose behavior was likely to be at least as strange or threatening as their own. The therapeutic milieu of doctors, social services, groups, school, testing, activity, and above all community, meant hours of intense and stressful interaction a day. When kids *did* want adult attention, they had to negotiate for it. And they had to share it with a whole bunch of temporary siblings, all troublesome, all demanding, some scary, and some just really, really weird.

One way or another, almost all of the Center kids had poor social skills. Some were agonizingly shy. Some piled chips on their shoulders and went around daring people to knock them off. Some sat by themselves in corners, watching or rocking. Some were so needy that other people avoided them to keep from being eaten alive. Some rocketed around until everyone in their vicinity was exhausted. Some spent their lives in eternal control struggles. Some treated every encounter as a tryst. Some had extremely well-developed antisocial tendencies. But at the Center, one smart-aleck remark or one piece of inappropriate behavior—"inappropriate" was staff shorthand for anything they didn't want the kids to do—could lose a trip to the caf for the whole group. That was bad enough in itself; little outings like those were the only relief from the interminable boredom of the units. But it was nothing compared to the punishment of rage, contempt, and humiliation that infuriated peers would mete out in retaliation for the loss.

So the community at the Center was a very complicated place for these kids, most of whom knew nothing about cooperation. Staying away wasn't an option; "isolating," as it was called, brought loss of privileges, and that just meant closer confinement. There was no escape from unit society, because unit society—for the kids who could learn to stand it—was the basic instrument of the Center's healing work.

*　　*　　*

IDEALLY, A HOSPITALIZATION brings with it relief as well as anxiety—the awareness that an acknowledged problem is being properly addressed. At the Children's Center, rage was a much more usual reaction, and these kids were enraged already. They were often on very bad terms with the parents who had initiated or enforced the admission. Sometimes this was because their own behavior had really been intolerable. Sometimes the parents themselves were a fundamental part of the problem. Mostly it was a combination of both. But it was the kids who ended up at the Center, and they usually felt, at least at first, that they were taking someone else's rap.

Some parents were so frantic, guilty, grieving, or furious, so frightened for—and sometimes of—their children, that they resorted to trickery to get the kids to High Valley. A few were so desperate to find a legal way of divesting themselves of their kids that a long stay in a hospital and then a residential school looked like a dream come true. (Their kids were not unaware of this.) Often they were no more expert than the kids at handling difficult feelings, so it was very hard for them to talk directly about admission and what it meant. What many of the Center patients heard from their parents as they set off for High Valley on that first day was that they were making a pleasant afternoon trip to see a new doctor at a place like a camp, a beautiful place with meadows, woods, tennis courts. Not until it was too late did the kids find out that they would be left there—locked up there—for weeks, or months, or years.

Even when the parent-child relationship was fundamentally sound, there were often hard feelings over the hospitalization. Sometimes the kids knew they were in trouble and went along with their parents' plans willingly. But that didn't spare them the eventual realization that the new environment, far from being an escape or a pastoral idyll, was much stricter in its demands than the homes they had left, and much less forgiving when its rules were broken. Panic and rage would set in as the new patients, dropped by familiar if infuriating families into unknown surroundings, suddenly had to learn to obey an army of powerful strangers and to live in a society of other kids as distraught and as ruthless as themselves.

They had abstract challenges to deal with as well. Along with the pain associated with their own private problems, they were often (overtly or covertly) held responsible for the pain of their families—a lot of responsibility for a troubled kid. They had to deal with the stigma, still very real among teenagers, of being sent to a psychiatrist—even worse, to a hospital full of "loonies," "sickos," and "retards." Finally, many of the kids were living with the aftereffects of abuse and betrayal, experiences that colored their views of everything, especially this appalling new place.

HOWEVER THE HIGH VALLEY MYTHS had it, a stay at the Children's Center was no indulgence. It was one more misery to balance on top of the precarious heaps of previous miseries that brought young patients to its doors. The kids wouldn't have been at the Center if they hadn't been in very deep trouble already; in the beginning, they tended to feel that being there was more trouble still. Upset themselves and seriously upsetting to others, they were thrust with little preparation into the crucible of an all-powerful institutional community. They met the challenge in different ways. When they left (usually to go home or to therapeutic residential schools), some had enough new skills to keep themselves relatively safe and out of hospitals or jails. Some didn't. The narratives in this book show how four of them managed to build new lives after a formidable crisis. We're hoping that they will help us to help other troubled kids do the same.

3

Reading the Stories

THE NARRATIVES THAT FOLLOW PROVIDE SOME pointed clues about how four kids managed to transcend adversity and begin to grow again.[1] These extended excerpts are not intended as "complete" stories. The narratives are works in progress, and they are best read as dynamic elaborations of important themes. When fourteen-year-old Rachel Somer's interviewer asks her what kinds of things give her trouble in the hospital, Rachel says: "I think it's—Sometimes when the kids get upset on the unit they'll say stuff to me and I'll take it personally. . . . I'm very sensitive when it comes to things like that, and I get upset." This is a brief statement, but it offers a context for the trouble she gets into, an acknowledgment of how she contributes to it, and the beginning of an inquiry into her lifelong problems with peer relationships. That's a vital storyline for Rachel, one that she expands and refines steadily over the next dozen years.

Why did Billy Mayor, just turned twelve, suddenly start having trouble in school? "I just had too much on my mind, I guess," Billy says. Like what? asks the interviewer. "What was going on at home." This answer, like Rachel's, is incomplete—but it, too, delineates an important storyline. What was going on at home, and how that's on his mind, are subjects to which Billy returns over and over again in his quiet but persistent efforts to get a handle on his life.

Rory Carroll is one of the contrast group, surviving but not flourishing at age twenty-five. Here's how he talks at fifteen about his early days in the hospital and the problems that landed him there. "Did some vandalism," he says. "And B&E's [breaking and enterings]." The interviewer asks him to say more, but Rory refuses. "No," he says. "I try to keep those memories out." This is the first hint of a very dramatic developing story—of Rory's frantic efforts to "keep the memories out," and (many years later) of his courageous struggle to face them.

In these narratives the kids concentrate on what matters to them, with an occasional nod to the interviewers' interests. In most cases they tell the truth as they see it, but historical ideals of correctness or completeness are not the point. Sometimes they avoid or prevaricate when they feel threatened, but their evasions are often more revealing than the truth would have been. These narratives are the stories that the kids are telling themselves—or someone else—at one particular moment. Their parents would tell the same stories differently; so would their siblings, their teachers, their buddies, the cops. And the kids modify their own stories as time goes by; Pete Hamilton's accounts of what he did with the gun he stole from his grandfather vary over the years as his ways of explaining himself to himself change. These are the tellers' ideas about their histories and the uses they make of them.

So in these narratives "truth" follows a private logic, not a consensual one. Jeff Mosse, one of the boys in the contrast group, spent a year and a half at High Valley, first as an inpatient and then in a halfway house. He was fifteen and a sophomore in high school when he nearly crippled himself by shattering the bones of his right foot with a rifle shot. His father had killed himself violently not long before.

Jeff is a young man of superior intelligence, thoughtful and articulate. His narrative has two central themes: the psychological disruption that resulted from his father's suicide, and an angry conviction that his mother never gave him the "free-flowing," "unconditional" love he needed to feel worthy and valued. A countercurrent in his narrative suggests that even to Jeff things aren't quite as simple as that. Sometimes he lets himself suspect that his feeling of never having been loved enough might have as much to do with his own personality as with his mother's. He knows that since early childhood he has cherished a mysterious and pleasurable investment in remaining at cross-purposes with her and foiling her efforts to be close to him. He remembers setting up tests for her to fail—not telling her when he was upset, for example, and waiting silently for her to notice. On the occasions that she didn't, he'd get angrier and angrier until he turned to violence, breaking his favorite possessions. (This is exactly what he was doing when he attacked himself with the gun, only that time he turned his rage upon his own body.) He knows that his mother was strictly taught by her own parents that a lady is always cool and distant, and he admits that her reserve is probably more a habitual style of expressing herself than a measure of her caring. He knows that he himself is intolerant of emotion and wary of intimacy. But none of this changes the way he *feels*. His mother tries desperately and guiltily to make up for her "failures," but to the anguished frustration of both of them it doesn't make any difference. Jeff has already lost one parent traumatically, and his belief that the other one never "really" loved him is very painful to him, yet he clings to it. He doesn't look for a deeper understanding of his relationship with her—a larger context that might include his ambivalence as well as her weaknesses. His mother's "coldness," like his father's death, is how he explains to himself what he feels.

Reading the Narratives

As we read the narratives, we looked for hints of processes that might enable the turnarounds of resilience to occur—attitudes or skills present in young people in incipient form *even before their resilience is apparent.* Those are very different from the sorts of accomplishments by which adults are usually judged, and we had to keep in mind that resilience and maturity are not the same thing. Youth and inexperience are unmistakable in the narratives of all the High Valley kids. They make rash decisions. Their fantasies are grandiose, their criticisms harsh. After Pete gets out of the Center, he spends several years trying to establish himself as a desperado. Rachel marries at sixteen. Billy drops out of a first-rate high school. But rashness, grandiosity, and a certain absolutism are markers of adolescence, not of psycho-pathology. The kids' anger, which is pretty intense at times, isn't necessarily inconsistent with resilience either. On the contrary, the capacity to tolerate anger is a sine qua non of emotional ma-turity, and the patients at the Children's Center had plenty to be angry about. But in the resilient kids, aggression is contained and tempered over time. Pete's murderous fury at his father eventually evolves into an irritated but compassionate accep-tance of Mr. Hamilton's limitations and his "awkward love." Billy's rage at his controlling mother subsides into recognition of the burdens she bore and a friendly willingness to help. In the resilient kids, self-assertion and the communicating and negoti-ating skills that go with it gradually replace less useful forms of aggression—violence, revenge, self-destructiveness, defensiveness, blame. Human development doesn't stop at twenty-one, and the most competent young adult in the world has a lifetime of psychological work ahead.

So we were not particularly expecting to find "successful adaptation" or "competence" per se in the teenagers' narratives. What did emerge in our analysis, however, were attitudes that appeared to be harbingers, or forerunners, of the short list of protective factors on which resilience studies have converged: according to Masten, "connections to competent and caring adults; cognitive and self-regulation skills and positive views of self; and the motivation to be effective in the environment."[2] We are hoping to show practically how these abstract factors manifest themselves in speech and behavior. Connections to competent and caring adults are more likely to develop when such connections are valued; cognitive and self-regulation skills and positive views of the self depend strongly on the ability to confront and deal with what one feels; the motivation to be effective in the environment requires the belief that effectiveness is possible. So we have chosen to approach these factors a bit more concretely than Masten does, and we will concentrate on three themes—relatedness, agency, and reflectiveness—which we found tightly woven into the narratives of the resilient teens.

Reflectiveness is curiosity about one's thoughts, feelings, and motivations, and the willingness to try to make sense of them and handle them responsibly. *Agency* is the conviction that what one does matters, that one can intervene effectively in one's own life. *Relatedness*—engagement and interaction with others—may be highly valued even when there are no helpful others around, and this may predispose youngsters to be able to use supportive connections when they are available. These are themes that can be followed in the content of the stories. So can the structural attribute of *narrative coherence*—the quality of attention, organization, focus, and responsiveness that characterizes both well-processed emotional experience and well-told stories.

HERE'S AN EXAMPLE of how these themes look in one narrative. Pete Hamilton, in his first interview, is talking about the problems that brought him to the hospital. He stole a gun; he's been kicked out of half a dozen schools; he's fucked up all his life. The interviewer wants to know why he's been so difficult. "I just didn't like it," Pete says. "I wasn't going to work with it."

That attitude has just earned Pete a long stretch on a locked psychiatric ward, and brought him uncomfortably close to imprisonment. There's plenty of defiant stubbornness there. But it's not *only* defiant stubbornness. Note that Pete hasn't blamed anyone else for his troubles. He speaks as the motive force in his own life, and he assumes full responsibility for his behavior. He can look at himself honestly and think about what he sees. He can *rethink,* too: from his vantage point at High Valley, Pete can look back on behavior that at the time seemed to him like a good idea and reframe it as "fucking up." That's important, because without flexibility, growth is impossible. Later on, this reframing will itself be challenged as the adult Pete recognizes at last how constrained he really was by the frightening circumstances of his childhood. Still, he would rather take the blame for things he couldn't control than feel helpless. He is no victim.

Pete doesn't talk much about relationships at first; he has other things on his mind. But he makes very strong and intense connections with his interviewer and other receptive adults within his purview. He's looking for a fighting chance to feel safe—in fact, "a fighting chance" is the organizing metaphor of his narrative, and it induces him to think in ways that potentially lead out of helplessness and into something better.

THESE THREE INTERESTS—in reflection, agency, and relationship—are intricately intertwined. The growth of one encourages the flowering of the others; to suppress one is to stunt the rest. Honestly recognizing your feelings as your own is a prerequisite to taking responsibility for them and acting effectively upon them. Unless you take responsibility, it's hard to feel like a person whose actions can make a difference. Responsible behavior is both a cause and a result of these skills; so are humor and curiosity and persistence—and good relationships, which reward emotional growth but depend on it too, and which are one of the biggest and most important mastery challenges of all. Reflection, agency, and relatedness are seeds of change.

Sandy Carlson's breakup with an old boyfriend contributes to the suicidal behavior for which she is hospitalized. A year later she describes her current relationship with him: "I get little pangs, like, you know, maybe we could get back together. Then I just pull my head together and say no, it's not possible. He hasn't changed, and I have. . . . He has to be tougher than anybody else. His whole family's like that."

In this brief narrative, Sandy reflects on her feelings and Paul's nature, looking back on their old selves with tolerant goodwill. She accepts her longing for him, but she knows that her needs are different now, and so she chooses not to act upon it. She is reconsidering a once-central relationship in the light of her new experience as master of her own life.

Billy, who can't stand the stifling domesticity in which his mother's neediness entraps him, loves the idea of a buccaneer's existence. Still, he refuses to be seduced into the local bike-stealing ring that is proving very lucrative to his neighborhood pals; the stakes are too high. He doesn't want to end up in Juvie—that is, in the grip of the juvenile justice system—even if it costs him some money. He knows he's risking his buddies' disapproval, but he manages to convey his feelings to them in a way that maintains their respect. His narrative of that decision is a perfect miniature saga of temptation resisted, and in its dénouement (the acceptance of the other boys) it also reflects a significant level of relational skill.

Note the differnce between Billy's decision and this one by Charlie Sanders, from the contrast group. Charlie talks about the last time he did drugs: "I got in trouble with the boy who started me off on drugs. . . . He just called me and this time conned me into it. . . . I thought he was just being a friend, but then I didn't think twice, really." Charlie "didn't realize," "didn't think." He takes no responsibility for his own decisions; he lets another kid "con" him even when he knows him to be trouble. Billy thinks; he opts out of the bike ring; he doesn't end up in Juvie. Charlie doesn't think; he succumbs to drugs; he gets into trouble again and again; he ends up on probation.

These distinctions are not absolute. Charlie's comment that "I didn't think" could be just an excuse, but it could also be an initial act of reflection. If it isn't, though, Charlie's story is going to narrow his opportunities and diminish his freedom of determination. Billy's story keeps his options open.

RACHEL IS PURPOSELESS in her early days at the Center. She doesn't think about anything; she has no interests. She acts as if her behavior has nothing to do with her—it just happens and then it's gone. But one day she notices that she isn't quite the same as she was when she arrived, and for the first time she sees herself as a person for whom change is possible. This is a huge reframing and a psychological watershed that organizes her thinking in a completely new way. She no longer thinks of herself as helpless. She learns to reflect, the better to know what she wants. She establishes goals and takes action to achieve them. She assumes responsibility for the consequences; when she has a setback she goes back, rethinks, and tries again. From a position of almost complete passivity she comes to understand herself as an agent, and from there she bends her efforts persistently and ever more effectively toward establishing a life that makes sense to her.

Jeff resists change. To the great detriment of his happiness and his relationships, he holds fast to his view of himself as a boy insufficiently loved by his mother—even though he distrusts it. He knows, for instance, that he enjoyed childhood occasions of being sick because "you get to feel sorry for yourself." But he has no curiosity about what role the wish to feel sorry for himself might play in his psychological life. Rachel's curiosity and her openness to change allow her to rewrite her troubled history. So far, Jeff has remained trapped in his.

PETE DESCRIBES IN HIS first interview how he felt when living with his depressed and furious father. "I was scared shitless of him and I wouldn't say boo. . . . I was almost always depressed. . . . Sad, because I didn't like living there, you know? . . . I was pulling a lot of really stupid, stupid shit, and I think one of the reasons for that was because I just heard that I was going to be there for a third year." Looking back on what he was feeling then, Pete describes a close relationship between his feelings and his behavior. As he gets older his emotional awareness becomes more detailed and sophisticated, but even very early on he is doing his best to make sense of the interplay between what he feels and what he does.

Vick Sansom is one of the contrast-group girls. Her parents brought her to the Children's Center when she was twelve and a half because she had been acting extremely fearful, asking all the time about acts of self-destruction and causes of death. She's two years younger than Pete, but that doesn't account for the difference between their accounts of their admissions. Why did she come to High Valley? the interviewer asks.

"Because some old shrink guy told me I had to. . . . School sent me."

Why did they send you?

"I don't know."

Do you have any idea? Did anything go wrong during that time?

"No."

That's kind of amazing, that they would send you here with everything being okay. Did you want to come?

"No."

Why did you?

"Because somebody told me I had to."

Did they explain to you why they thought you should come?

"No."

They just said, Vick, you have to come?

"Mm-hmm. I didn't know I was coming until the day I came."

How did it happen?

"I was staying at Carrington Hospital, and my father told me I had to come."

You were in a hospital already? How long had you been there?

"For about three days."

I see. Why were you there?

"I was resting."

From what?

"I don't know. Somebody said I was resting."

Vick knows more than she's letting on, of course. Still, her passivity and indifference contrast sharply with Pete's intense analytic interest in his own pre-admission history. She doesn't care about the concrete details of how she got to High Valley, let alone the feelings and experiences that brought them into being.

Magda Bruno, also from the contrast group, was fifteen when she was admitted. She was acting very wild and talking in desperate ways about doing herself harm. Her parents had divorced and her mother had moved out, leaving Magda with a lot of responsibility for her brother and her father, a needy man embittered by his wife's departure. In his hurt cynicism he was fiercely discouraging of Magda's age-appropriate interest in boys. She recognizes this and will talk about it, but that's as far as she'll go. Her father's the one who should be in the hospital, she says. "I'm as normal as any other teenager, and I got put here."

Well, how did you get here? Who made that decision?

"My father. . . . For a year he's been telling me I'm mixed up. And so then he gets everyone else to tell me that I'm mixed up. . . . I don't understand this."

What did they mean by mixed up?

"I don't know. I don't know."

But you believed them. So what do *you* see as mixed up?

"I had to believe them. If that's all you heard for a year, you'd believe too. Shit," she goes on, "I'm not like any of these kids. . . . I thought my father was the only person with problems. Then I come here and *everyone's* got them. . . . Theirs are worse than mine. I don't care."

Rachel is also powerfully struck by her encounter with the other kids' problems, but ultimately she finds it reassuring—she's not the only one. Magda doesn't make such optimistic use of her situation. This is another characteristic difference between the two groups. And while she's less passive than Vick and more forthcoming, Magda is just as incurious. Three years later she still doesn't know why she'd been sent to High Valley. "I think it was all because they said I was just a real nut or something, because I was going out with somebody so much older than me. And they thought I was all screwed up because of my parents being divorced. When actually it was them who was screwed up. . . . I was growing up, I was an adolescent, that was it. . . . All my friends have gone through it and they are normal— *they* didn't have to be sent away."

Magda seldom looks further than her own resentments, and when she does she can't rouse herself to take constructive action on her own behalf. As an adult, she talks about how anxious she feels living in her boyfriend's house, knowing that she might be kicked out. "When [we] fight or something, I'll just always say, 'Well, I'm just going to leave.' I don't want—because I'm always worried that someone's going to leave me for some reason. That's the thing that has stuck with me probably, and I'm really trying hard to get over that, but it's not as easy as I thought. And like I use it for an excuse and that's tough, but I'll do it."

She is articulating an insight that eludes Rachel for a long time: that she's afraid of being left. But once Rachel grasps this, she purposefully sets about increasing her emotional independence. Magda, several years older, knows that she would be better off dealing with her fear directly; but discovering that it's not so easy to act on the knowledge, she sticks to her old technique of being the first to leave. She knows she's evading responsibility—"I use this for an excuse"—but "that's tough." And she doesn't require honesty of herself. "I always want to be the first one to say, when we're fighting, that I would go first, so that I don't seem like I would be rejected."

Magda is defiant in her refusal to change. Jeff's stance is a futile "That's just the way I am"—he perceives himself as helpless. But while Vick and Magda are passive in the face of their demons, Jeff is holding actively to an old story. He knows he does it; he even calls it a "mental fallback." "I tend to . . . avoid getting committed to people, for whatever reasons from my childhood. I don't want to use those as excuses, but maybe I guess that's just the way I am because my parents were both, just weren't, were a little, weren't that open, loving." Like Magda, he knows it's an excuse. Like Magda, he doesn't challenge it.

HONEST REFLECTION CAN be painful. In Rory's early days at the Center, the interviewer comments that he seems to see all problems as outside himself: it's the hospital, it's his parents, and so on. "No, I have my own problems," Rory interrupts.

What are they? asks the interviewer.

"I don't look at them. They're just there."

Jeff is more articulate than Rory at first, and his fluency highlights some of the more subtle difficulties of reflection. When he's anxious, the connections between what he says, what he thinks, and how he feels get very shaky. In his first interview, he talks about why the staff on the unit didn't trust him when he arrived. "I hurt myself before I came in."

What did you do?

"I almost shot my foot off," Jeff says. "I didn't mean to shoot myself that bad, but it came out a lot worse. I had to get—My bones got broken, you know. I didn't really mean to, but they got hurt a lot worse than I had planned to and they didn't trust me at all."

A year later he's still thinking about this. He didn't like being trapped on the unit. "I couldn't leave, you know, and I had to have dinner on a tray. I couldn't go to the caf or anything." As he pursues his remembered frustration, it's clear that there's a disjunction between what he "understands" in his head and what he grasps with his feelings. He says that he can see why people would worry about him after he hurt himself so badly, and why they would restrict him so as to keep an eye on him. But he can't, really. "If you had nothing else to go by but the fact that I hurt myself, I suppose you could call me suicidal. But I didn't really feel suicidal at all. . . . I went there expecting to be able to go to everything—the art studio and stuff like that, school and what not—and no matter how much I talked to my doctor, she wouldn't change it. . . . I could have gone back home the next day, and now I am here in this locked-up place and I can't leave."

Jeff can describe his self-destructive behavior, but he seems not to have any sense of the feelings behind it. Nor does he "get" the horror and concern that responsible adults feel when a fifteen-year-old (whose father recently killed himself) makes a serious attempt to shoot off an extremity. His capacity for reflection stops where feelings begin, and all of his thinking does little to improve his emotional grasp. "You just think about [feelings] so much that you can't really—You just don't let them flow and let yourself feel what you're feeling when you try to think about them."

In fact, Jeff isn't really interested in what goes on inside people, himself or anyone else. He's been preoccupied with the meaning of his mother's behavior toward him for his entire thinking life, yet when asked as a young adult why his parents might have behaved as they did during his childhood, he dismisses the question with a scornful laugh. "That's an almost ridiculous question, you know? People are people. I don't know. You mean a *reason?*" He dismisses in the same way the question about what he's learned from his own history. "I don't know—I could probably pick something up. It's such a crazy question, too." Mostly Jeff wishes he could forget. But he can't allow himself to. "I wish it wasn't an issue. I wish it was just a few feelings and whatnot." Alas, his wish can't make it so.

Magda, too, would rather not care; her alternatives to reflection when the going gets rough are alcohol and pot. Where do you turn when you're upset? the interviewer asks the twenty-five-year-old Magda. "I cry a lot for a while. And then it gets me to feel better, you know, if I smoke a joint. Sometimes that makes me just forget about it and then I don't care. Sit back, I don't care, I'll think about it later." She doesn't.

But when Rachel realizes that she is doing things on automatic pilot, blocking thoughts out of her head, she tackles the problem head on. "I have to start thinking more," she says. "Because I really wasn't thinking that much. I was just doing things —and that, I think, was wrong."

ATTITUDES CAN CHANGE, however. Rory's do. His skill with feelings is just about nil while he's at the Center. The interviewer asks him how he's feeling, and Rory says that he can't label feelings at all. "All I can label are sadness, happy, and angry."

What are you now? asks the interviewer.

"What am I right now???" He has no idea.

Together they identify a "craving" feeling, which Rory understands concretely to mean that it's time for a smoke. The interviewer offers to explore with him the possibility that the longing might be about something other than cigarettes. Is Rory feeling any of those *other* feelings, perhaps, like happiness or anger or sadness?

Rory is completely out of his depth, but he's fascinated. *"At once?"* he asks.

I don't know, says the interviewer. Do you ever have these feelings at once?

"Oh, no," Rory says. "I thought they just came one at a time." So far he can handle feelings only in action, or in cigarettes. Ambivalence isn't on his radar—yet.

A FIERCE PROTECTION of their own agency is characteristic of the resilient kids. If they don't have a sense of themselves as movers at first, they claim it passionately as soon as they grasp the possibility. Pete got hold of this early, although he often used it in alarming ways in his efforts to feel less helpless. But Rachel felt for a long time like a pawn, first of her parents and then of the hospital. Her family thought she was sullen, but she later says of herself that she was lost. "I never did anything. . . . I didn't do anything." A year out of the hospital, she recalls the helplessness of her post-discharge days and the epiphany that changed her life: "I [had been] calling all the people up here and asking them for help. Like, 'What do I do? What do I do?' And then I started thinking, 'They're not going to do anything for me.' So I started doing it myself." Rachel's ways of working toward the future, like Pete's, are scary sometimes. But they're *hers*, and she learns from all of them.

Vick, too, arrives at High Valley unable to imagine changing her circumstances, and a year out of the hospital she still doesn't really know what it was all about.

Boy, that must be hard, the interviewer says. To be at a place like this without knowing why. Did you ever ask?

"No," says Vick.

The interviewer tries very hard to engage her interest. He offers a lot of different ways of thinking about it, and even some comments about how he might feel in a situation like that. But all Vick says is, "I don't remember."

You don't remember, or you don't want to talk about it?

"I don't remember anything. I don't want to. . . . So I blocked it out."

Why?

"I didn't like it."

She's been in two psychiatric hospitals, yet she has no curiosity about why. She keeps her attention very narrowly focused on what's right under her nose. Her actions are *re*actions. "This weekend I went home on pass and burned my hand trying to make cookies," she says her first year. "I touched a hot pan."

And what happened then, says the interviewer, once you burned yourself?

"I sat there screaming for ten minutes."

Did anyone come to help you?

"My mother."

What did she do?

"She turned the cold water on. Told me to come stick my hand under it."

This is not the behavior of a person accustomed to taking charge of her own life. But it could be that that burn really did seem as unprecedented to Vick as she makes it sound. She may not have noticed earlier ones enough to learn anything from them. There are many aspects of her experience that she *doesn't* notice enough to learn from, or give much thought to changing.

Her style is to opt out. She's a master of avoidance, and even her actions have a passive quality. For a while she does her best to get suspended from school. Why? "Because I don't like school very much. And I wanted a little vacation." She doesn't like to work, and her way of handling pique at her science teacher is to skip class. So by the time she's twenty-three, her cherished idea of becoming a nurse has come to naught. This wasn't an idle dream, either. Vick has spent years as an expert and confident candy striper, and loves taking care of people and animals. She seemed well on her way to a nursing career when her derailment occurred. She'd like to revive the plan, but she hasn't, because— she says—it's too noisy to study with kids in the house. But every time the her baby reaches a certain age, Vick gets pregnant again. She has five children now, and the goal she most convincingly expresses is to be a grandmother. This is a dismaying ambition to hear from a twenty-three-year-old, as it gives her nothing to work toward over her adult life, and its realization depends entirely on the activities of other people.

Passivity and action without agency are common among the contrast-group kids. Charlie in an early interview says he needs money. So what do you do? the interviewer asks. "I don't do nothin'. There's nothin' I can do about it." When he does do something, he acts with little purpose and less hope, like going out drinking after a fight with his girlfriend. "It seemed to make things better, I thought. Yah, I felt more relaxed."

But a powerful sense of agency doesn't always make for smooth sailing either. For a long time after Rachel starts charting her own course, she hits every rock in the channel. Her decision to conceive a child at sixteen is really alarming. The other resilient kids have their moments, too, and so do plenty of teenagers who never set foot in a psychiatric hospital. Still, the belief that one can influence things is an important hedge against helplessness and hopelessness, and an inducement to master the skills (emotional, relational, practical) of a satisfying life.

EFFECTIVE AGENCY DEPENDS heavily upon reflection. Just about all children look for ways to maximize their clout. When nothing else is available they fall back on whining, and any cagey kid with a little ingenuity can do much, much better than that. *Really* cagey kids understand that it's just as important to avoid the things that minimize your clout, the ones that get you ostracized or hospitalized or locked up. But many of the kids at the Center haven't grasped this. They're too impulsive to anticipate consequences, and they're not reflective enough to contain their impulses. The resilient kids, on the other hand, are looking hard for the points of leverage from which they'll be able to move the world. When can you change something and when can't you? When do you keep trying and when do you cut your losses? They immerse themselves in questions like these and modify their behavior accordingly, always keeping in mind their two prime considerations: *This is what I want. How can I get it?*

They learn to tolerate delay, for example. To be effective, you sometimes have to give up an immediate pleasure in the service of a long-term goal. The contrast-group kids have a hard time with this. Magda as an adult wishes that she had money of her own; she knows that her financial dependency greatly exacerbates her fear of being abandoned. "I feel like, 'Oh my God, he's my boss, he pays me, I live here, he pays my rent.' You know, I wish that I could be a little bit more independent. But then I always want to keep my own money to go spend on clothes, so I don't know which one I'd rather . . ." She giggles and trails off. So far she's remained dependent, and she has no plans for ten years down the road. "Usually I don't even know what I'm going to do tomorrow."

Vick as an adolescent worries about life after graduation, but she doesn't think in terms of acquiring skills that will increase her confidence. There's a melancholy cast to her wish to acquire a pet raccoon. It would be happy in a cage, Vick says. "Because it is not out there, and it doesn't have to look for its own food and water." But cages aren't for Billy or Sandy, no matter how much foraging they may have to do. Ten years later, asked if she has dreams for the future, Vick says that she hasn't thought that far ahead. But the others are always thinking about what's around the next bend.

SIXTEEN-YEAR-OLD Rory has been skipping classes. This is a violation of his probation, and the vice-principal is getting ready to turn him in. "That's a *school???*" he complains. "They're supposed to *help* you, and the guy's trying to screw me up the ass really bad. And I said, 'Well, if you do, that's gonna cause problems.' And then the next day a letter was sent to my parents saying that I threatened his life and the principal's life, and I did nothing of the sort."

Okay, so Rory didn't threaten the guy's life. But he takes no responsibility for the threat he *did* make, or for skipping the classes he needs for probation, or for being on probation in the first place. He doesn't acknowledge, probably can't see, that he contributes anything to the situations that enrage him. So—for the time being—he is condemned to a cycle of getting into trouble, lashing out blindly against a perceived enemy, and ending up in deeper trouble still. "I . . . don't think I have a problem," Rory says. "My problem is High Valley."

Pete gets into big trouble when he's caught with a gun in school. But he doesn't blame anyone else. He knows he did it, and he knows *why* he did—to feel less helpless against his violent father. That assumption of responsibility makes a big difference. While Rory's cycle makes him more vulnerable every time it repeats, Pete can work on breaking out of his. He already knows that his aggression is his own, so he doesn't have to get angrier and waste his energy fighting with other people about whose fault it is. He can think about what to do with his feelings instead. He gets better at sticking up for himself in constructive ways, and eventually discovers that he doesn't have to be on red alert all the time. He relaxes a little, and soon he has some attention to spare for other things—like what he wants to do with his life. As his mastery of his ferocity becomes more certain, he worries less that he'll hurt the people he loves. Relationship becomes a possibility for Pete again. But as long as Rory sees himself as the victim of other people's efforts to screw him, he's stuck; there's nothing he can do about all the anger in his life until he can recognize the part of it that is his own.

The resilient kids grasp very quickly that if they don't take responsibility for their own behavior, other people will. In Sandy's first session, the interviewer asks her how she gets anger out of her system, and she pithily says that she doesn't—not at the Children's Center, anyway. Four points are not for her. Not a sophisticated piece of anger management, perhaps, but it's beyond many of the Center kids; if it weren't, the QRs and restraints wouldn't be necessary. Charlie isn't as good as Sandy at keeping out of harm's way. A year after discharge he's picked up for drunken disorderliness and put on probation again. He was drinking the last time they picked him up, the interviewer notes. Did he realize that he was heading for trouble? No, Charlie says, because he was drunk at the time. The interviewer suggests to him that maybe getting drunk was a factor in the getting-into-trouble process.

"Yeah, I thought of that."

But you weren't able to stop drinking? Or you didn't care?

"No," Charlie says. "I wanted to drink."

THE BIG ISSUE for most of the kids is rage. Many can handle it only by acting on it, and this is constantly getting them into hot water. Even the extremely passive Vick acts on anger. "There's this lady I don't like, and [one Halloween] I painted all her windows black, so she thought it was morning and slept late and got fired from work." Wow! How did you feel? the interviewer asks.

"I laughed for a week." Several years after her discharge, she destroys the mailbox of the psychiatrist who referred her to High Valley. Boy, that's a long time to be mad, isn't it? "He'll get over it," Vick says. Yes, *he'll* get over it, the interviewer agrees. But will you? Will you ever stop being mad at him, do you think? "Uh-uh."

When the boyfriend of eighteen-year-old Magda tells her that he wants to date other people, she vandalizes his brand-new car, his pride and joy. Outraged, he takes her to small claims court. She has to pay damages for months, but she has no doubt about her own bottom line: "I owed this to you, you know, for hurting me."

Pete admits to having broken another kid's toe in his misspent youth—he stomped on it to keep his chief rival out of a race. But by the time he gets to High Valley he's working hard on self-restraint, and working out his feelings in gruesome fantasies instead of destructive actions.

ACKNOWLEDGING YOUR PART in what happens to you is one aspect of responsibility; doing something about it is the other. Magda has just been fired from her job. "I got canned . . . because I didn't wake up one morning and go to work." Just one morning and they let you go?? the interviewer asks. Well, not exactly, Magda says. When they called her up to remind her, she just turned over and went to sleep again. "And they just said, 'Forget it.' . . . I was sort of disappointed."

A couple of years later she's still disinclined to relinquish short-term pleasures ("I'm a flirt, I admit it—I can't help it"), even when she knows they're not in her best interest. She elaborates this theme progressively as she gets older, and at twenty-five she gives the most detailed version of all. This time, the problem is her tendency to be "too honest." There's a girl at work who's "just not really into hygiene, I guess. You know. I just couldn't stand it anymore, so one night I just really told her, you know, 'Don't you ever take a bath?' and stuff. I really felt sort of bad after, but—" Is that how you told her? the interviewer interpolates. Like that? "I said, 'How often do you take a bath?' She said, 'Once every two days.' I said, 'Well, you should try it once every day.' No—first I asked her if she used the same bath water." She laughs.

"It's not like I don't like to be that way," Magda goes on. "It's just that I get myself into trouble so much." She knows that she doesn't really want to be any different, that she enjoyed putting her colleague down, and that the issue is not too much honesty—it's too little kindness. But in calling it "honesty" she evades psychological responsibility for her impulses and frees herself to act upon them—a perfect example of the way in which narrative can influence behavior.

Jeff's narratives influence his behavior, too. For Jeff, thinking is often a way of *not* knowing what is going on. He focuses on abstractions that divert his attention from his own experience. So he gains nothing from his ruminations, and uses this to justify his contention that thinking about "psychology" isn't worth the trouble. That same smokescreen quality shows up in the way he handles responsibility—for not having friends, for example. "I don't know anybody that really does [have friends] in adolescence." That explanation relieves his anxiety, but at the expense of his sense of efficacy. Having attributed his loneliness to something beyond his control, he's not motivated to do anything about it. He takes a similar view of the depression for which he was admitted: "It's a biological, chemical disease." He knows that that's not the whole story—"There's got to be something to cause it"—but that's the part he concentrates on. "Once you get depressed, you sort of can't, you know, control it, really. . . . I mean, it becomes almost a disease."

By the time he's grown, Jeff can clearly see how much he's losing by his "rational" and "academic" approach to feelings. But he still prefers external explanations to internal ones. He doesn't think about heavy emotional stuff, he says, because his best friend Fred doesn't want to hear it. "And I wouldn't either, if I were him. . . . Life is now. So I avoid any of those family and past things, my emotional life. So. That's about it. I wouldn't tell him any secrets, either." Jeff doesn't ask himself why he's chosen a best friend who forecloses (if indeed Fred does) on exactly the subjects he claims he'd most like to be able to share. Jeff is an extremely intelligent young man. His powers of thought are prodigious, but he can't always use them on his own behalf. Narratives that deny responsibility (it's chemical, it's adolescence) and agency (you can't really help it) also deny him the opportunity to cope.

ADULT LIVES DON'T RUN WELL on childhood convictions about how the world works—that you get what you want by crying, that thoughts can kill, that vacuum cleaners can swallow you up. Early ideas about emotion can be equally perilous, and they're harder to spot. Yet the capacity to reframe them can be lifesaving, especially for children who have grown up with their self-esteem under attack.

Rachel has been out of the hospital for a year, and her great new awareness of change now pervades her life. For a while, she feels at a disadvantage because of her neediness. Then she notices that she's not the only needy one. Eureka! She's not permanently one-down anymore; she can offer other people support in return for what they give her. That small insight makes a big difference.

Sandy worries at first about what people think about her hospitalization. She knows there were rumors when she suddenly disappeared from school. "I figured they'd all think I was crazy." But a year of wider experience teaches her that her hometown was very conventional, and that broader and less provincial people don't think that a person is a "sick loony" because she's been a hospital.

Billy revises his view of himself after he earns admission to a competitive high school. "It surprised me. I was smarter than I thought I was."

Rachel and Sandy and Billy come to these reframings of their self-image early. But the kids are not all so open to change. Jeff is the most articulate about how hard emotional flexibility can be. He acknowledges in his second year that his mother will never be able to prove her love to his satisfaction, but he holds on to the struggle nonetheless. "It's like I'm sick, it is almost a disease, almost a mental fallback, you know, and you can't really try to make it better." At twenty-five, he gives a longer version of the same dilemma, adding: "I didn't think of it in those terms when I was young, but that's what it seems like now." But he *did* think of it in those terms. In fact, he talks about it exactly as if he were still the five-year-old who couldn't bring himself to ask for his mother's attention. "I have great expectations for every single person in the world," he says as a grownup, "and I'm usually let down." He can't mourn the perfect mother he never had and move on to more fulfilling relationships. He can't rethink his view of his mother or of himself with regard to her. He can't find a more compassionate context for the mutual pain of the child who needed his mother and the mother who couldn't satisfy her child's need.

This kind of flypaper situation is not for Billy, who at sixteen tries one last time to connect with his abandoning father. His father can't do it, and Billy decides he's had enough. "The hell with him," he says. He cuts his losses, goes home, and picks up his life. When the time comes, he sets out to be the best father he possibly can to his little stepson, keeping his own experience in mind as a vivid counterexample.

BUT EVEN ATTITUDES about change can change, especially in teenagers. Rory and Charlie hang onto old ideas for a long time. They struggle with fears and anger that they handle over and over in their same old self-defeating ways. But when they come back as adults, the resemblance between them is gone and Rory is sounding much more like Rachel than like Charlie. He now sees his youth in the light of his grief over the death of a brother, which he suffered essentially alone. Much more aware of the inner source of his pain, he's no longer fruitlessly raging against the whole rest of the world. He's relinquished some of his old anger, and found a more comprehensive and kinder understanding of his younger self. Where once he insisted that "my problem is High Valley," now he says with understanding and regret, "I—did dumb things to forget."

SKILLS IN REFLECTION and responsibility help us to think accurately about others as well as ourselves; they're solid foundations for relationships. But relationship has themes of its own —ways of thinking not about individual persons, but about connections *among* persons and among relationships. Perhaps the most important theme about relationships, and a central divide between the resilient kids and the others, is how much they matter.

Relationships are endlessly complicated and fundamentally uncontrollable. They demand patience, tolerance, and a conviction that all the trouble will be worth it. That is not an obvious conclusion for people whose early relationships have been inadequate or traumatic. Yet the resilient kids have this faith, and even when they are preoccupied with other things, even when they are fearfully or angrily avoiding other people, relationship is always on their minds.

Billy is wild to escape his appointed role as his mother's wife. All he wants is to be out of there, living out a twelve-year-old's macho fantasies. Still he notices, and ponders, the different ways his mother and his grandmother wield their influence: one dictates; the other persuades. Billy has no trouble discerning which way is better, and why. Pete leaves home at sixteen out of fear that his rage threatens his mother. The whole time he's away he works on that fear, trying to find the crucial balance between being dangerously vulnerable himself and being dangerous to the people he loves. Whatever disappointments the resilient kids encounter, they do not give up on relationships permanently. And they keep trying to get them right. Even when he's enraged at his father, Pete tries not to hurt him. One day at High Valley, when his father's been giving him an especially miserable time, Pete is sorely tempted to refuse to go out on pass with him. All he has to do is say no. "But I didn't say it," he says. "It would hurt his feelings. He's a very feelingful person, as much of an asshole as he is sometimes."

Billy's reaction to his father's abandonment is to look for relationships with people who want them more than his father did. Jeff's reaction is never to try again with anyone else. "When he killed himself, . . . that sort of has made me leery of opening that up again." Magda enjoys her friendships, but she's careless with them. When there's tension with her best friend Stell, she says at twenty-five, "I don't do anything. I wait for her to call me and tell me what's wrong. And then I'll listen to her. And if I think she's right, then I'll say I'm sorry." She giggles. "And if I don't think she's right, then I'll hang up on her."

For a long time Rory, like Pete, wants nothing to do with his critical and abusive father. He feels so strongly about it that he refuses to go to family therapy sessions, a very serious violation of Children's Center rules, and punishable by restriction and loss of privileges. In his first interview, Rory says that he's begun to talk to his father again. But "that's only so they'll think I love my father, and let me out of this place. I don't know what they want out of me. If I knew that, I would have gave it to them." Pete has an instinctive understanding of ambivalence, but Rory can't see that he might have more than one feeling at a time (his old bugbear) about the old man, or that the old man might have complex feelings about him.

At least not yet. Rory's first-year statement about the limits of his reflective capacities—"All I can label are sadness, happy, and angry"—is in itself an act of reflection, and a meaningful one. His wonder at the idea that a person can have more than one feeling at a time is a real, if rudimentary, engagement in psychological exploration. Rory is inexperienced, but he's not indifferent. Among our sample kids, he's the embodiment of the theoretical construct that resilience and its precursors are not a yes-or-no attribute.

For a while Pete avoids closeness deliberately, feeling, like Jeff, that it brings nothing but trouble. But in the midst of an anger and unhappiness so pervasive that even his idealized mother falls under its cloud, he finds himself noticing that connection can be a hedge against the very experience that he most dreads: his savage rage. He reports in an interview what happened one day when he and his mother drove together to a family session and he tried to talk to her about how he was feeling. "You know, you don't have to agree with it. You don't even have to like it—just listen," he said to her. "She did. And so when I got here, I was much calmer. . . . Maybe I'll be friendlier next year."

Charlie has no such sanguine expectations. "Two of my sisters are already divorced," he says. "About five people just on my street just got divorced." You think you'd end up divorced? asks the interviewer. "Yeah," says Charlie. He's decided that he'll never marry. He can't hope to feel different in a year, and he can't imagine being able to influence his marital fate.

Once the resilient kids do start to seek relationships, their anticipatory work stands them in good stead. They reflect on others as carefully as they do on themselves, and they reflect on themselves in connection with others. How do you act in a relationship? What is too close, and what is not close enough? What feels good and bad? What works and what doesn't? What do you do when something goes wrong?

Sandy observes that her friendships change as she does. The boyfriend she has at sixteen is someone she couldn't have valued before, and this tells her something about herself as well as about the other person. But Charlie, at twenty-five, doesn't see his friendships changing at all. "They're all the same. . . . Most of them I knew since first grade, too." He seems pleased with his consistency, and while there's nothing wrong with old friends, this is another area in which Charlie's life seems to have gone into permanent contraction.

Rory hangs very tough for the first two years, but in the third he makes an unexpected admission: he's been paying attention to the interviews. "Just come and talk—I see you once a year, not gonna do any damage to me. . . . Also getting trust—I can tell somebody something and they can't screw me." Despite his worry that talking is dangerous, he has noticed that the interviewer has been safe so far—in fact, Rory seems to be hinting at some vague satisfaction with the situation. And, not coincidentally, he reveals that there's a second new thing on his mind this year: girlfriends. They're a dicey proposition, Rory says. "They learn a lot about you, and they also know that something's wrong, and if you don't want to tell them, they keep at you. You just get to the point where, 'Ah, shut up.' Get into fights and everything, just like in the family." What's the problem? the interviewer wants to know. Why not be more open? "Just the idea of getting hurt. Just can't have it happen anymore."

But a few minutes later he contradicts himself. "I just want somebody I can get close to, go out with for a long time, and finally break down and tell them about me, somebody else to know about me besides me." And having perceived and expressed one utterly fundamental ambivalence about relationship, the kid who used to wish that feelings happened only one at a time goes on to recognize—and marvel at—another. "How the hell can I love somebody that used to beat the hell out of me, and the court had to have him stop it?" Rory is asking much better questions now, and his stories are reflecting a more useful view of the world.

Magda at twenty-five has shallower vision of relationships than the wistful longing Rory discovers in his mid-teens. "Friends are important because you always have someone to spill your dirt to that you can't tell at home," she says. "Because some of the things, if you told them at home, you get in trouble for. And you have to tell someone." Has she learned anything from her relationship with Stell? Magda laughs and says she hasn't. "That's sad to say, but I don't think so. I really don't." "Telling" is more important to Magda than knowing another person and being known; in truth, she doesn't appear to notice much about the people in her life. What does she like about her boyfriend? His brains and his success and his looks, Magda says. Either she doesn't look, or she can't see, further than that.

Vick's vision of friendship is even starker. "Somebody to talk to, do things with. That's about it." What kind of things bring her together with her husband? That's a good question, Vick says, but she never answers it. Jeff takes a characteristically abstract approach: "I think it's biological, so an explanation isn't required. But, um, as social creatures, you know, I think we have an innate desire to be with some certain group of people."

But if Rory can do it, so might Jeff or Vick or Magda or Charlie when the time is ripe. That's why it's not absolutes that we're looking for in these stories, but potential: things like Rory's tentative manifestations of interest, or Sandy's delight in her own expansion, or Pete's idea that next year he may feel different— the seeds of crucial habits of mind.

Coherence and Breakdown

Narrative coherence, unlike reflection, agency, and relatedness, is a quality of narrative structure rather than content. It is a clue to how well an experience has been integrated. Can a teller focus on emotionally taxing material without vagueness, avoidance, confusion, or changing the subject? Some things are just beyond our powers to talk about adequately, at least for a while. But as we do the psychological work of coming to terms with them, thinking and talking get easier, memories become more accessible, we are less deflected by anxiety and confusion. Rory at twenty-five is remembering one such struggle when he explains how his ability to deal with his beloved brother's death has evolved over ten years: "I can talk about it now. I don't glaze over into a daze and start having pictures in my brain of the scenes that I really don't like to picture."

Here's an example of "glazing over" in action—a loss of narrative coherence under emotional stress. The adult Magda tells about a breakup with a boyfriend two years ago. He left her in a fury, convinced that his relationship with her had contributed to the failure of his business. Magda thinks there might be some truth to this. She's living with another man now, but, she says, Sam's departure and bankruptcy put a damper on her life. As she tries to talk about it, her story starts to lose shape and becomes harder and harder to follow. "I drank a lot after that, you know, I just drank every day and that, to tell you the truth, it took me a while to figure it out, but it was making me feel worse to drink, instead of saying 'Yes,' I'll drink, and that, and swear it will be better, I won't remember. Forget it, I'd be out in the middle of a bar and I'd just lose it. [She screams.] And the guy next to me, like, 'What's wrong?' 'Shut up, leave me alone!' So."

The coherence of all the kids depends on what they are talking about. Although Rachel is eloquent in her passionate descriptions of her friendships, it's many years before she can talk about her family in an organized way. But all the resilient kids demonstrate early on a real appreciation of how helpful a story can be in containing and conveying feelings, and in giving you a sense of a continuing plot even when you can't see it yet. They work to get it "right." They have high standards, and they reject glib generalizations that don't really say what they mean. When Pete struggles to describe why things have been better since he stood up to his father, the interviewer offers him an easy out: He had to respect you as an adult? *"No!"* Pete says. "He was scared to death!"

Sometimes the kids manage an incipient form of coherence in a fantasy before they can really "talk" about something, as in Pete's lurid revenge tales and Billy's epics of conquered danger. The resilient kids show a respect for context and meaning even when they are too confused to put it all together. Here's Rachel in her first interview, describing how she came to High Valley: "I didn't do well in school. . . . A lot of kids were on my back and I was having a hard time with that. So my grades started slipping and I was doing really bad. . . . And then when I went to junior high it was a lot harder through the eighth grade. I just couldn't take it any more."

She's thought about this. She knows she's in the hospital because of something that was going on *in her*, even if she can't yet put that completely into words. She also knows, if vaguely, that the thing that was going on had something to do with conflicts with other kids. She can see that her emotional discomfort was reflected in her schoolwork, and she gives the whole story a historical context. Her summary—"I just couldn't take it anymore"—may not be the definitive description of her emotional distress, but it's true as far as it goes. This is only a sketch but it covers a lot of territory, and Rachel fills it out methodically over time.

The less feeling a person can tolerate, the harder it is to keep an emotionally intense narrative organized. Here is Jeff at twenty-five, trying to answer a question about how childhood experiences have affected his adult personality. "Well, I think they are, you know, they are the adult pretty much. I changed a lot, I think more than most people through adolescence to now. I don't know if most people think they have changed a lot. But I don't know, I assume there're some, your personality is formed by, who knows, two maybe, age four. Certainly by the time you're ten, you're pretty much who you are, although it is possible to change some more. I feel like I really changed a lot when my dad died. That threw everything out of kilter. . . . It seems like there was a real split in my life that time my father died, and I'm certainly a different person than I would have been. But compared to my next door neighbor, I'm sure I'm much more of the same person as I was when I was young." Like all of Jeff's narratives, this one is willing and open. But it never addresses the question the interviewer asked: How have your experiences affected you? It morphs almost immediately into very confused abstractions about how people change. That's typical of Jeff's style when he is anxious: his words obscure reflection more than they enhance it.

That question gives Magda trouble, too. With her, it shows in a series of internal contradictions. How have childhood experiences affected what she's become? "It's not that I blocked out what happened, because I don't, because it still—Sometimes I use it for an excuse. Well, you know, just, I don't know, in what context, but I do use it for an excuse sometimes, and um, but I'm just glad that it really would, it still to this day bothers me, you know, but um . . . my mom leaving and all that. But I really came out of it pretty much unscathed, I think. I've done really well."

Here's a more complex example from Jeff. The interviewer asks how his relationship with his mother has changed. Jeff says that he wishes he knew. "I don't know how you ever figure anything out about psychology. I hate to say I don't have much faith in it finding anything really deep, but I don't know. I've been thinking about it for so long, and um—maybe I'm too subjective about it. . . . How could you figure anything out, when I haven't a clue on it and I've been thinking about it for twenty years, you know? Anyway, the—um, I don't know, I get confused. I have—There's so many different angles and ideas and thoughts about it.

"In some ways I, you know, really like my mother," Jeff goes on. "I don't even want to say I love her, you know. I don't feel that." Jeff has finally organized himself to tackle the question, but as soon as he does, confusion sets in. Is he distinguishing here between liking his mother and loving her? If so, the distinction is unclear. It seems more likely that he has made a slip of the tongue—another sign of confusion—since the rest of this passage is a statement of how he *doesn't* really like her, or at least won't admit it. "I mean, maybe if she died it would hit me like a ton of bricks—I'm just denying this love I have for her. But it doesn't feel like it. And, um . . . but there's some—Most of what I think is, the big issue is that, like, that her emotions are, don't show and don't come through and that everything's sort of, I don't want to say it's just a social consciousness that keeps them out. . . . And I'm annoyed at her for being that way."

Sometimes he gets completely lost. The interviewer asks the adult Jeff about the power dynamics in his relationship with his best friend Fred. "Sometimes, when it's reasonable, I mean, it's reasonable, we know, I know not to rely on him for things. I know I would never say hi, or agree to do a painting, a house-painting job with him, he just can't deal with things like that. I, ah, I have fun with him, we have fun together, and that's what we do together, you know, and I'd like, I'd love to go on a long vacation with him, and he's a writer, he writes all these, he writes for a paper for a living. But he writes other stuff, and I, I pretty much paint for a living. So, um, you know, I could definitely—I would love to go and for a number of months, and you know, paint while he's writing and I'd like to write also and do that kind of thing. I can't remember the question now."

IT IS THE TELLER'S engagement with his or her own feelings that gives a story its impact on other people, and the emotional distance reflected in a poorly coherent narrative seems to influence its capacity to engage a listener. It's hard to feel keenly what Jeff is trying to convey in the story about his mother; even his description of his terrifying assault on himself is lifeless and impoverished compared with Pete's muscular summary of his in-

trinsically less dramatic troublemaking. There's a lack of immediacy, a one-dimensional quality that fails to grab the listener the
way Pete's earthy directness does. The stories of the resilient kids
are rich, lively, and dynamic; they are connected with, and reflections of, powerful feelings. The other kids have less access to
their feelings, and so have fewer to share. They pay less attention
to themselves, and their own lesser interest evokes a proportion-
ately lesser response in us. Perhaps one way that resilient children find the supportive relationships they need is by telling the
stories—moving, horrifying, poignant stories—that attach nurturing adults.

An extensive menagerie is the center of Vick's early teenage
life, and in her second interview she talks about her mice. She
has six in a tank in her room, she says, so she's never lonely at
night. She plays with them in the evenings, lets them run around
on her bed, talks to them. "I tell them their fur's nice. Because
they have wicked shiny fur." The interviewer, clearly speaking
from his own mindset, comments that it's unfortunate they
don't talk back. "They squeak," Vick protests. But she doesn't say
anything about what their responsiveness means to her, or challenge the interviewer's narrow view. He doesn't recognize that a
rift has developed, and although the subject means a lot to Vick,
she drops it, perhaps detecting a lack of interest. But the resilient
kids take their listeners willy-nilly where they want them to go.
Any mouse of Billy's would be three feet long, with laser eyes
and a tail strong enough to lasso a steer. It would speak at least
three languages, and it would be damned hard to dismiss.

AS THE REFLECTIVE PROWESS of the resilient kids increases,
they can stand more intensity of feeling about more things.
Their narrative organization holds up better, and their stories
become broader and deeper. They relinquish generalizations in

favor of descriptions full of intimate and immediate detail. Rachel's bland references to her "close," loving family steadily give way to a much more particular portrayal of the complicated relationships within it. From the early comment that the kids at school were on her back, she unfolds ever richer perceptions of *why* she had such a hard time with the other kids and what kind of a hard time it was. Rachel moves easily between an increasingly subtle grasp of why they might have behaved as they did, and an expanding awareness of why she is so vulnerable to other people's behavior. In her last interview she is still deeply interested in this theme, and the prospect of understanding it even better in the future gives her great satisfaction. But Jeff's story of his frustrating relationship with his mother does not change discernibly over the years; nor do Magda's accounts of her frustrated wishes and goals.

The resilient kids are flexible. Their narratives have a dynamic quality—new information, new ideas, new emotions are constantly being assimilated. They attend to details; they make distinctions; they look for similarities. They adjust their thinking when necessary; they don't fall back automatically into old familiar patterns. Once Pete realizes that it's more efficient to keep someone from challenging you in the first place than to have to fight them afterward, he incorporates this principle into his sense-making and quickly expands its application to nonphysical threats. He becomes a master of preemptive intimidation: the way to deal with snobs is to be snobby. "If you're not, you're lower than them." He laughs. "But if you show them that *they* are lower than *you*, then they feel too low to be snobby to you."

Rory too is trying to get a handle on his rageful explosions, and he's making some headway: "I can probably just pin them, instead of hitting them. Just pin 'em on the ground and let 'em have the embarrassment."

This is definitely a start. It's better to pin people down and embarrass them than to tear them limb from limb and end up in jail. But there are big differences between these two approaches to the problem of self-restraint. Pete's is based on psychological savvy, not willpower. It requires less effort in the moment, and it's easier to sustain. Once he grasps that outsnobbing snobs is more effective than punching them, he no longer has to struggle not to attack. He can move a whole category of potential fights out of the physical realm and into the psychological one. He can even relax enough to laugh about it. His understanding grows out of his increasing grasp of his own vulnerable self-esteem. His narrative is more coherent than Rory's, which probably reflects greater comfort with his subject matter. It's also more engaged and more engaging—sharp, observant, funny. Rory is trying and he's hurting, but he doesn't (yet) give his stories the emotional Velcro other people stick to; he's still afraid that being open means being hurt. The power of a story depends on the teller's willingness to speak from the heart.

COHERENCE IS NOT THE SAME THING as literary talent or a gift of gab. Sandy loves to dispute, and so does Jeff, but Jeff gets too tangled up in his thinking to tell a gripping tale. Rory's not a talky kind of guy, and his stories are pretty sparse at first. Billy's not a talker either, but he gives up his beloved shaggy-dog stories as he becomes able to talk about *himself.* In the early interviews, he fills in the gaps with jokes and preposterous anecdotes that entertain both parties but keep them at a distance. He doesn't need the wild tales once he starts talking about real emotion. Barring an occasional riff just for the fun of it, his interviews develop slowly into engaged and engaging discussions of how a boy grows into a man. Billy has little patience with words for their own sake, but he doesn't need complex rhetoric. His honesty and straightforwardness are just as successful and just as engaging, in his conversation and in his life. And funny thing—that's how Rory is starting to sound too.

The Seeds of Resilience

These narratives are full of twists and turns, digressions and dead ends, retreats and escapes. For stories of success, they include a lot of failures. But as Pete, Rachel, Billy, and Sandy steadily learn to think in ways that work well for them, and as a sense of efficacy takes the place of bravado, helplessness, and despair, their coping improves dramatically.

The narratives of Jeff, Charlie, Vick, and Magda evolve less. As adults, these people still cling to the same coping styles that failed them as teenagers. They seem to go through the same experiences over and over again, suffering from them but learning little, seldom opening themselves to something new. Yet it cannot be said that Sandy is resilient in some absolute way and Magda is not. The kids who appeared resilient to us at the time of this study might look very different ten years later if a new catastrophe were to come along and overwhelm them, and the contrast-group kids might prove more successful at a different time or under different circumstances. That is why the point of this study is not to identify resilient kids, but learn to recognize the seeds from which resilience can grow, and how to nurture them.

When he was in his twenties, Rory scored right in the middle on all our tests, earning himself a place in the contrast group. But by his late teens he is already starting to sound as though he's getting his feet under him, and as the years go by, his attitude, his narrative, and his life increasingly resemble those of the resilient kids. At thirty, Rory may be an official new member of the resilient group, and even now it sounds as though he is well on the way.

RORY HAD SEEN a lot of trouble by the time he got to the Children's Center. Underneath his wild behavior and his legal woes lay a heap of daunting losses. A cross-country move at age ten, when his father was transferred, cost him his friends. (Billy was uprooted at the same age and in the same way.) His extended family went though a series of dangerous and frightening crises that upset Rory greatly and further burdened and distracted his parents. A girl he cared for moved away unexpectedly in the weeks before his admission. And in the weeks after, his older brother died in an automobile accident.

Rory was very attached to his brother Rich, who had worked his way out of troubles of his own and could understand what Rory was going through. Rich never attacked Rory's self-esteem the way their critical father did, so Rory was willing to talk to him, and to listen. It was Rich who got Rory out of his "B&E and vandalism" phase. "He talked sense to me. He didn't start calling me a thief, a liar, bullshit artist, and shit like that. He goes, he said, 'Hey, what the fuck you getting out of it?' . . . And, like, I could tell my brother the truth."

Rich's death during Rory's first month at the Children's Center is a disaster for Rory, an unbearable loss that undermines his entire emotional foundation. "That was the end," he says of himself ten years later. Helpless grief piles up on top of the staggering rage that Rory is already carrying toward his father, and it completely swamps his capacity for containment. His family, alone in their individual griefs, can't find a way to talk about it.

"I don't think anybody has ever gotten over it in my family," the adult Rory says, including himself in the remark. He does still seem depressed. He echoes some of Jeff's painful beliefs about the endlessness of cataclysmic loss. But something has changed in Rory. He's had an insight, has noticed that he associates love with pain, and he's found a psychotherapist to help him sort that out. He is really thinking about his feelings. And when the interviewer asks him if his very difficult romantic relationship (on which he is now working hard) has taught him anything about himself, Rory says, "Yah. Relationships are damn important, and you'd go through anything just to keep what little you have."

This is the dour vision of a lonely man who has suffered a lot. But it is also a greatly expanded and conscious recognition of the importance of connection. Rory is aware as he has never been before of how loss has hurt him. His adult interviews are very reminiscent of Rachel's teenage ones, and they leave us with real hope that Rory may at last be on a better track. The interviewer asks him where he sees his life going in the next few years. What would he see as an improvement?

"Better and more mature relationships," Rory says. "Relationships."

He is beginning to make sense of the world in a way that increases his options instead of narrowing them. He is finding places and people that can be a source of strength for him. This is what resilient people do. But how do they do it? How do they think about what they do? That's what the narratives show.

4

Pete

You've Got To Want To

PETE HAMILTON WAS ADMITTED TO HIGH VALLEY at the age of fourteen and a half, after he stole a gun and brought it to school.

PETE WAS THE SECOND of four children. His father was a successful securities lawyer; his mother didn't work. Pete had been a very difficult child since his nursery school days, when he became notorious for attacking other kids. He started stealing at age five. By the time he was eight, he had been diagnosed as "hyperactive," although the team who evaluated him at High Valley thought his problems were more emotional than neurological. Pete had also been a fearful child, dreading separation from his parents, and prone to severe homesickness and night terrors. He slept with a night-light until he was twelve.

Pete was very aggressive in school. He didn't get along with his teachers, and he induced other kids to do what he wanted by a combination of cajolery, manipulation, and threat. By the time he was a junior, his parents' futile efforts to find a place that could "handle" him had led to brief enrollments at nine different schools.

His home life was chaotic as well. When Pete was eight, his parents ended their painful marriage. Mr. Hamilton had a family history of depression and drug abuse, and suffered from drastic mood swings. He attempted to medicate himself with drugs and alcohol, but they only shortened his fuse and increased his violence toward his wife and children. (Pete began emulating Mr. Hamilton's drug use very early, stealing from his father's supply.) At the time of Pete's admission, two of his siblings had documented psychiatric problems, and one was also in trouble with the law.

For a while after both parents had remarried, things were calmer. But Pete's aggression, stealing, and drug use were getting worse, and so was his schoolwork. The family didn't follow through on a psychotherapy recommendation. Finally Mrs. Hamilton sent Pete to live with his father for a year, in the hope that that would settle him down.

It was not a success. Pete thought it meant his mother no longer loved or needed him, and that hurt him deeply. And he and his father had been at war for years. The angrier he acted at school, the more restrictive and punitive Mr. Hamilton became, thinking Pete needed "taming." But Pete only rebelled, and their struggle escalated.

For a long time Pete had handled his rage at his father with fantasies of revenge and destruction. But when he realized in his mid-teens that he had grown big and tough and fierce enough to make the fantasies come true, he was as terrified as he was relieved: What would happen if he really did fight back? Suddenly his most reliable way of containing his fury felt too dangerous to use. He kept himself together for a while, but when his parents reneged a second time on their promise to let him return to Mrs. Hamilton's, Pete was beside himself. He ran away, back to his mother, and stole a gun from her father on a holiday visit. He brought it to school with him, where he showed it to classmates and played with it in a variety of threatening ways. He didn't shoot. But the police were called, and Pete was charged as a delinquent child in possession of a dangerous weapon.

The court committed him to a state hospital for evaluation before trial, but a lawyer colleague of Mr. Hamilton's negotiated a plea agreement whereby Pete would spend an extended period in treatment at High Valley; this kept him out of a juvenile correctional facility.

By the time Pete got to the Children's Center, he saw relationships with adults as desperate control struggles. When he couldn't manipulate his way around the rules, he exploded into fantasies of violent and bloody revenge. He demanded total admiration and total control, and withdrew into silliness or rage when he didn't get them. The only feelings of warmth he expressed were toward his mother.

But the staff and patients on the unit also quickly recognized Pete's lively intelligence and musical talents. He very slowly began to settle down as the family therapy sessions and the pass system gave him at last some control over the time he spent with his father. For a long time he remained verbally abusive, physically rough, manipulative, disobedient, dishonest, and sometimes threatening—but he was not assaultive.

Ten months after his admission Pete was discharged to his mother's custody, with the understanding that he would attend the hospital-affiliated high school and continue his therapy program at the Children's Center.

The First Interview

At first Pete talks mostly about what he does and doesn't like to do. The main thing is that he wants to be the boss. "I basically like to do my own thing," he says. "I like to do what I feel like doing, whatever that turns out to be." Alone or with others? the interviewer asks. Pete says, "Sometimes I like to do it alone, and sometimes I like to do it with other people. I like to do things alone more. I find that when I'm doing something that I can do alone and other people are helping me, I don't like it. I like to do it all myself."

THIS WISH TO "do it all myself" is an organizing principle for Pete and displays the double power of narrative to give meaning to the past and shape the future. Pete has had long experience with a controlling and intimidating parent, and has come early to the belief that the best way to stay out of threatening situations is to keep to himself. Another child in Pete's shoes might have constructed a different narrative—one that emphasizes cooperation, for example, and the pleasure of family activities when everyone is getting on well, or the joy of making others do what he wants. But this is Pete's narrative, and as he learns to notice his feelings in more detail, it evolves. When he realizes that he gets lonely sometimes, he begins to look for better ways to deal with intimidation than to attack, to hide, or to succumb. He recognizes that what he really wants is to feel less threatened—not more alone—and he refocuses his attention and his narrative on making himself less vulnerable. He grows physically stronger, and relationships start to feel safer to him. He becomes more open to them, lets himself use them more freely, and even eventually—as he rather dryly admits as a grownup—

lets himself depend on them a little. His narratives reflect this evolving sense of himself. They grow out of his past experience, but they also inform the decisions he will make, the new experiences he will seek out (and avoid), and the new stories he will end up telling about them. This process of recursive sense-making is characteristic of narrative. The contrast-group kids use it too, but the new experiences and stories to which their narratives lead them are at best repetitive, and at worst destructive.

PETE SAYS THAT HE loves the attention he gets from his guitar playing; he wants to be "number one," to perform at a certain local coffeehouse where musicians play and sing and get all kinds of free food—"a whole shitload of cookies and things"— in the service of a worthwhile cause. ("Being number one" is another important narrative line that Pete will elaborate and rework over the years.)

They talk about the approach of Christmas. Pete says it doesn't bother him that he spends the holidays one year with his mother's family and the next with his father's. It didn't bother him when his parents separated, either. "'Cause my feelings are getting a lot better, but they're not too friendly towards my father. He's just pulling a lot of shit. . . . Oh, just doing all kinds of rotten things, towards me, my brothers, my mother, my sister. . . . Well, it's too bad that it had to turn out that way, but he won't give me any shit now 'cause I guess he's kind of scared that I turned up with a .32 automatic, after I'd been saying if he touched me again I'd kill him."

The interviewer asks Pete what he means by touching.

"Well, he was always punching on me and my brothers, mostly me. Beating on me, throwing me down the stairs, throwing me against the wall, grabbing and throwing you."

Did you ever get hurt? asks the interviewer.

"Me? Never seriously. I was a pretty tough little kid. But from the earliest years that I can remember, about from the year eight, I vowed that I'd put him through a wall someday. And then, as I got older, I told him—I didn't tell him directly, but I'm sure he's heard it, 'cause I told enough of his friends and enough of his relatives that I'd kill him if he touched me again." He turns to the crisis that preceded his admission. "One time it got so bad I couldn't hack him any more. I just went to Bob [the social worker at his school, Bob Jenkins]. I said, 'You gotta do something.' . . . And I ended up staying in the emergency care shelter for a week to two weeks. . . . I had a lot of incidents. Somebody saw me walking a younger kid into the park at knifepoint, 'cause the kid made me mad. I don't know why I did it, and that's why I went to the emergency care shelter. Because everything was driving me crazy and I would have killed myself, but maybe to get it stopped, to stop myself from doing it I told Bob I was going to kill myself. . . . A couple days before that, I showed him a pill which turned out to be a sleeping pill, which I knew it was. . . . The main reason I showed him, in my head, was to stop myself."

Pete had stolen the drugs from his father; he takes pride in plundering the old man's caches. Not in "doing the chemicals" per se, he makes clear—"Who in their right mind would be proud of doing chemicals?"—but he wants to have them available. Maybe just to have them, maybe to do some dealing, maybe to kill himself. "Drugs were a good escape," Pete says. He talks for a few minutes about how important his father's friends are, treating their power as if it were his own, and admiring their prominence and influence.

Pete starts to describe how he came to be in the hospital. He knows that he was sent to live with his father "because no school system would take me. I've fucked up all my life. I've been kicked out of three, four schools, and I've had a really hard time in four others." Why? "I just didn't like it. I wasn't going to work with it." (This desperado theme is an important one for Pete, who would rather see himself as an active agent than a victim even if it means taking a lot of flak for bad behavior.)

That was how he felt about living with his father, too. It was bad enough at the beginning. "The first year I was scared shitless of him and I wouldn't say boo. . . . When I was living with him I was almost always depressed." But it got worse. "I felt sad because I didn't like living there, you know? . . . I was pulling a lot of really stupid, stupid shit, and I think one of the reasons for that was because I just heard that I was going to be there for a third year. 'Cause you know that originally started out with my mom saying, 'You're going to go live with him for one year.' And then she said two years, and then I was hearing rumors of three." That was when the "kill-myself shit" happened. And that was what pushed Pete over the edge, making him desperate to get out from under his father's thumb and back to his mother.

Are you heading in a better direction now? the interviewer asks.

Yes, says Pete. "I was really fucking up my life before."

This first interview has to be cut short because of a time conflict, and the session ends abruptly.

WHEN PETE RETURNS to complete his first interview, discussion immediately turns to his relationship with his father. They're getting along better now, and Pete has a theory about why: "He doesn't try to push me around, mainly because I won't take it now—I won't be quiet about it." He describes again the crisis that brought him to the hospital, this time in slightly different terms. Now he suggests that his own open threats to his father's friends alerted the old man, and that the "bust" for possession of a weapon a week later gave weight to his declaration of intent. Pete maintains that since then, Mr. Hamilton has taken him more seriously. (This is the central theme of Pete's early narratives, and it remains an important one throughout: The best way to deal with threat is to out-threaten. That way, no one gets hurt.)

The interviewer asks Pete where he got the gun, and Pete replies without evasion: "I stole it from my grandfather." He felt some uncertainty about whether to take it, but he did because he likes guns. "I just like them—they're about the ultimate power." He knows that he got caught because he displayed the gun in public; it's not clear at this point whether or not he intended this to happen. He handled the gun carefully, he says—unloaded it and left the safety on—but he made very sure that people knew he had it.

Pete and the interviewer talk for a long time about scariness and being scared. Pete has been doing a lot of thinking. His possession of the gun certainly got his father's attention, and Pete still thinks that "the only reason that man would listen to me is because he's scared." But he's not sure yet whether he's "enough in himself" to enforce his father's good behavior, or whether he needs external reinforcements like firearms. "I never had any intention of shooting him with that gun, but I'm not going to tell him differently. 'Cause as long as he's scared of me he'll stay off my back. . . . Like at the family meeting last Thursday, I went on pass with my mother and he was saying, 'Why can't I go? Why won't you go on pass with me?' No, he didn't say that. He was saying, 'Well, I don't drive so many miles just for this.' You know, blah, blah, blah. And I just said, 'Too bad.' And when he realized that I was not going to change my mind, he practically—he didn't really, but he almost sounded like begging me. . . . 'Cause if he had kept on much longer, I would've said no."

That's a new experience for you, says the interviewer—you tell him no, and that's it.

"From that day I split in February [when he ran away], I was no longer scared of him, and I was ready to do whatever I had to do if he tried to fuck with me anymore."

But at the same time that Pete is pleased with his new capacity to hold his own with his father, he is nervous about the aggression that makes it possible. He also can see that anger isn't all that he feels, and he doesn't want to hurt the people he loves. Even while he's thinking that his soft heart got the better of him, and that he should have rejected his father's request about the pass after all, he can't bring himself to do it, because it would hurt his father's feelings.

But he does get angry at the interviewer, who he feels is interrupting him. This brings on some talk of nervous breakdowns and other such terrible things that can happen if you get too mad. Pete gives a vivid description of what would happen if he *acted* on his anger—he'd wreck the office, throw the typewriter through the window. But that's only make-believe, he makes clear. That's what he'd do *if* he really got furious. He tells a number of other stories, including a really scary one about the state hospital from which he came to High Valley: "When they first told me that I was going to be locked up in there and I couldn't get back down, I got bullshit and somebody talked me down and I waited and my mother came, and then after talking with her I just got more mad. I said, 'I'm not staying here,' and I grabbed my mother and I said 'I'm going out of here with her,' almost using her like a hostage. At which point I hear this 'All available help to Ward D,' right? And the next thing I knew I was holding my mother like this, I had my back against the wall, and there were ten or fifteen people there. . . . I backed against the wall into a doorway and I took this belt off, and I said, 'Come on and I'll kill the first mother that comes after me.' . . . And some guy comes forward and *wham!* I let him have it right across his face with the belt and the metal end, and he was down on the floor."

He was meaner then than he is now, Pete adds dryly. He's been tamed since. (This is Pete's second main theme: balancing the defensive and destructive aspects of aggression. It's worth noting that there is no evidence in either of his hospital charts that this battle ever took place. There are many observations, however, that when Pete gets anxious he has recourse to stories in which he defeats foes much larger and more powerful than himself.)

They go on to talk about relationships. Pete says that he doesn't have friends. He's lost some in all his moving around; some have fallen out of touch; some are scared of him. And he's very competitive. He can't imagine having a family, and when he goes out with girls he doesn't get very involved, although he enjoys it. Still, as they prepare to end the interview, Pete is disappointed: "I can't see you any more till next year?" (This is his third big theme: the balance between the risks of relationships and their comforts.) On that note, they part.

The Second Interview

When Pete comes in for his second interview, he's sixteen and a bit. He's attending the hospital-based high school, and he's enrolled part-time at an acting school in the city. He demonstrates his technique of voice projection and his suave new clothes. "That last time you saw me I was probably wearing blue jeans. Now, you know, I'm wearing these—Italian tweeds. Some nice Italian shoes. Dark socks, dark shirt. You know, all that."

He's got plans for after his graduation from the High Valley High School in May. He knows the names of all the big theatrical agents, and he's psyched out the best ones to approach. Soon he'll be making $250,000 a year and driving a Lotus. He laughs. "I happen to have more motivation than a lot of people." He's given up his goal of playing the guitar for a living—acting is a better career. Who's going to come to his graduation, a huge ceremony to be held at the city opera house? "I don't know," says Pete. "It doesn't matter to me."

Who would you *want* to be there? the interviewer persists.

"I don't care. No, this is *my* deal. I don't care what they do." His parents are paying for the acting classes, though. He's the second youngest in the school—most of the students are much older. The one he likes best is the oldest in the class. What he likes about acting is the ego trip. "When you're up on stage, a lot of people look up at you and they say, 'I'd like to be like him and I'd like to look like him.' . . . They admire you and they envy you, which is an ego trip in itself."

Pete knows that he hasn't yet won this coveted envy and admiration. In fact, people tend to be snobby with him. But he's learned how to handle that—give them a taste of their own medicine and attack *their* self-esteem. (This is the technique Pete discovered for controlling his father: fight fire with fire. It's also a refinement of his theme about doing what he wants to do. He still wants what he wants, but now he aims to get it by psychological means—prestige, influence, money, mind games—rather than through violence.)

Psychological pecking orders matter to Pete. He worries a lot about how people think of him, he says, and part of this is feeling that he has to come out on top. So if he doesn't think acting will do it for him, he'd like to work in "home customizing, which would be essentially interior decorating, but I won't call it that. That's too strange." Why? asks the interviewer. "It usually comes with a very feminine guy, if it's a guy. And I'm not feminine."

(Another theme: what masculinity means.) He laughs. "I'm quite the opposite. And as for the acting, I'm gonna make it because I know how to handle competition. I've done it before. I broke a guy's toe just to keep him from beating me in a Junior Olympics semifinal when I was about twelve."

He expands on this episode. He knew he would lose if he ran against this guy. But he's smart; "I study up on my competition." The interviewer asks what he would do if he were competing with a rival actor. "Shave their head," says Pete. "I'd shave his head and tell him, 'Go ahead and say who did it! Go ahead, I dare ya!' And I'd shave their eyebrows. . . . If they were already bald, which some actors are, you know what I'd do then? I'd take ink which does not come off ever, and I would put a line, a black line so that you couldn't cover it with makeup, from the tip of their nose all the way down the back of their head and put big whiskers on their face. Big cat whiskers. Because I won't stand for it! I'm gonna be the best." You really *are* determined to be the best, says the interviewer. "Yup," says Pete. "I don't think there's anything wrong with that, because I'm not gonna physically hurt anyone. I'm just gonna get them out of my way."

The interviewer tries to suggest that there might be other ways of handling competition, but Pete doesn't let him. If the competition isn't important, he'll take his chances. But if it makes a difference, "then you better believe I'm gonna do it. Because you just don't hire actors whose face is covered with black ink."

You're probably right, says the interviewer.

"So they just have to wait about six months for it to wear away." He laughs. "Aren't I the evil person?"

(Pete spins out this vision with relish. He's a master of blood-curdling fantasy, and he knows it. But fantasy is all it is. There's no evidence that Pete has ever, since his admission, attacked anyone who wasn't looking for an enjoyable scuffle. He's developing an operating principle that will eventually keep him from scaring himself to death with his own aggression, and he explains it: the more menacingly you present, the less likely you are to have to fight.)

The interviewer tries to get Pete to talk about friends, but Pete is still preoccupied with competition and his plans for success and big money. He demonstrates his stage presence and talks about how important it is to learn to look one's best. And he's developed an interest in classical music. It has class. He likes it. But also it means that he could go to a cocktail party and fit right in, except that he doesn't drink. He's given it up. "Drinking and my personality don't get along. And so, rather than fuck up my life, I fucked up drinking." (An intense focus on appearances and an imperious need to think well of themselves are typical of adolescents. In Pete they are exaggerated; his family circumstances didn't give him much chance to practice smoothing out ups and downs in self-esteem. He's not quite as free of drugs yet as he would like, either. Still, he's concentrating on something substantive: What do you have to do to grapple with life, to make the kind of things happen that you want to happen?)

How does Pete feel about his time in the hospital? the interviewer wants to know. He doesn't care, Pete says. He's going to keep his eye on the place, and if he ever finds a reason to do it, he'll sue them to rags. He's already got a rich and powerful lawyer to do it for him (the one who got Pete sent to High Valley and so kept him out of state custody.) He doesn't need to be violent anymore because he's found a better way. Money and a good lawyer will get him what he needs.

When the interviewer presses him about the hospital, Pete retreats briefly into uncharacteristic compliance: the Children's Center helped him a lot, he says, especially "the shrinks—you guys." But he soon reverts to type. He's gotten rid of his doctor, "discontinued his use." And since the doctor "tried to be a jerk with his family meetings," Pete has discontinued those, too.

He thinks it's working out well. "I still have a lot of flaws, and a lot of things have to be straightened out, but I'm doing my best." He has made resolutions to better his personality and his inner self. "I'm growing up to be another conformist," he goes on. "I'm smart enough to learn quick that there ain't no way to buck the system. Just no way. So you gotta do the system, and you gotta bend it a little like the businessmen do. . . . I feel that I'm gonna go a lot farther by contributing and abiding by the rules and things. And basically I don't have to give up my wildness inside totally. But I am, I did, I gave my wildness a lobotomy. I took out maybe three-quarters of it. . . . I'm stronger than people take me for. . . . I'm using it for my benefit. I'm working on controlling my temper because I found physical violence would never get me anywhere." (Pete develops several major themes here. He still won't give up his "wildness," but he's coming to see for himself that there is at least some value in conformity. He knows he has to control his temper, and he's working on and fantasizing about what he needs to do to feel less helpless.)

He imagines going to an elegant party, conversing impressively with the adults about classical music. He'll drive up to the Center in his new Lotus and shock Jill Gonzales, his favorite nurse, into a heart attack! But he adds a wistful afterthought: "She's always there—that's why I say Jill. Who's ever there that still knows me?"

They talk about his family. No *problems*—they just don't talk. His stepfather is the nearest thing to a human computer. "I respect him for how intelligent he is, but I disrespect him for his lack of emotions. . . . Homosexual men may be feminine but at least they have feelings." His own father has fallen for the "Thou shalt be manly" command, which has not done him any good. They don't talk. Pete knows he'll lose any arguments they get into, and he hates losing. But he *does* talk to his mother. "My mother and I talk more than anybody in the world. Nobody talks to their mother like I do. . . . And I would literally kill for her. She's the only one I would go to jail for life for. Because if anyone hurt my mother . . . I would kill him. I would make it the most painful death ever known to man. Because I've got so much love and respect for my mother that I would just make that goddamn bastard pay."

He'll take care of her when his stepfather kicks off, he says. No other man would take as good care of her as he would. ("There's never problems between me and my mother, ever. I like my mother too much," Pete says here—ignoring, among other things, the way she relinquished him to his father and his fantasy of using her as a hostage. But although he may be protesting a bit too much, his connection with her is real and important to him, and he uses it to help him control his ferocity.)

Pete says that he no longer wants to hurt either of the fathers in his life. He makes clear that he feels very competitive toward both of them, and very resentful of any attempts on their parts to control him. But it appears that he is starting to see them in a more balanced way. He counters his idealized view of his father's career—"He's a very, very, very brilliant man. I would say he's one of the best in the country"—with a typically hard-nosed assessment of his character: "But when it comes to raising a family or being a person—zip." When the interviewer asks him to describe something in his life that *hasn't* gone well, Pete says straightforwardly that he ripped off his stepfather and got caught. He had to sell his guitar to make up the money, otherwise he would probably have gotten thrown out of the house.

He wanted to avoid a confrontation with his stepfather not, he makes clear, because his stepfather could beat him in a fight—Pete has been studying martial arts. But Pete knows that he has to keep out of very aggravating situations or he'll lose his temper.

They reminisce a bit about how that used to be, and Pete points out that the worst he's done recently is throw a few chairs. "Now, usually, things that make me angry are things that I could have avoided. Now I'm just trying to avoid things."

The Third Interview

When Pete comes back the next year, he's seventeen and singing a different tune. He has dropped out of high school, and acting school too; the whole thing turns him off. He doesn't think that how you look is so important any more. The main thing is "getting the hell out of this state!"

"Everything wrong or bad that's ever happened in my life has happened in this state," Pete says, and he's sick of it. He's going to leave it (he means the constituency in which he's been living, but it's an apt metaphor for his unsettled feelings as well) and get a new start.

Now he can admit that he is not as good a guitar player as he would have to be to fulfill his musical ambitions. And he's not practicing. He's unstrung his guitar. The interviewer expresses some concern over this, but Pete reassures him: he didn't slam it against the wall this time. "I unwound the strings properly!" (Here are the first softenings of his grandiosity. But Pete is still an all-or-nothing kind of guy—if you can't be the greatest, forget it. A comfortable and constructive balance between these two extremes still eludes him. This is not uncommon among adolescents, however.)

Other themes are developing, too; it's as if a whole spring-time of shoots is suddenly peeking up out of newly thawed earth. Pete is pissed off at his current therapist and has given him the sack. His view is that the shrink was picking at him, dwelling constantly on Pete's past. To shut him up, Pete told him some very embellished violent stories, and the shrink said to Pete's mother that maybe Pete should be committed. Pete says that the stories were bullshit; when the doc took them literally, he felt misunderstood and betrayed. They are definitely on the rocks, and Pete is very angry indeed. Another reason to split and start over.

He goes on to tell some more bullshit-type stories, but (at least in this interview) the context has changed: Mr. Hyde and Dr. Jekyll are now cohabiting. On the one hand, Pete is an honorary member of a biker gang. On the other, he's been going to the symphony with some people he knows. Both of these sides of himself are okay, Pete says. Rock and symphony. But no disco, which to him represents "pompous assholes and queers."

He elaborates: the rock/biker and classical/symphony sides of himself are both real. So neither should be completely suppressed. They are just going to have to coexist. "It's like three-dimensional rather than one-way, you know? I mean that it's cool that I can listen and tolerate, or watch or do, more things than one particular lifestyle." (With that word "real," he acknowledges—that is, reframes and takes responsibility for—his love for classical music. Before, considering it at odds with his ferocious wild self, he had presented it primarily as a device to be used manipulatively, for what it could get him. But Pete is seeing more and more clearly that his fundamental problem is not his conflicts with the rest of the world, but his own conflicting desires.)

There's one side that he isn't dealing with yet, though, and that's the "disco" side, the one for queers and assholes. It turns out that Pete's dissatisfaction with acting school has a lot to do with having been branded gay by some of the people there. He gets very angry, and lest he blow up, he leaves. (This too is a developing theme. Taking off before hostilities explode is now Pete's preferred technique for keeping out of trouble. As he said at the end of the previous interview, there are some things he's learned to avoid.) He's been fighting with his family about the kind of job he should have. "I don't want to go to jail, and if I stay around much longer I may go to jail, because I may seriously beat the fuck out of my stepfather. . . . He thinks I'm a lazy slob and I think he's a computerized motherfucker! . . . And my mother, she's such a fuckin' hypocrite, 'cause for years and years the extent of her work was maybe a few house chores and fuckin' tennis all day. So fuck that shit, man!" He adds, with a grimness that rings all too true, "Going through school for me was worse than any job *they* ever had."

Pete's stepfather needles him, calls him a little thief. Pete thinks about kicking him in the face with his heavy boots. "You know what a pair of boots like this would do to someone's face?" But, he goes on, "I know as soon as I beat him up my mother's gonna have that resentment, and that's something I have to deal with." (Pete is tolerating even intensely angry feelings much better now than he used to. He doesn't act on them, and he can even allow himself to be openly angry at his mother while still remaining concerned for her and for himself. And he retains some objectivity and a lot of humor.) His stepfather is smart, he'll admit. But "as far as life goes, you could unplug him every night with all the rest of the computers."

Pete's doing okay with his real father, whom he recently visited. It's more of a chum relationship than father-son. They went to bars together. "I like the old man," Pete says. "I know what's in the tapes, but . . ."

What brought about the change? the interviewer wants to know. "When I finally stood up to him," says Pete. And he had to respect you as an adult? asks the interviewer. But Pete rejects this piece of "therapese." "No! He was scared to death. I told him I'd cut his fuckin' throat! Ha!"

But even that looks different to Pete now, because he is seeing his belligerence in a new light. It still interests him greatly, but it's not his only recourse, what he does when he's out of control, for lack of alternatives. He enjoys fighting and doesn't see anything wrong with it. But he also has "a civilized side. . . . I like two, three, four different lifestyles."

He'd like to go to music school; his playing isn't good enough and he'd like to improve his technique. He couldn't get into Eastman or Juilliard, and they aren't his kind of place anyway. The local school would be fine. He *was* upset about losing a job, though—his favorite one so far. The company folded. He choked up when he was laid off, he tells the interviewer.

So you *do* get attached?

"To some people, yeah," says Pete. "I'm still pretty much a loner." But he's not as easy about that as he once claimed to be. "I look out at the sky—it just bums me out. Been surrounding myself with drugs and people and booze and things like that." And hanging out with the bikers to avoid the pressure of his feelings. "When you're with a bunch of rowdy people, man, you're just not depressed." It's two steps forward and one step back. He dropped out of high school, but he took the necessary steps to acquire his GED, the General Equivalency Diploma. (This is a new development of the loner theme. It's a great advance in self-awareness for Pete to know that he's avoiding feelings, and to connect that awareness with how he uses relationships. It's also notable that when foiled in one path, Pete looks for another one. He couldn't tolerate the stresses of the hospital high school, but he did get the academic credentials he would need to pursue a career.)

The interviewer wants to know what has made for all this turmoil, and Pete says, "I think it's just the way my family life is, the way it's situated. I haven't been getting along with anyone in my family at all. And they're not happy with me and I'm not happy with them." (This is a very different kind of statement from the "I don't care what they do" of the year before. Pete isn't quite ready to admit that he's lonely and looking for connections. But he now acknowledges that the lack is affecting him. And as he goes on, he delineates his anxieties about relationships in a way that he's never done before.)

He hasn't got any close friends. Some of his friends are closer than others. But, he admits, having friends is hard. Because when you're with people, you have to balance some very complicated things. If you only feel safe when people are scared of you, they might not want to hang around. But if they *aren't* scared of you, then maybe *you* don't want to hang around. Also, relationships raise issues of sexuality. Those came up at acting school. He could go back if he wanted, but for now, "I just got sick of it. I got tired of it, and people were getting the wrong idea and I couldn't deal with that too. . . . Someone calls me a queer and I'm liable to turn around and play with their face, you know. I was really drummed out of that by peer pressure. Also, it was some of the teachers involved. I mean, I've never gotten along with teachers, especially ones that think they're God Almighty holy, and there was people there that thought they were the next best thing to gold. . . . I'm a paranoid person. I'm insecure, I know that. I'm always looking around my shoulder, making sure no one's coming up on me."

But more and more now, Pete's fear is not that someone will do something to him, but that he'll get so angry that *he* will do damage. He tells some violent tales of fantasied revenge on his ex-shrink, and he and the interviewer talk about the "paranoia" that Pete was famous for on the unit. How tough do you have to be to feel safe? Can you handle it by lessening your own vulnerability, or do you have to have other people, like Pete's 250-pound biker friends, to protect you? Pete says that he wants to leave his protection behind, see if he can be a new person. Start fresh.

The interviewer asks him to think back to the time in the hospital. Pete says he thinks that some of the discipline was good, but that it was too much. "I don't think it's right to try and take someone's spirit away, which is what they do by locking you in." He rejects the interviewer's suggestion that somehow his thinking changed during the course of his hospitalization.

"Anything that's good about me now I've done myself." He thinks that the place should be looser, less full of rules and quiet rooms. "There are better solutions for people's aggravations than QRs. Discussion, man! Even when people aren't capable of discussion, if you've got a room, they can go—as an adult, so to speak—and talk. I think I'd like to have an unbiased person there, someone who wouldn't take a side, you know, one way or another." And there should be fewer groups. "I wouldn't group everyone together. Nobody likes to be grouped. I'll tell you that right now from present experience. Nobody likes to be put in a group."

The interviewer asks about girls, and Pete says, "I can't deal with relationships. I don't want any new relationships. I haven't looked for any new relationships, because I'm not happy with the ones I've got." He likes sex, but the rest is too complicated, and he worries about how angry he gets. He has a favorite fantasy of waking up one morning in a time capsule, to a world that is all forest again and where fighters and killers are needed and valued.

The interviewer asks if there's anything Pete wants to talk about, and Pete says, "Well, I'm sure you've read that I've got a lot of hate. I hate a lot of things. I hate a lot of people. And I'm absolutely sure you can read that, but don't make me out to be a maniac. . . . It's just lately I've had a lot of hate, I've been depressed."

But he's beginning to have some inklings about how to deal with this, and they come from conviction now, not hospital propaganda. He's been testing out "talking about feelings," and he finds that it both helps him feel less hateful and strengthens his relationship with his mother.

The interviewer asks if it was coming back to the hospital that made him feel so full of hate again. No, Pete says. "I hate this place, but no, I don't think that's what caused it. I mean, people like that doctor make me hate. People that think they know what's going on in your head. . . . Maybe I'll be friendlier next year. I'm not being unfriendly to you, but . . ."

"No," the interviewer agrees, and the meeting ends.

The Fourth Interview

Pete is now eighteen and back from his year "out of the state." He lived on the streets of San Francisco for a while, and then spent some time renovating derelict apartments in Washington, D.C., both as a job and as a public service. But now he's trying to get into music school. He wants to start practicing, because he would like to be a professional. And he wants to quit smoking.

Pete's tone is quieter now, although he's talking about heavy things. He still works hard to convince himself, and his listener, of his strength. He likes the harsh realities of cities, he says, even in the worst neighborhoods. He's been working hard writing songs about his experiences. This last year was something he wanted to do. "I like the slums."

The interviewer thinks it must have been scary. "No," says Pete. "Nothing bothers me. I'm pretty good at martial arts. . . . I conceal weapons and I can kick about seven feet in the air. . . . I'm not violent—I just know how to. I am the wrong person to screw with." He tells of some close encounters of a very threatening kind, and again the interviewer says that it sounds scary. Again Pete rejects this.

"I like it. It's fast; it's exciting. I don't get in trouble because any of the people I get violent with are looking for violence. It's an acceptable setting for people who like to get rough. I like to get rough. I don't go looking for trouble." For a while, he says, he worked on a subway guardian squad, but he quit when he came to think that the squad cared less about guarding people than finding excuses for mixing it up. "I thought they would overdo it. You feel awfully macho when you walk around with twelve guys who know how to kick."

He tells the interviewer that he found the money he needed by hustling in the Tenderloin. "You get blown, and you get fifty dollars." (In a later interview Pete contradicts this statement convincingly, saying that he could never quite nerve himself up to prostitution, which of course is more about blowing than being blown. He seems to be indulging in some macho exaggeration to disguise the fact that he had found someone to take care of him a little; he can't admit this until several years later.) He worries that he might have contracted a venereal disease. His parents aren't giving him money, but he's still insured under their Blue Cross until he turns twenty-two.

He has a new attitude toward fighting now. "It's a sport to me, it's boxing. . . . I'm not angry anymore." You used to be, the interviewer says. Pete agrees that he used to think so. But now "my whole past is irrelevant—it's behind me." (That had been one of his goals when he left the "state.")

How did you leave it behind? the interviewer asks.

"Because I don't deal with it anymore," says Pete. "This is the only place that I come to that I have any past at."

How is that for you? asks the interviewer.

"Well, I really don't like coming here, but I agreed to do this for four years. I can't guarantee I will come in a lot." But when the interviewer asks if he would prefer that this were the end, Pete says no. "Let me see how I feel in two years or a year or whatever."

Then he makes a revelation. "I guess you probably know this. Yeah, I'm gay. But it doesn't mean anything. I have proved it to a lot of straight people—that's why I fought Lou [a biker he knows]. He didn't like gay people, so I gave him a hell of a fight. Now he doesn't think gay people are a bunch of fags." He tells some more stories of his toughness, and then goes on to a description of sexual experimentaion at the Children's Center that would have given the staff heart attacks if it had ever come to light. He can admit that he's gay now because people recognize his strength.

He doesn't want to go to college, Pete says, but he has to. He's still working both sides, and he has to give the civilized one its due, especially if he wants money. If he doesn't make it in music—"I like the attention"—he'll go into child psych. The biker side is there too, but now he talks about it in the context of his never-quite-satisfied need for relatedness: "The gangs—they're technically not real gangs. They're kids who hang together."

He's living in an apartment away from his parents. He's on good terms with them, especially his mother, "but they don't have any say in my life anymore."

Pete goes back to his year on the road. He made an effort to do a lot of things. He's seen a lot of things, too—a lot of crimes. He also saw his father beat up two girlfriends. "Claims he didn't, but I saw it." (This is the first time that he hints at the reason for his passionate loyalty to his mother, despite her derelictions. His father beat her up, too.) And Pete has learned some things about himself.

"I'm greedy." He wants money, power. "I like it, I really do. That's what being in the gay scene and being a hustler is all about. You get sugar daddies." He goes on to detail a list of powerful sugar daddies in all ranks of government. (This fantasy, which is what it later turns out to be, is the first open acknowledgment of Pete's long search for strong and nurturing older men. As in the passage about hustling, "sugar daddies" here is an exaggeration and a tough-guy dysphemism. For the time being, he would rather be seen as a heartless hustler than a needy kid.) He's still conflicted about how violent to be, especially if the only alternative is passivity; he still believes that "I got picked on a lot as a kid because I was afraid to fight."

But in this context Pete can now say that his father "didn't beat on me as much as I used to think he did. It always seemed in my mind to be magnified. We don't get into that anymore. I don't like adult male authority." The only people he'll listen to are the police, "and that's only because they are more violent than I am." Living on the street? "I wouldn't recommend it to anybody."

This is their last meeting, the interviewer points out, unless Pete agrees to continue in the study (which Pete does). What did the Children's Center do for him?

"Nothing, really," says Pete. "Well, I can't say *nothing*, but not a lot. It made me more aware of myself." He details what he's aware of with his characteristic mixture of perception, bravado, and humor. "I like my own way, and I really don't like ultimatums. I get frustrated and I get anxious and I lose my temper and I say, 'Fuck this!' I'll pick something up and I'll hit somebody with it, be it a chair or a typewriter."

Pete has not actually been hitting people with typewriters lately. But the interviewer asks, What happens? The moment before you hit, do you think: Maybe I shouldn't hit?

"No," Pete says, "I think, 'Smash that motherfucker!' I think, 'Blood!' . . . I don't usually go out of my way to fight, but that's the difference. Back then I probably would have hit somebody without even thinking about it. But now you've got to hit me first."

He doesn't think the hospital helped him that much, nor did his psychotherapy. What did? asks the interviewer. "You've got to want to," says Pete. "You've got to want to." The discipline was good for him in some ways, he goes on. But damaging in others, "because it made me hate a lot. But I don't hate really nearly as much as I did. I'll tell you what, most of anything that has happened to me good, I've pretty much done for myself, though. I won't give the credit to this place. This place is just a holding facility for nuts."

There are some last-minute negotiations about money and transportation reimbursement, and then they thank each other politely. Pete's last words are, "Take half that violence off that tape. I don't know how."

The Follow-Up Interviews

Pete returns at twenty-five for new interviews on family attachments and peer relationships. "Here goes the can of worms," he begins wryly. His sense of humor has not diminished over the years, nor has his hard-headed realism. "I was a terrible, terrible child," he says. "I was thrown out of so many schools that whole counties wouldn't take me." But this conviction has softened a bit. Pete can see now that he was fighting to survive, and he gives himself points for that. He has some real appreciation of what he was up against, and respect for what he has accomplished in spite of it all. "I graduated with honors from a top school—I put that on my [study intake] form. It said 'Education,' and I was very pleased to put that. So."

These two interviews are about relationships—for a long time Pete's least-favorite subject. But that's not true anymore, in large part because Pete has learned to tolerate the mixed feelings that characterize intimacy. That has made all the difference in the world. He can call his father a "perfectly dreadful man," and then immediately soften the judgment by offering exonerating details of his father's awful childhood. His father took drugs to cope, Pete says. But "*his* mother was a lush. . . . And his father was a cocaine addict. . . . So I mean, the guy has had it. He was screwed to begin with."

Pete's description of his father now encompasses both the terror the old man once evoked in him and the other feelings between them. "I know he wanted to show love, and I know that a lot of times—and I have to give him credit for this—he tried to be a good father. . . . Inability for him to express it right. Inability for me to accept it the way he was expressing it. And so, awkward love."

Pete knows now that "I always loved him on some level." He

can see how much the rage of his childhood had to do with fear, and why he so longed for the support of a loving older man. Is there any satisfaction in his relationship with his father now? "Yeah. I get a great deal of satisfaction from spending the least possible amount of time with him. . . . I grant you that some of it is oversensitization. But with reason. So."

Pete always maintained that his beloved mother was "a genuinely loving person," and he has come to see that they bonded as the chief victims of Mr. Hamilton's rage. But he can also acknowledge now that he and his mother were allies only in that they fought his father side by side. She did not protect him from the huge man who was "destroying the house, hitting people, screaming, breaking things." He has recently seen his mother confront some of her own insecurities, and this has shown him in a new way that in spite of her inner calm, she struggles with her own limitations.

The interviewer asks why he thinks his parents behaved as they did. "I think my father behaves the way he does because he's crazy," Pete says. "I think my mother behaves like she does, or did, to defend herself. . . . She defended herself by locking a lot of it out. I always call her the Queen of Denial, you know, because she just doesn't want to know about it." But he and his mother go back over some of their difficult times now, sharing their feelings, putting them into context, and connecting them with things that happened later. And Pete remembers there having been "a real friendship, a bond between us. A real exchange of that need for some security, or whatever it was."

He mentions in passing a fifth-grade teacher who "remained in my life for a long time"—an early expression of what seems to have been his lifelong search for supportive relationships with adult men. But even this man came in for a share of Pete's violence. Pete no longer experiences himself primarily as a violent guy, and when he goes on to detail some of his attacks on the people he *hadn't* cared about, he takes himself a little aback. "I was a very lovely child, you know," he says sardonically.

He's still looking—he may always look—for a more comprehensive perspective on his rage. He knows that long ago he needed his anger: it was the force that finally enabled him to take a stand against his father and conquer the fears that fueled his violence. But he also knows that it's exhausting and costly in the everyday world. "I don't like to be intimidated. . . . When someone tries to intimidate me, 99 percent of the time I will rise up in their face, and it won't be a game." He doesn't mean fighting; he means making clear that he is taking a stand. "That's something I don't think I would have incorporated in my being if I hadn't been so threatened as a kid. Because I think it's abnormal to be so defensive to the point of confrontation, you know? . . . I have a better handle on it now." He thinks that the defensiveness is what his experience with his father has given to his adult personality. He knows he's scared people away all his life by verbalizing his violent thoughts. And that's been a loss; his mother instilled more loving, caring, sensitive feelings in him, and it's been hard for him to put those to use. "I mean all those people I would have liked to have been friends with growing up, and I scared them all away, because I was so afraid that they were going to do something threatening to me."

He talks about the older men who have been important to him: the fifth-grade teacher, with whom he was in touch until just a few years ago; his maternal grandfather, who was (in Pete's childhood view, anyway) "the dude my father was not." A cold fish, but a man of refinement. His mother has some of this, Pete adds, demonstrating once again his new and less stylized view of her. Except for his mother, though, almost all the people closest to him are what he calls "mentors"—men at least fifteen years older than he is. "I don't have a lot of girlfriends, you know, [but] I'm very good friends with my mother. . . . I don't like my father very much, so I find all these guys I do like that have qualities I respect." One of these—surprise!—is the computerlike stepfather who used to enrage him so. He now thinks it likely that his stepfather *had* wanted to show him some feelings, but that Pete himself, in his own wariness, had prevented this.

Pete's mother and stepfather asked him to move in with them after he graduated from college. They needed a housesitter during a long trip abroad. Pete was wary, but they prevailed upon him to do it, and since then they've all gotten along well. He has come to respect his stepfather as kin to his grandfather. "He's a gentleman." Not by wealth or background, not "whoopdedo, you know? But he's got a lot of class."

One of the other exceptions to Pete's concentration on mentors was a woman who was a big "growing place" for him, the only "relationship" he ever really had. She got married, but Pete still misses her. She told him that he was a big growing place for her, too. But "unfortunately she wanted scads of babies and I couldn't do that. Not yet." So his best friend now is Herb, who let Pete move in with him for a while during Pete's years on the street.

Herb is a former alcohol counselor. His steadfastness was a cushion for Pete when the streets got "evil." Pete can admit now that although he had scoped out the fringes of the male prostitution scene in San Francisco during his *Wanderjahr,* he couldn't actually bring himself to get involved, no matter how bad things were. There was a period when he was living on Wonder Bread and trying to steel himself to do what he had to do to find a sugar daddy. But eventually he gave up and called Herb, who came a long way to pick him up. Herb was the one who bailed him out in the days when he was still getting into trouble. He's "not the sharpest guy in the world, but he's got a good heart and some knowledge, and the two of them together, you can get some good advice."

When they first met, Pete says, he was out for what he could get; he'd been deliberately cultivating an attitude of exploitation. But Herb never asked for anything back, and over time they grew closer. Pete maintained the friendship in the face of his mother's disapproval, and eventually she came to like Herb. But that doesn't mean that he and Herb don't fight. "I don't give in," says Pete. If they've reached a mutual understanding and agreed to disagree, if they find common ground, that's one thing. He doesn't need to win. But "I don't give in."

Pete has another friend—less close than Herb, but someone he spends more time with. Stan had problems when he was growing up, and has not tried to make much out of his life. His passivity frustrates Pete, but it has not destroyed the relationship. "I am trying to convince him to find some little things —nobody's asking him to go be an executive—but some little things that turn him on and go for it, just do it. You know, he likes to draw and paint. *Do it!* . . . But he still has the sensitivity of a fourteen-year-old." Stan is so easily hurt that he won't engage.

This doesn't jibe with Pete's own "usually sanguine perspective." He laughs when he says this, but he means it. "As far as I'm concerned, I've come back from the dead, and for [Stan] to sit there and mope at me, you know . . . I've got a lot going for me, but I also had a lot *not* going for me, and so I know what it is to climb back. . . . If I had believed you aren't able, I wouldn't have made it. I would have been dead." Stan doesn't have things integrated, Pete thinks. He goes on to say with his characteristic tough clarity that this is not his own great wisdom speaking, but the collected wisdom of a lot of people. "I have really collected the best of all these people that I've known. And I continue to do it. I look for the best in a person and I try to learn something from that."

He doesn't hold onto fights, he says, and he'll admit it when he's wrong. But to him, "giving in" means surrender. "I *never* surrender," says Pete again, except to preserve his life. He mocks himself for his warlike imagery, but he is very aware that relatedness opens you up to hurt, and he knows his preferred way of dealing with that—at least, he thinks he does. "Most people for me are expendable. . . . If someone hurts me or if something becomes unbearable, I'm more apt to cut it off. I may go back eventually, but . . ."

He describes a painful experience of having once been "expended," as he puts it, by a group of older men he had trusted. He won't let that happen again. "I guess I was replacing my father like ten times over. So that hurt me, and I think I've sort of hardened up to the point where I'd rather cut it first and be in control of it."

But as he and the interviewer begin to consider the complicated vicissitudes of dependence in relationships, Pete recognizes that this is no longer really so. He feels 100 percent independent in his relationships, he says, and yet he knows there's a level of dependency, because sometimes he feels lonely, and when he feels that way he'll call Stan, or he'll call Herb. He thinks some more about what he just said about expendability, and he has to admit that he really *wouldn't* "expend" Stan, even if Stan really pissed him off. He'd forgive him. He'd do it dramatically, or maybe even melodramatically, because that's how he does everything. But he'd do it. "So there's dependence there. That's as near as I can come to independence."

The final questions of these two interviews are: What has Pete learned above all from his own childhood experiences? And what does he look forward to in the future with regard to friend-ships? His responses are the mantra of a person committed to agency. To the first he says, "Get over it. Get on with it. Cognitive therapy. You know. Recognize it. Accept it. Mourn it if you need to, but get the fuck on with it. . . . Don't be a victim." To the sec-ond: "Relationships. New and exciting and better ones existing and to be discovered. . . . Meeting people out there [who are] just sucking the marrow from life. . . . Those people turn me on. Be-cause, Jesus, that's the way it should be. . . . Not moping around waiting for the end."

WHEN PETE CAME to High Valley he was dangerous. In the 1970s, children who brought guns to school were unusual even at a place like the Children's Center. Yet in spite of his real ferocity and his long and creative history of antisocial behavior, Pete's early stories show seeds of true psychological strength. He pays attention to his emotional life in the best way he can. He tries to understand himself, to do what he can to make his life work, and to protect—and find—relationships that matter to him. From his first days on the unit, Pete strives for what he later comes to call *integration*. He takes a tough-minded and honest approach to himself even when he's lying through his teeth to everyone else. He never stops struggling to figure himself out; he never de-nies responsibility for his own doings; and he is always looking for new ways to think about things or make them better.

It's relationships that are the hard part for Pete. He is caught in perhaps the most painful of all the dilemmas of children of violence: the people who should be protecting them from dan-ger are the very ones who endanger them most. He can conceive of only two ways to deal with the situation, but they're just as scary: to fight to the death, or to drug himself into indifference. Still, he is devoted to his mother in spite of her many and manifest failures to protect him from her raging husband. He perceives rightly that with all its imperfections there is something solid in his relationship with her, and he carefully protects it from his ruinous rage. She is the only person in the world for whom Pete's realistic and cynical spectacles get a bit rosy: until he's sure he can contain his rage, he doesn't let it touch her, even in thought. Pete's narrative influences his behavior pivotally here. His exaggerated regard for his mother motivates him both to contain his violence and to protect an important relationship. A narrative that concentrated on his mother's failures (as Jeff's does, for example) would likely have increased rather than diminished the pressure of his violence. This is an example of how a choice of narrative can be a fork in the road.

Similarly, although it takes Pete years of work to get a reliable handle on his violence, he never loses sight of its potential for harm. By the time we get to know him, he has already become relatively adept at making sure that the worst never happens. When his newfound and successful strategy for controlling his father's violence—out-threatening him—starts to scare Pete himself, he carefully, if indirectly, enlists reinforcements. Perhaps he was not always in quite as much control as he would like to believe, but here again his narrative—that he enlists help before something goes seriously wrong—both makes constructive sense out of some very frightening episodes and points him in the direction of establishing helpful relationships. As Pete's self-confidence grows, he can face directly the important truth that he has been looking for, and finding, supportive older men for a long time. But even before then he finds a story that encourages him in his search.

Pete doesn't waste effort denying or ignoring his problems. He takes to reflectiveness naturally; he has a real sense of what he calls his "inner self." And he has quite a notable faith in his reflections and will fight for their validity, even when they are challenged or discouraged by adults who are more conventional, more sentimental, or less brutally honest than he. Fantasy is another form of reflection for Pete—a way of becoming aware of what he feels. His dramas are disconcerting to his audiences, but they do no harm and they give him room to exercise his emotional imagination. Inside his own head he can work with the full force of his rage in a safety that the "real" world cannot offer, learning to contain it and eventually mastering it.

Pete never does, after all, knock his father through the wall. As an adult, he can look back and see that some of his furious talk was like a snake's warning rattle. It made clear that he was dangerous and warned away potential attackers (and victims). It also alerted well-disposed bystanders, if any were around, to take the countermeasures necessary to protect him and everyone else. This is another way that Pete's narrative both explains and influences his actions. It consoles him for his childhood helplessness, and gives him a goal: increased agency and self-determination.

Pete's view of his "wildness" is unusual and striking. He never relinquishes the conviction that it is a necessary and intrinsic part of him, to be preserved and nurtured and never suppressed. This is not a point of view that goes over very well at a place like High Valley; a lot of pressure can be brought to bear about such things in a psychiatric hospital, often in the guise of teaching self-control. But Pete resists it with the fundamental clearheadedness that stays with him even at the hardest times. He knows that there's a difference between self-control and compliance. He accepts the party line about needing to control himself and he believes it, partly because when he loses control he scares himself. But he also knows that he needs his wildness, so he sets himself the demanding task of integrating it. And he works on this task steadily and with dedication for the next ten years.

As soon as Pete is out of the Children's Center, he begins to grapple with the future, and his view—his narrative—of himself as agent comes to the fore. Even the complaints people made about him before his admission—that he lied, stole, threatened, manipulated to get what he wanted—speak to his sense of agency. "I never surrender," the adult Pete says. He will do, and he looks forward to doing, what he has to do to make his dreams come true.

Some of Pete's dreams, the early ones especially, are unrealistic, but that's business as usual among adolescents. And his ambitions have been shaped by his distorting early experience: either you're the cock of the walk, or you're nothing at all. He's stuck with a bad pair of alternatives until he becomes able to envision a third one, and Pete, who never surrenders, goes with the first for survival's sake. Eventually he is able to imagine a life beyond killing or being killed, a life in which you can try to fulfill your goals in relative autonomy and peace. But in the meantime his fury and grandiosity are reactions to his helplessness at his father's hands. He supports himself with dreams in which he feels powerful, and these serve his desire for agency—the antithesis of helplessness.

His extravagant visions keep him energized, and Pete remains excited about his future even when he is depressed. He confronts it actively at every turn. This is an indispensable aspect of psychological life to him. Stan, his friend of many years later, gave up that excitement when he was a kid and, as Pete sees it, doomed himself to a life of despair. Despair is not Pete's bag. He sets out to achieve his goals, and the main one is to avoid being helpless.

Pete's violence is the flip side of his preoccupation with safety. He concentrates on getting bigger and stronger and better able to defend himself (agency again: "I got bigger than my father on purpose," he says later), and the physical part of his fears begins to subside. He reframes his view of himself as a ruffian and begins nurturing his "other" side, the elegant and classy one. As he appropriates in fantasy the power of the lawyer who kept him out of jail, he envisions an alternative way of life within the system, a life where expertise, rather than violence, is the source of power, and where you don't have to be an outlaw to succeed.

After his discharge, Pete returns to the world of "real" relationships, and all the old pressures come back. But he protects his important connections, even when that means keeping away from them. His withdrawal is not indifference. His decision not to refuse his father's visits is an early glimpse of the empathy that flowers in him later.

As he fears violence less—his own and other people's—Pete lets himself experiment with closeness. Here, his use of his own narratives is especially striking. If you're a tough guy who can take care of yourself, you feel safer. And eventually you can even feel safe enough to look—at last—for older men to give you the stability and the support that you never had before. Pete's "sugar daddies" are a fantasy, as it turns out, but his narratives about them are the expression of a wish that he eventually realizes in his long and important relationship with Herb.

When Pete's optimistic view of his future falters, he's haunted by visions of inexorable failure. That's not unusual among adolescents, and it's very common in kids who need an exaggerated sense of their own power to counteract experiences of terrible helplessness. Pete's reaction is to remake himself into someone better. He'll get away from everyone else and concentrate on himself; relationships are feeling to him like much more trouble than they're worth. But for Pete, unlike some of his fellows at the Center, this is a temporary stance: a *reculer pour mieux sauter*. He is giving way a bit to afford himself a stronger advance later.

Sure enough, a year on his own renews his sense of adventure. He has tested out his central narrative—the stronger you are, the less you'll have to fight—and proven its reliability. He feels sure enough of his control now to let himself experiment with love and with anger *within the context of relationships*. He's not stuck anymore with the old dichotomy of surrendering to his rage or wrestling it into submission. He can allow it on his own terms. He can also allow himself the admission that he's been tiptoeing around for years: that he's gay.

This announcement may have less to do with sexuality per se than with the fact that Pete is now admitting how much he wants supportive relationships with men. People use sex as much as an avenue to relatedness as for its own sake, and Pete knows that he's working on his need for relationships with *males*—he already has his mother for a female figure. In acknowledging his homosexuality, he is also laying claim to feelings and the right to have them. He doesn't seem to feel particularly deeply about sex at this time. In fact, he says explicitly that he enjoys it with both men and women. But he *does* feel deeply about the newfound capacity to be open about his gayness after years of defensiveness. It adds to his confidence. He has reframed a past (perceived) weakness into an assertion of strength.

By the time Pete is twenty-five, the work of ten years is bearing fruit. He has earned a *cum laude* degree from a fine university; he's strong and physically confident; he's at peace with his history and with his family, and his sexuality isn't causing him grief in either direction. His early capacity for reflection has evolved into real empathy for himself and for his parents, and this has allowed him to reframe many of the most painful aspects of his childhood. In consequence he feels much less like a "fuck-up," with all the compensatory aggressiveness that failure has always evoked in him. He's at ease in his life. Now his central dilemma is the tension between his wish for closeness and his fear of it. Once you stop being haunted by the threat of imminent death, you have to worry about other kinds of hurt, like the vulnerability that comes with attachment.

Pete talks less about his sexuality now. He's still interested in both sexes, and love isn't really on his mind. But relationship is. For the first time, he is more engaged with the delicate pushes and pulls of intimacy than with gross struggles of physical strength. Perhaps when these are more comfortable for him he will be able to focus explicitly on what he wants in a romantic and sexual partner. "I couldn't do that," he says of the marriage and babies he didn't give the girlfriend he still longs for. "Not yet." But he *can* admit that he wasn't really hustling that year in San Francisco; the "sugar daddy" he found was more his rescuer than his victim. He's less afraid of his neediness and less ashamed.

Taking responsibility was always one of Pete's strong suits, and it still is. "When you meet three people in a row who are complete raving assholes, you better look within," he says in one of his adult interviews. And he does, in a huge and very sophisticated piece of reframing. "All these people I would have liked to have been friends with growing up. . . . I was so afraid they were going to do something threatening to me that I had to put this barbed-wire defense up." As Pete sees these things, relatedness becomes easier. Having taken responsibility for putting up the barbed-wire fences, he can consider taking them down.

The adult Pete knows that relationships are the psychological work that remains to him. And he looks forward to it. He knows what relationship can give him, if he will let it: *I look for the best in a person and I try to learn something from them.* This is exciting to him: *Those people turn me on.* And then his battle cry, and the battle cry of resilient kids all over: *Because, Jesus, that's the way it should be. . . . Not moping around waiting for the end.*

5

Rachel

I Started Seeing Things Change

RACHEL SOMER WAS IN EIGHTH GRADE, NOT quite fourteen, when she came to the Children's Center after slashing her forearms with a razor blade.

RACHEL'S MOTHER WAS a housewife while her children were growing up. She took her first job, as secretary to a local pediatrician, while Rachel was at High Valley. Mr. Somer is an engineer, the co-owner of a small business. Rachel is Mrs. Somer's daughter by an earlier marriage; neither she nor her mother has seen Rachel's biological father since Rachel was about a year old. Rachel's mother married Mr. Somer when Rachel was two; he adopted her a year later, and the new family celebrated with a name-changing party. Rachel has three younger half-siblings, two sisters and a brother, who are the children of Mr. and Mrs. Somer.

Rachel's parents reported to the High Valley staff that their daughter's early years had been unexceptional, but over time a less rosy picture developed: Rachel never really had friends. She was always uncomfortable around her peers. Her parents blamed this on the other kids' "meanness," but by their own testimony they themselves were not always at ease with outside attachments. Mrs. Somer said of her growing up that she had married her first husband as a way of getting out of her clingy family, and Rachel herself came in time to the conclusion that her adoptive father's family routinely rejected outsiders and kept its members sequestered in a tight circle. Rachel was a responsible and reliable girl—she was much in demand among neighborhood parents as a babysitter—but she had no outside interests or connections, and she kept very close to home.

Although Mr. and Mrs. Somer described their family as very close, happy, and normal, there was plenty of anger under the surface. Rachel's parents had established the same kind of highly centripetal family they had grown up in, and there wasn't much acknowledgment that a fourteen-year-old daughter should be well embarked on the adolescent journey to psychological autonomy. Both parents had grown into forceful people, but they seemed to be more concerned with keeping Rachel focused on the family than on helping her take on the world outside.

When Rachel was in the fourth grade, two good friends of the family died, people who had been "like grandparents" to the children, and her favorite uncle divorced and left the area. That was also the year that Rachel began to deal with the fact that she had been adopted by her father. For the first time, she got behind in her schoolwork. But it was not until eighth grade, according to the Somers, that things really fell apart. Rachel was failing in all of her subjects. At home she was withdrawn and unresponsive, coming out of her room only to eat. She seemed to have changed from a caring and loving child who was especially close to her father into an indifferent and "mouthy" teenager.

A lot of strain developed, and after Rachel was suspended from school for forging her parents' signatures on a bad report card, her guidance counselor arranged for her to spend a month at a local residential shelter. That move was intended to gave all parties some room to let off steam, and Rachel began at the same time to see a psychiatrist. But shortly after she returned home, she began the self-mutilation that eventually brought her to High Valley.

Rachel's behavior wasn't nearly as wild as that of many of the other kids at the Center; in fact, she was unusually quiet. But in the staff's eyes, that made her situation all the more ominous. She couldn't concentrate on anything for more than a minute or two at a time. Even among the distracted kids on the units she stood out as one who completely lacked awareness of her own feelings. Many stressed kids deal with their emotions through social activities or athletic or musical interests, but Rachel had never established any such resources. When her feelings got so strong that she couldn't ignore them, she would withdraw for hours on end or get involved in any quarrel that might cross her path. Unit staff noted that while Rachel paid almost no attention to herself, she exercised a constant and paradoxical vigilance over other people and over her surroundings; she scanned the horizon endlessly for patients and staff, waving at people a long distance away, always on guard lest she miss any comings or goings. She never left the unit voluntarily, and at school she was often seen roaming the halls as though she were looking for someone. The staff thought that this was another way of distracting herself from what she was thinking and feeling; but they also wondered if, in her perpetual reconnaissance maneuvers, she might be looking for her lost father.

Rachel was very angry. This was her reason for cutting herself, she said. But she did not reflect on her anger or evince any curiosity about it. She wasn't violent. It was just that when she got angry, she got angry. She slammed doors, cursed people out, and struggled with the staff. A staff member observed that she treated her rage like a natural phenomenon, like a thunderstorm—something that came and went and had nothing to do with her. She blamed whoever was around for the consequences. She paid no attention to her own behavior, the ideas that provoked it, or the results it produced. She expressed only one thought about it directly: that she might lose her family as she grew older and more independent. Indeed, her family did seem to have a hard time with autonomy, and did not understand or encourage it.

Rachel's lack of emotional awareness kept her from planning effectively—when it came to schoolwork, for instance. Her intentions could be instantly derailed by any feeling that might happen along and engage her in a struggle with a nurse, a teacher, or another patient. She would occasionally ask with real bewilderment, "What's wrong with me?" But she never tried to answer the question.

Rachel seemed to take delight in fomenting trouble. She involved herself wholeheartedly in any unit unrest that arose, whether it concerned her directly or not. Sometimes she was close and clingy, demanding friendship and approval; at other times she would lash out unexpectedly in ways that brought restrictions from staff and ostracism by peers. Soon she felt as isolated and scapegoated as she had at her junior high. This clingy quarrelsomeness also characterized her behavior toward her mother, and seemed to be a rather unsuccessful technique for distracting herself from her own feelings and for regulating interpersonal space. Family meetings confirmed that the Somer family had great difficulty with negotiations of closeness and distance and expressions of "negative" feelings. In this family, closeness was desired but overwhelming; distance was safer but lonely and depressing.

Rachel at first refused to participate in unit activities, but she did want time with individual staff members. The staff designed a program in which she could earn that time only by doing exactly what she was supposed to do, on the unit and at school. This settled her down. And in fact, despite all of Rachel's struggles at the Center, soon she didn't want to leave. She hated being there, but she hated being home more. Mr. Somer's medical insurance made a long hospitalization possible, and Rachel remained at the Children's Center for ten months, preparing for discharge to a residential school.

The First Interview

When Rachel comes for her first interview, she's fourteen, and six months into her admission. She knows that soon she'll be going to a "resi" (residential school)—a prospect that she loathes. The very first thing she says to her interviewer is that she doesn't know what the interview is for. Are the kids forced into answering a lot of questions? She just wants to know what she has to do. The interviewer explains, and Rachel begins to talk about her school problems. "I didn't do well in school. I could have, but a lot of kids gave me pressure. A lot of kids were on my back, and I was having a hard time with that. So my grades started slipping and I was doing really bad. . . . And then, when I went to junior high, it was a lot harder. . . . I just couldn't take it anymore, so I went to Brooks Village [a community center for troubled adolescents and families] and when my time was up there, I went to a psychiatrist that they recommended. He put me in here after about six weeks."

She didn't really know then what her problems were, and she still doesn't. "I don't really know what started it, but starting in fifth grade through the eighth grade it was just like a lot of kids were giving me trouble. . . . They were always threatening fights. . . . They didn't say much about how they felt about me or anything—just fights and things for no reason. I don't know to this day. I don't know what was wrong with me." (Here is one of Rachel's central themes. She doesn't really know what was going on and she couldn't take it anymore; other people sent her hither and yon, and now here she is. Rachel will spend the next ten years figuring out what was going on, but her days of leaving her fate in the hands of others are strictly numbered.)

Still, for the moment she's at the Center. At first Rachel paints a rosy picture: Everything's really going good now. She talks more with the staff than with her doctor because, she says, "they're closer. They spend more time with you than your doctors do." The staff is around all the time, like family, but the doctors aren't—they're more "foreign." Rachel prefers the people who are around more. She likes the people who have been here since she came in. "'Cause they can see, they can tell me how much I've changed, and point it out to me what I was like back six months ago." She laughs. "And it's really good." Her favorite person to talk to is the oldest member of the ward staff, a woman, who listens to her but feels free to disagree. It was she who first pointed out to Rachel the possibility that her own behavior might have something to do with her not getting along with the other kids. "Like the rowdiness. I used to cut myself a lot, and a lot of things used to happen. . . . I'd do things and get sent off the unit, put in locked-up seclusion and stuff. . . . I don't do much of that anymore now."

But when the interviewer asks Rachel *why* she was rowdy, she doesn't know. She's new to talking about her feelings. "I never used to talk to anyone." Even in your family? asks the interviewer. No one, says Rachel. People in her family don't talk about their feelings. She begins for the first time to ponder a contradiction: "Well, I think our family is really one close family [this is her parents' fantasy], but I don't really think that they talk about their *problems*. . . . They keep things to themselves." (Another theme: What is a close relationship, really?)

Nonetheless, when the interviewer asks what happens when things *don't* go so well, Rachel offers a reflective comment: she's too sensitive and takes things too personally, and then she gets upset. (This is an early move away from the denial of feelings that had been so striking at the time of her admission, and a first step in her growing self-awareness.)

What happens when she gets upset? Rachel says that at first she'll go to her room, and then maybe go for a walk or talk to someone. Her first reaction is still to withdraw. She tries to talk about this, to explain why she doesn't stay away as she used to at home. But her explanations are chaotic and hard to follow; she's only just learning to put together how and what she thinks about things. She tells the interviewer, for instance, that "I'm friends with just about every kid here." But she leaps from there to a description of her closest friend and why she likes her. "She's really understanding and if there's any problem she'll come and ask what's wrong. She's not quick to jump on your back or anything. She's really nice. I like her. Which you can't say that much for a lot of kids here." She doesn't notice the inconsistency.

Rachel still tends to fade out when the interviewer probes for her feelings. She's glad to be at the Center right now. "I like this place. Just being around a lot of people makes me feel good." (Soon Rachel will have some different things to say about the Center. But this is the first instance of a very consistent strength: she makes excellent use of rose-colored glasses to help her tolerate anger while it's happening, and then looks back on it after the fact, from the safety of distance. Still, it's true that she wants a lot of people to be around—something that she's just beginning to understand.)

When the interviewer asks about her family, Rachel offers the party line. "It's a nice family." But the interviewer wants to know more—What are the people like?—and tries to give her a way to think about it: How would you describe them to a stranger who has never met them? Rachel can't do it. She tries her hardest to answer, but she just gets more and more flustered. "I think my parents are a little bit strict. I guess they don't want to see me growing up, or whether—I don't know—whether they can understand just how people grow up. . . . I don't really know what to say about that. I'd never really talk to my family. . . . They always try to make you, but I never did." She's having a terrible time with this, and the interviewer tries to make it easier, but Rachel keeps falling back on "I don't know." They finally give it up, agreeing that talking to her family is one area where things still haven't changed all that much.

They move on to her parents' strictness. How do they react when Rachel breaks their rules? "They're upset, but you know, I don't really know how they *feel* if they don't say anything; it's just that they get mad." Her best friend "outside" is a schoolmate, a guy her age who's been in some trouble with the law for stealing. But he's getting some help now, and he can be sympathetic to her ups and downs because he's had his own. (This is an expansion of Rachel's what-are-relationships theme, and her first foray into an area that will take on great importance to her—the need for people to *share* feelings with her as an equal. Just someone to talk to is not enough.)

She flounders again when they talk about her relationships on the unit. "It's more or less like a family—but not really—just like in a family setup, sort of." She can't think of relationships out of the context of "family," and she loses what articulateness and reflectiveness she has when that loaded subject comes up.

But even in this interview, as she cautiously practices looking at herself, she shows that she is developing some real insight into relationships on which she has more distance. Once she got used to the kids here, she says, she could see "exactly what was on their minds." She clarifies: she now believes that the behavior of the kids at her old school—the scapegoating that was so hard for her—was a reaction to their own private worries about being left out.

When the interviewer tries to bring her back to her family, Rachel again reverts to monosyllables, except for asserting three separate times—when she feels that the interviewer is not grasping this—that she does not know her parents. (These are not her usual overwhelmed "I don't know"s. They're a clear description of a real situation as she understands it. Already Rachel has a sense for when intimacy isn't really there; she may not know much about it, but she knows when it's missing.) The one family member she talked to, she says, was an uncle about eight years older. He has moved away, so she doesn't get to see him much anymore. This makes her sad. (It also gives credence to her parents' belief that losses in the family may have precipitated Rachel's decline.)

Plans for the future? Rachel talks readily about the plan, not hers, that she go to a residential school. She's thinking of being a childcare worker. (Childcare workers are unit staff, often quite young people without professional degrees who are thinking about careers in psychology. They are usually the people who are most around for the kids to talk to and be with, and usually the closest to the kids in age.) But, Rachel goes on, she doesn't want to do it in a place like the Children's Center, where there's too much "unlocking doors and locking this and locking that. It's too much of a hassle. You don't really get enough time to spend talking with the kids." (Rachel is openly preoccupied with how kids can find the people they need to talk with—but even at her time of greatest need, she is not willing to pay any price for it. She wants closeness and independence both.)

Rachel doesn't really know what kind of further training she'd need, but she'd get it if that's what she had to do. Yes, she's had troubles in school, but she thinks it would be different now. It would be easier. *This* time, she would know what she's doing.

She still can't support that wish with detailed self-awareness. She acknowledges that she still doesn't *really* know what was going on back in her old school. She wouldn't write a paper if she was asked to then, but now she probably would. The interviewer points out that that's quite a change, and asks if there are other things she'd like to change. "Well," says Rachel, "I don't even know what I'm looking for. Like five months ago I didn't know what I wanted to change, but after I look back I see what I *have* changed. So I don't really know what I'm looking forward to." (This will become Rachel's most reliable tool in building the life she wants: her faith in her capacity to change, even when she doesn't understand how it happens. She is not reflective enough—yet—to discern what is going on inside her from one moment to the next, but she can look back, she can see, and she can learn.)

The interviewer again approaches the question of changes Rachel would like to make with her family; again Rachel withdraws. She says only that she doesn't feel connected with them, and that even though they try to connect with her, something gets in the way. As they spend a few minutes anticipating the part of the study where the family will be interviewed together, Rachel withdraws still further. She says anxiously that she's heard that "they get you set up so that you're in a fight with your parents—that you people sort of set it up that way." The interviewer tries to explain, but Rachel is lost in this fantasy for the time being. The interview ends.

The Second Interview

Rachel is a bit shy of sixteen at her next interview. She left High Valley as planned to go to a local residential school from which she has recently been expelled. At first she blows this off—"It didn't work out"—but as she settles down, she acknowledges more robustly that she was breaking the rules and cutting classes and "having too much of a good time." They warned her and warned her, but she kept doing it anyway. The interviewer asks what she thought about that, and Rachel, who on her admission had blamed anyone and everyone else for the trouble she got into, says flatly, "I was surprised they let me stay as long as they did." She'll be going to another school now, and if she does well there, she can go back to this one next year.

At first she was bothered about having to change schools, she says, but now she realizes that she can still see all her friends. And although she's had to talk a lot about all the things that went wrong, it's okay, because she herself can see so clearly the difference between the way she was a year ago and the way she is now. "I think it's mostly the way I feel about myself and my family and stuff. Me and my parents get along a lot better now. . . . Everything's straightened out a lot. It's like I used to be afraid to say things, talk to them, tell them how I felt. Now it doesn't bother me to say things. I can explain myself better. And we get along. They understand me and I understand them a lot better."

Rachel offers no details; her feelings about her parents still don't find much expression beyond generalizations. But she does go on to recapitulate explicitly something she said in the first interview that seems to be very important to her: she can see very clearly that *she herself* has changed. The interviewer asks her what caused this. Rachel doesn't know, but she knows what she sees; she guesses that "just growing up" is the reason. Have *they* changed? asks the interviewer. "No. I don't know. *I've* changed a lot. I don't know about them."

She goes on. "I used to depend on people. When I got here, I used to depend on people more than I should. . . . Here, everybody used to do everything for you. Like I really got used to it. . . . I didn't know what to do. It was like I could never see myself. . . . There's no way, I wouldn't believe, you know, my self-image has gone up so much. More dependent on myself, a lot better about myself, it's easier, life just seems to be easier."

Now she makes her own decisions. "I never noticed it," she says when the interviewer asks about the process of the change, "but then when I went back I could see. . . . *That's* when I can see changes."

She returns to her previous theme of independence. For three weeks after she left the hospital, she had a terrible time. Everybody had been making decisions for her, and when she left, she was suddenly lost. *This* transition, the one after her expulsion from school, is very different, because this time she knows what to do with herself. "I didn't know where to turn, you know. All these people had been doing everything for me, and they sent me out, and they said, 'Well, here you are.' And I just had to start looking for my own life. . . . After a few weeks, I started realizing that things had to be done and that I was the one that had to do them. It was easier after I started thinking that way, you know. It was fun for a while because I'd never been able to do things on my own—people were always doing them for me. And then that started changing. I could control my own life. It was something else. I enjoyed it."

The interviewer asks what it was like in those three weeks, before she started taking control, and she describes a period of frantic dependency and then a realization: "They're not going to do anything for me. So I started doing it myself."

"I think this place is a big mistake, you know, the way they run it," she goes on. "They really make you depend on them, like you don't move without making sure that they approve first. So it was very hard for a while." Almost like a new family, says the interviewer. "Yeah, it was. It was really just like that." (This is an astute and subtle recognition of the existential paradox of psychiatric hospitalization, which enforces profound dependency as a condition for growth. It's also a commentary on Rachel's own early environment. In exercising the right to make more and more of her own decisions, she is challenging both the traumatic aftermath of the hospitalization and the stultifying confinement of her controlling family.)

Now, she says, she does things her way. When the interviewer asks if doing things on her own was a problem before she came to the hospital, she replies: "I never did anything. I just like went to school, and was totally withdrawn from my family. I just came home and sat around. I didn't do anything. I wasn't happy. . . . I wasn't in control of myself. I could never understand how they kept telling me, 'Things will get better,' and I couldn't see it, you know. I never had seen change before, and they kept telling me, 'You *will* see it,' and I didn't even know what it was. And then I started seeing things change and stuff, and it really made me happy and it made me keep going."

The interviewer goes back to Rachel's comment that "this place is a big mistake," and asks why Rachel thinks she shouldn't have been here. But Rachel, who once didn't know what she thought, recognizes the misunderstanding right away, and is quick to make herself clear. "I don't think it was a mistake to come here. I just think it was a mistake the way they made you depend on them, 'cause it was hard for me after I left. And it was also hard for me while I was here. Because after they started saying, 'Well, depend on us,' I did. And then when I went on my own, I couldn't take it." (Again, Rachel delineates this quandary with delicacy and subtlety. The hospital staff are trying to foster self-awareness and independence of thought, but as they do so they are exercising extreme control.) Rachel can see the contradiction in this. She sadly mentions a friend from High Valley who stayed there for two years. "She depended on them so much that she wouldn't leave."

Rachel's been paying attention to this. She made a lot of friends at her school, and for the first time she experienced herself as the equal of other people. She started seeing things differently. "I wasn't dependent on them, you know. It was like we were good friends, a lot of us, and I never really had that before. It was really something special to me, and I was just as good to other people as they were to me, like I could help them as much as they could help me, and that really made me feel a lot better. . . . [On the unit], we all depended on them, they didn't depend on us, and it was just the opposite when I got out. You know, people depended on me as much as I depended on them, on an equal basis. It showed me a lot. It showed me that I was just as good as other people."

They explore her troubles at school. Rachel maintains her own theories about those troubles, despite apparent skepticism from the interviewer, who seems disposed to accentuate the negative—for instance "copping out" of schoolwork. Rachel agrees that she did that occasionally. But she insists that it's more accurate to say not that she did less schoolwork, but that she did more of other things. Schoolwork is less important to her now than having friends. (This is interesting in several ways. Rachel, the girl with no friends and no interests, now has a very gripping interest indeed: friends. Her priorities for the moment are clear, and she will pursue what she values even in the face of a lot of pressure from the elders who advise her. But she doesn't yet anticipate how tough it can be to attain the balance she seeks between connection and autonomy.)

For now, she insists that the way she managed her friendships "was good for me and for them." But she does go back to reconsider her statement about whether or not she copped out, this time in a more discerning way. She had been thinking that she didn't know what to do with her life. So she'd just *do* things, and block the thoughts out of her head. (This is the technique that the High Valley staff had noticed, the one they considered responsible for her very serious cognitive problems. But as her next comment shows, she's aware of it now and paying attention to it.) "After a while, it started catching up on me: 'Well, I have to start thinking more.'"

You *have* to think, Rachel goes on. If you aren't thinking, even friendship can be a problem, because you have to keep yourself and your friends separate. Otherwise you'll break your neck trying to help someone else. She likes that aspect of herself, but she knows it's a potential problem: "I didn't adjust myself at all . . ." She trails off.

The interviewer asks, Is it like you lose yourself in their problems?

No, says Rachel, "I just don't pay any attention to *my* problems." (This is a really acute piece of self-analysis. Rachel has discovered for herself what the staff had been so concerned about: that she distracts her attention from her own feelings by a painful and defensive preoccupation with other people.) Still, she says now, she's not going to change it. Why not? asks the interviewer. "Just the fact that they're my friends." (She can see the problem, but she's not willing to solve it by being less involved. This is reminiscent of Pete's unwillingness to give up his "wildness" on anyone's terms but his own. In Rachel's relationship narrative, this is also one of the points from which she looks both backward and forward. When her first relationships get out of balance, she recognizes it and begins to imagine a more balanced way of relating. Having imagined it, she sets out to look for it.) They talk about whether she's working on this in her therapy, and that shifts the conversation back to High Valley.

Rachel hates coming back to the hospital for doctor's appointments. "It's like I've changed so much, and people look at me as a person like I used to be. . . . They treat me like I used to be treated, and that really bothers me," she says, confirming the staff's hypothesis that her problems had something to do with her parents' denial of her growing teenage need for independence.

She is testing out her fears that "negative" feelings destroy relationships. "I don't lose friends," she says. "People just stick with me. . . . If they don't work out one way, then you're always friends, you know?" She's been seeing a guy off and on for two years; they both see other people. She's a little surprised that they're still friends, because they used to take all their angry feelings out on each other. That doesn't happen anymore? asks the interviewer. "It does, but we always get over it," Rachel says.

The interviewer asks if she's noticed any changes with her family, about whom Rachel had barely been able to say a word the year before. She's more able to say what she wants now, Rachel says. "It's like they say things to me, and I'll be able to say something back if I don't agree, or something. Before, I couldn't do that. But I don't talk to them as far as my problems and my feelings. Never have.

"Never have," she repeats emphatically. "Just doesn't fit me, you know. Some people do and some don't." But if she has an argument with her parents, she can now say how she feels about it, whereas before she couldn't answer them. What would you do? the interviewer wants to know. "Just sit there and listen to them. I mean, they could talk for *hours* and I couldn't say anything."

They're getting ready to stop. The interviewer asks if there's anything she wants to talk about. Not really, Rachel says, so they do a little comparing of this year's interview and last year's. Rachel acknowledges having held a lot back last year and laughs at herself. The new school she's starting at is smaller than the old one. She thinks that's better—she can get more individual attention. "I need help. That's why I'm going there, you know, not to fool around as I have done." And they make plans to see each other next year.

The Third Interview

Rachel comes for her third interview. She's seventeen and has just graduated from high school. She's married. And she's pregnant—the baby is due in three weeks. Rachel leaps excitedly into her tale: She and George didn't want to get married until after Rachel finished school, but Rachel was determined to have the baby right after graduation. So they conceived the baby before they got married. It was the only way to do it. The interviewer expresses some surprise—her parents did too, Rachel says—and offers the opinion that it must be trying to be expecting a first baby at seventeen. Yah, says Rachel, but this is how she wanted it. When the baby is twelve or thirteen she'll only be in her twenties, with plenty of time to do whatever she wants. She'll have her whole life ahead of her. (Other people may not approve of Rachel's plans, but they can't say anymore that she's incapable of making them. And she now has a very vivid sense of having a future.) The pregnancy has been good, she goes on. No problems, except that she misses going out at night.

What about the stressful side of it? asks the interviewer. She feels rebellious. "It's because I'm so young. I'm not used to someone telling me, 'You can't do this.'" A confusing statement ensues—there's a brief breakdown of narrative coherence—and it takes them some time to unravel it. It turns out that Rachel is speaking not of *someone else* telling her what not to do, but of having to tell herself. She's talking about the need for self-discipline and responsibility. "No more all-night this or skipping that or just taking off here and there." And she's making an effort not to let herself get overinvolved with people. "Because I just get myself too caught up in their problems. That is one of *my* biggest problems. . . . This year I just said, 'Wait, I am going to sit back and straighten out my *own* life and do what I want to do.'"

The interviewer asks her yet again (this comes up every year) whether listening to other people's problems keeps her from attending to her own, but Rachel makes the same distinction she has before. It wasn't the listening that was the problem, but that "I would lots of times put people's problems ahead of mine. But it's a lot easier now, too. I am not living with so many kids either, so it's easier to separate myself."

They talk about the glorious end of her high school career: Rachel has graduated a year early, with honors and extra credits. It was hard to convince her parents and her school that this early motherhood was what she wanted. They were all sure she wanted help with *not* getting pregnant, and they couldn't hear anything different. She stuck out the accelerated program to get everyone off her back, because she wanted very much for her parents not to be unhappy with her. (Her narrative about balancing the demands of relationships and the demands of the outside world has taken a new turn. She isn't yet tackling the problem of the conflicting demands *within* relationships.)

It turns out that the interviewer hasn't heard her either, and asks if there was any point where she wondered about her decision to keep the baby. But Rachel rejects immediately the implication that the baby was an accident: "No, definitely not. Like I said, this was something that we planned. It was a shock to a lot of people because I'm so young, but I have my own reasons. I would rather do it now than twenty years from now."

Why? the interviewer wants to know. Rachel repeats herself patiently. "Well, like I said before, I will still be young and be able to start over again. Most people don't get married and get settled until twenty-five to thirty, you know. I'll be starting then doing something that I want to do, and go to school, too. That was my main reason."

They talk about parenthood, and Rachel points out that as the neighborhood's most sought-after babysitter she has taken care of a lot of kids in her day. When the interviewer asks her what she thinks will be the hardest, she responds, "I think just making the right decisions. Every mother thinks, 'Well, you know, I am not going to do what my mother did; I am going to do it this way and that way.' But, like, everybody makes their mistakes. I think just knowing I am going to bothers me, but that's the only problem I have with it."

The interviewer wonders about her forethought. Is she seeing that there is a certain sacrifice that she'll have to make before she starts over at twenty-five or thirty? Of course, says Rachel. "You can't just get up one day and say, 'All right, I am not going to have the kid today—I am just going to go off and do what I want to do.' You can't do that."

How do you feel about that? the interviewer asks. "That's fine with me. I thought about it a lot beforehand. Like, a lot of people think I can run off when the baby is two years old and do what I want, but that is not the case. It's a lifetime commitment. But this way—I was really responsible for myself at twelve and thirteen, you know, and so I think my child will probably be the same way." (Rachel is still a teenager, with the teenager's great gift of seeing only what she wants to see. She also has the teenager's limitless faith in her own capacities. But her willingness not to be cowed by the fear of being less than perfect is an enormous strength.)

The interviewer asks her what she has, or wants, to give her child. Understanding and honesty, Rachel says. "I don't know if there is a certain way to do it. I think it's just feeling. Or just letting the kids know where you are coming from and not trying to hide all the time the things that you feel. And I think that my parents did that a lot, and I don't do that."

And how about what you want in return?

"Well, I'm not going to say anything. Because I don't think parents should say, 'Well, I want this in return.' Because a lot of times they don't get it, and if they are always looking for something, then you are always going to be disappointed with kids. . . . Just respect, and that's about it. And that is something I have always had with my parents." (In her anticipation of motherhood, she is putting her parents into a new context that makes their behavior with her more comprehensible.)

They talk a bit about finances. George is working; she would like to work, but she doesn't need to right now. They aren't looking for riches. They might move out of state where things are easier, but it's great not to be starting out with nothing. They are on their own financially, but Rachel's parents are emotionally supportive.

How has she been feeling over the past year? There have been ups and downs, says Rachel. She was down for a while after her last interview. She took off from home and school for three weeks, drinking and getting high. But after that, she and George started to get really close. "And it was something I could really hang on to, something I grew with. So I straightened out and mellowed out a lot. . . . I see people do it now and I say, 'My God, that's crazy.'" She attributes her mellowing partly to George's being older than she is, and partly to her new sense that the relationship gave her something to do. "Probably just something to put my energy towards, because I just didn't have anything before, other than going out and taking off all the time." (She knows now that one way to handle anxiety is to pay attention to something that interests you; she couldn't do this when she was in her early teens.)

She was sad, Rachel says, when her parents couldn't accept her plans at first, because she wanted more than anything for them to be happy with her. But "I just stood up and said to myself, 'Hey, this is my life and this is what I want to do. I wish you could accept it. If you can't, that's too bad.' Maybe I didn't mean it, but that's how I stood up and said it, and then they started to come around. Once they knew I was going to finish school, they knew I could get it together, then they felt better." So did she. (She is still very dependent on their approval, but she has found ways to negotiate on her own behalf and to mend fences when necessary.)

The interviewer asks about her previous year's experience of taking control of herself. "Well, I definitely got what I wanted. I just couldn't see where all these people were telling me, 'You can't do it,' you know, 'You can't be on your own,' you know, 'You just couldn't handle it with your emotions,' and this and that. And I just knew they were full of it. . . . I *have* done it, you know?"

They discuss the boundaries between dependence and independence. Rachel knows that she still needs people. She doesn't like being alone, and that makes her dependent on her husband. But she's not as sensitive as she was. And she feels that he depends on her as much as she does on him. Not in the same ways, but it's an interdependence, and that matters to her. She states again her belief that reciprocity and equality in relationships are important for self-respect.

The interviewer asks her what stays with her as she looks back over the past year. "I think it was just a year ago that I took charge of myself. . . . I feel good about myself. . . . Not being so dependent on other people, other people who wouldn't be there forever—that was one thing that took a lot of work." (Rachel is somewhat preoccupied with other people who won't be there forever, and she is still more fearful about this than she can acknowledge. But she copes with the anxiety in what has become a reliable way: by downplaying her weaknesses until she's in a position of relative strength, and then looking back on them and tackling them. Right now her efforts are more toward establishing "forever" people than toward learning to tolerate separateness, or even the flexibility of distance that characterizes more mature relationships. Pete did it the other way round. He found the risks of relationships easier to take as he felt surer that he could go it alone.)

Rachel goes on to describe a very painful experience of being left by someone who was very important to her—that was why she split from school for those three binge-y weeks. But she said to herself: "I am going to pick it up where I left off, and just not get so dependent on other people." And, she says, she took pains to learn to stand on her own two feet before she jumped into the relationship with her husband. (This is a continuation of the previous theme. She hasn't completed the job of learning to stand on her own two feet, of course. Very few people have, at seventeen. But Rachel's most striking characteristic is the steady alternation between her innocent hopes about how things could be, which give her the courage to take risks, and her later grapplings with how things really are. She has seen that being dependent doesn't forestall loss, and neither does keeping other people dependent on you. But the unexpected departure was a wake-up call to Rachel, and she is trying again to protect herself from unreliable relationships, this time by institutionalizing her connections through marriage and motherhood.)

She does make clear that her relationship with her husband involves a different kind of dependence than she felt for the mysterious person who left. "If I didn't see that person every day, and if that person didn't fill my needs every day, I was just like, 'What am I going to do,' you know? And when I got caught up in that . . . I just had to break, so that's what I did. That took a lot of work, it took a long time to heal, but once I did I definitely felt a lot better. That's when everything started pulling together. I was glad for that."

Rachel goes on to talk more specifically than she has before about the nature of her friendships. Most of them have been with older people. Her husband, too, is older than she is. "I just never went for kids my age. . . . I think it is trust. . . . Because I really didn't like kids my age when I was in school, so it was like older people I could trust not to turn around and stab me in the back. Which I found out not to be true all the time, but . . . you know, it was different."

The interviewer asks some very sober questions about money, and quarrels, and the statistics of divorce among very young couples. Rachel takes a positive view, as she has done about just about everything since her discharge from the hospital. Hopelessness is not for her.

Money isn't that important to her, she says, and she and her husband aren't into the fighting scene. As for divorce: "I know that I won't get divorced, even if I go through hell first; I know I won't, because I didn't get married to get divorced. . . . If there is things wrong, what we would do probably is take time away from each other, and we have done that a lot. . . . I think working things out is 100 percent better than getting divorced. . . . Trying to get things back together is very important to me."

What do you think you will have to work hardest on, to be successful at being a mother next year? To continue to change and grow?

"I think growing up," Rachel says. "Because I have to do that, just taking the responsibility of the ages as they come. The Big One-Eight is not going to be that big for me, because I have already done everything. So, I don't know, just adjusting to whatever plans there might be, and trying to make it better every day. . . . I take things as they come."

Rachel is very poignantly adolescent here in her sense of invulnerability and her all-or-nothing view of things: she's been there and done that; she knows everything she needs to know; she'll never get divorced. But when the interviewer asks if she's going to have to grow to handle the stresses of being a mother and a wife, she makes a very adult distinction between growing and "growing": "No, I don't think so. I definitely don't think so. Years ago, people got married and had kids, and their lives changed and they became the housewife, barefoot and pregnant and let's make supper. . . . I don't want to get older just to be a wife and be a mother. I just can't see that. I think not being outrageous in front of a kid, like not having big parties and stuff like that, is one thing that I would do, but I will not try to become older just to set a role, because I think that scares kids too."

The pros and cons of her own parents? "Well, they were always there. Even if they hated you, they loved you. I could always go back and say, 'I'm sorry.' And just to have them always there and never say to me, 'Get out and never come back,' and mean it, was really important to me. I think that is one thing I would like to do." (That is indeed very important to Rachel; in fact, it is so important that she can't really test it out until she is considerably older and braver. It's the expression of a very deep but as yet un-realized wish.)

The interviewer asks how she feels about the prospect of saying goodbye to childhood. Rachel has thought about this. "It happened so fast that I missed saying to myself, 'Maybe I should have waited until I was twenty.' But it's just something to think about. I mean, if you were twenty-five and did it, you might say, I wish I had done it five years ago. I think just the freedom of be-ing a teenager is going to change. But I don't know if I am going to miss it. I don't think so."

Jobs? Rachel hasn't had the true big First Job yet, not the kind that pays. She'll probably want to work after a couple of years, but who knows what will happen between now and then? What she looks forward to now is "pulling our lives closer together, I think. My family closer together. I think that's a major thing." She worries about being able to maintain her friendships, and the worst thing she can imagine is something happening to her parents. As they begin to wrap up the session, the interviewer asks what she thinks the key is for understanding the changes she's made in the last year. "I think just looking at myself. In the past, I have been really sensitive and really worried about what people thought of me. I think the most important thing to do is not to worry so much about what people think of you, but worry more what you think of yourself. And I think once I found that I'm number one, then I could really stand up and give to other people what they have been giving to me for so long."

Thanks for coming in, the interviewer says. "It was fun," says Rachel.

The Fourth Interview

At her next interview, Rachel is almost eighteen. She's been out of the hospital for three years, and she's the mother of a healthy baby boy. She and her husband have moved into their own house, and everything has worked out—childbirth, money, marriage, motherhood. George is happy as a father, and Rachel feels that with Danny's advent the two of them are really getting to know each other after the tensions of pregnancy. She doesn't even feel particularly deprived of free time. Her husband works a three-to-eleven shift, so he can watch the baby in the mornings if she wants to go out or if, as she is contemplating, she gets a job. "We always have free time," she says. "We never consider ourselves tied down, because the baby's really good and he never gives us any trouble at all. He never cries. When he has a problem, he cries like anybody would, but otherwise he doesn't." She feels okay about leaving him with his grandmothers, but she's not ready for babysitters yet. They have a weekend a month to themselves, and otherwise they take the baby with them everywhere.

What's it like having the baby totally dependent on you? the interviewer asks. I just take it naturally, says Rachel. She's looked after a lot of babies; she enjoys it. She repeats her assertion of last year: "I'm glad I was young." The interviewer asks what she's good at as a mother, and Rachel finds that a hard question. "I don't know. We take care of him really well, and we have a nice environment, and we both spend a lot of time with him. Being able to spend time with him and having him know who we are and be happy—it's good. We have a lot of patience."

There are some hard parts. George has a great job, but it doesn't provide quite enough for a family of three, especially now that they'd like to move to the suburbs. They think about it, but it's not an issue between them. When tensions come up they argue briefly and then talk afterward. Usually it's she who starts the arguments. "He sort of just says what he says and that's all he is going to say. But me, I like to go on and on." But they don't really fight that often.

As usual, she equivocates when the interviewer asks what she anticipates over the next several years: "I don't know, I really can't say." When pressed about whether she'll work, she says, "Oh, I'll definitely maybe be working." George might go to school, or he might not—he wants to be a programmer. He has a good job now, but he's afraid of getting bored, and if he wants to go to school, he can. Rachel herself still hasn't thought about what she wants to do as a job. She doesn't know about other children, either. Not for another twelve or thirteen years at least. (This is at odds with her idea of last year—that she would get her childrearing over early, so as to be free for school at thirty.) She's not sure. This is it for a while. But when the interviewer changes the subject to friends, Rachel as always reengages immediately. In fact, the richness of her discussion of her friendships makes apparent by contrast how little she has to say about her relationship with her husband, or about her marriage. What especially pleases her is that she has a closest friend now. "We just hit it off right from the beginning. That's it. I don't really know how to say why. It just happened, and she is really understanding and she needs me as much as I need her and that's what makes us stay, like others didn't."

Rachel still has very little to say about her family. But she has been thinking about her early troubles and the High Valley days. "That was a big mistake, and that is where it all started, coming here. Because once you are in a place like this, you really know all the bad things in the world."

At first it sounds as though Rachel isn't acknowledging the extent of the troubles that brought her to High Valley, but she is trying for something more subtle than that, and she goes on: "I had problems that could have been dealt with at home, not here. It would have been better dealt with at home. I can see people coming here, sure, but I wasn't one of the ones who should have, and I sort of learned how to swear, how to spit, how to be mean, you know? I just really disliked this place totally. I think it is wrong for a lot of people who are here to be here. . . . I think they treat you totally inhuman." How? asks the interviewer. "For one, my first day here they told me I was coming in here for an interview, and neither my parents nor I knew that I was coming here for good. And you just walk into the place and they lock the door behind you, and you feel like, 'What's going on?' You know, I think it could have all been dealt with at home. And it wasn't. So . . ." She trails off.

The interviewer asks how she thinks it should have been dealt with. "There should have been counseling, family counseling at home." And nobody tried that? "Well, I had gone to a psychiatrist. . . . He never worked out right. . . . He told me that if I tried to kill myself I could get out of my family life and not have any problems, and so that's what I did. . . . When you are twelve years old and someone says something like that to you, and you are totally confused . . . I just couldn't see anything else to do."

The interviewer starts to ask for clarification, but Rachel breaks in. "I'm not saying he's responsible, but I *am* saying when you tell a kid something like that—I wouldn't have done it without his help." And if you had gone to a different doctor, maybe it would have worked out? "Maybe it would have worked out, yah. He told me, and I think he told my parents, that this place was like a country club, and there is horseback riding and swimming and you walk around. You have friends. And he made it sound like . . ." (Here the tape had to be turned over and a piece of the dialogue is missing.) "I don't know, all of a sudden it was just like, 'Wow, you know, it was really weird and I was there for ten months, you know? Met people and grew.' I mean, I would have done that outside of my town anywhere—I don't see why I had to be in that institution. But I did all the growing things that I should have done somewhere else up there."

(Rachel forgets that it was she who had not wanted to leave the hospital once she settled down. But she may be right that with some real help she and her family could have resolved their problems at home. She's expressing her belief in herself as someone who could have been helped to do her growing outside the hospital. The authorities having failed her, she has taken it upon herself to do better.)

The interviewer asks if she tells people about her experience at the hospital. She has talked about it, she says, but she would just as soon forget it. Even driving back for the interview, she feels confined. "The thing I found the worst was seeing real young kids. For me, I thought, 'I can handle this, now that I am out,' but what really bothered me was seeing young kids being put in for reasons that they really don't have anything to do with." She tells a story about an episode with a very young patient that she dreamed about for a long time; she doesn't think young kids should end up taking the responsibility for their parents' problems. (This is the first clue to Rachel's feelings on that subject.)

A complicated discussion ensues. Rachel says that she got

worse before she got better at High Valley. She saw other kids kicking people, and "after a while, that was like the only thing I could do, you know?" She needed to grow up. But "it happened too fast. And I wasn't really ready for it. It was something that would have happened anywhere." She agrees that she needed someone to talk to, but High Valley was "too much for me." Some people need a place like that, she admits, but some don't. "It was just something, one thing, I wish that I had never gone through. But it happened. And I don't really think about it too much anymore." They go on talking about the pros and cons of hospitalization for different people, and Rachel shares some very perceptive observations about the way the unit is run. But the interviewer challenges her view that she could have made her changes elsewhere: How do you now deal with the kinds of things that used to be enough of a problem that you had to come here, when those same kinds of stresses come up in your life?

"They don't," says Rachel.

They don't even occur?!?

"No, it was definitely just adolescence and getting space, and I think it was just having real friends and knowing that people enjoyed being with me. . . . Now if someone comes up to me and says 'I can't stand you,' I say 'Hey, that's your business.' But if someone had done that to me five years ago . . ."

It changed, Rachel says, when she recognized that her problems and experiences were not so different from those of people she liked and respected. That meant that "other people can open up to me, and that they respect me and care for me, and that other people have gone through things that I have and picked themselves up and done well with their lives. And I think that is really important. People don't know that other people have had problems; they are not going to think that is helpful for a lot of kids." (This is the culmination of Rachel's growing conviction that her parents' inability to present themselves as uncertain or imperfect kept her from putting her own problems into perspective, and so from learning to respect herself despite her difficulties. She is using her now-reliable tendency to simplify a problem for a while until she has enough distance on it and enough emotional energy to cope more decisively.)

She's pretty happy now, Rachel says. She has everyday worries and concerns—sometimes money, sometimes boredom—but she's content. When she has a problem with someone, she sorts it out right away and then doesn't think of it anymore. "But if I don't tell them, then it is in the back of my head until I do." The baby gives her joy, and so do weekends with her family. Does she have frustrations or angers in her role as a mother? "Nope, none of those. It's weird. I don't have any problems with him—he is really too good. Maybe he's going to have a bad adolescence or something, but he's really good now."

When you think about your own adolescence, says the interviewer, what kind of parent do you want to be? As usual, when asked to speculate Rachel backs off. "Oh, that is so hard to answer." The interviewer tries again. How will you be different from your own parents? "Maybe I won't be—I don't know. I just can't answer that."

You haven't thought that out, or planned it?

No, says Rachel. "Everyone thinks that they are going to be the greatest parents, and 'I am not going to be like my parents, and I am going to do this right and that right.' But I have sort of figured out that he is going to do what he has to do, and I am going to let him know that we are there. That is all I can do. I am not going to drive myself like my parents did." But she adds immediately that she's only saying that now, and that when it comes down to it, she probably *will* drive herself.

You think it would have been better in your case if they hadn't been like that?

No, says Rachel. Better for them. (Rachel's psychological acumen is growing. She can see her parents as separate from herself even when their behavior affects her painfully, and offer them real empathy for their own troubles.) Things are going well with her family, she goes on. They are content with her and happy *for* her, and she's content with them. Her main goal is to move out of the city. The interviewer asks if there's anything she dreads. No, Rachel says—she's not dreading anything.

This is the last interview for the teenage Rachel, and the interviewer asks her if there's anything she wants to talk about. She says that she can't think of anything. Anything they haven't hit on that's important in her life? Nope, says Rachel. Any feelings about the interview? Nope.

They talk a little about the study. Rachel wants to know whether, when it comes out, it will have anything to do with the hospital itself. The interviewer prevaricates a little. "Certainly they are interested in finding out ways of dealing with kids better, and I think a lot of people here will be interested in seeing some of the suggestions you've made. They're always interested in finding new approaches."

"That I'll believe when I see it," says Rachel.

The Follow-Up Interviews

Rachel's frame of mind when she returns for the follow-up interviews at twenty-five is very different from the tolerant and placid one of eight years earlier. Despite her earlier prognostications, she's divorced. She's involved at last in a stable and satisfying relationship—with a woman. She's in school, pursuing a professional degree. And she is absolutely furious at her father.

This last causes her some trouble. The adult interviews deliberately raise stressful issues about early relationships with parents, and this has never been Rachel's easiest topic. The crisp articulateness of her late teens fails her for a while.

She tackles the task gamely, however, and after some struggle she manages to say that she had never realized how much was really *not* "there" for her. "It was uncomfortable to have emotions," she goes on. "It was uncomfortable to be angry in my house. And I *was* angry and I *was* frustrated, and it was very difficult because I wasn't allowed to express that at all." Her mother got angry at her when she did. Rachel has gained some perspective on this. "Now I see that she probably felt uncomfortable with my anger and couldn't deal with it herself. . . . I think that went for both of my parents." Still, it gets to her. "A very angry relationship," she says. "A very angry family, I think. Although it was not a good emotion to have in my house, it is there all the time." (Now it is possible to see the disorganizing fury beneath Rachel's respectful platitudes about how "they always loved me." They did. But there was real anger there too, and it has taken Rachel a lot of years to let herself know it and risk its effect on her parents.)

Even now it makes her nervous. She trails off after this brief spurt of fluency and retreats briefly to the "always there" bromides, in a last-ditch contradiction of what she's just said about how much was missing. When Rachel has spoken of anger before, it's been an abstraction. Now *experienced* anger is pressing on her. Finally she gives up and takes it on awkwardly. She starts out to answer a question, ends up someplace else, and has no idea how she got there. Underneath her confusion, she is seething with fury at her father, and she speaks in a way that she never has before: "He really has a real evil side of him, too. He can't deal with emotion at all, or change, or anything that deviates from his little mindset. . . . I could not speak out to him. I couldn't argue with him, I couldn't fight back with him. . . . I think there was a fear of physical stuff. I think there was a fear of physical violence."

It's hard to follow this part of the interview as it moves back and forth. There's a lot of confusion. "The anger was definite, though." And fear. "I think he shook me a lot, and I think when he got frustrated he would shake me, yah, and I despised it and I really despised him, having that over me. You know, he could be a really fun guy lots of times, but those really aren't the memories that stick out in my mind. I was afraid of him, and I was afraid to talk back or anything. It wasn't like I had a right at all." The interviewer asks if she can remember any specific day when she got upset around her parents. Rachel starts to respond but gets more and more lost, and finally coherence gives way under stress. "I remember lots of days that I just withdrew. I had started on, like, an eating disorder type of thing and I would compulsively eat, I think, and, uh, didn't gain a lot of weight at that point, but it was like what I wanted to do. It was almost like a freedom there. I was also very responsible—I was responsible for my sisters. I don't remember your question?"

She can think better about her mother. What used to get her really upset was "just having no control. When I first went away or almost away, the thing that I always used to say to the counselors was I felt like they were too strict. Well, it wasn't that they were really too strict. It wasn't that I was told, 'No, you can't go there or do this.' It was that they were too overpowering. You know, my mom was especially overpowering, very controlling."

As Rachel regains her cool, she relates her mother's need for control to her own ways of doing things. "If I was upset, it upset her that she somehow felt responsible, she couldn't fix that. . . . And I picked up a whole lot of that myself."

High Valley comes up in the context of the interviewer's question about childhood experiences of separation. "I think I really went down from there," she says at first. "That was a really wrong place for me to be."

But in fact she's of two minds about this, and as usual she strives to make herself clear. "But I also think that I opted to go to the hospital. . . . *I* made the move that brought me there, and I knew it ahead of time. When I sat down with the doctor and he said, 'The only way you can get out of your house is if you hurt yourself or injure yourself,' I immediately went home and did so. So that was my move." This is a piece of reframing that she had begun in her last adolescent interview. How concretely true is it? Who knows. What is important is that Rachel now sees clearly something that eluded her before. She recognizes that behind her behavior lay ideas, wishes, and fears, as well as decisions for which she now takes responsibility and assumes agency.

And how has all this history affected her adult personality? That's a big one. "I've been very self-conscious all my life. I've had a very, very poor self-image, up until the past couple of years, I'd say. Not able to achieve the goals that I want to achieve. Feeling that I can't. Needing people always to fulfill the gaps that I have. Many things. Not knowing what to do with my anger. Not, you know, wanting to have it. Being really afraid of anger. Not being able to deal with other people's anger towards me. Anything that people are uncomfortable with somehow becomes my responsibility to change it or fix it. I don't know, lots of things, lots of things."

She goes on. "When I was in the last school, that I graduated from, there was someone there that I was very close to, and when she left I ran out the next week and met my future husband. And it was just that quick. There was so much fear of ending up being alone that, you know, I just couldn't do it and I had a baby right away."

Rachel knows now that she catapulted herself into marriage and motherhood at sixteen as much out of anxiety as her avowed wish to plan effectively. Her old skills of retrospective reflection and reframing are still sharp. But for the first time she appreciates that her reliance on retrospection has to do with just how difficult "knowing things" in the moment can be. "My family is really dysfunctional. I really didn't know that before, and I didn't want to know it. I kept seeing kids that were burned on radiators or abused, or they had drunken parents or drug-addicted parents, and I always thought, 'Well, my family is really good, and I live in a really nice house with a pool in the backyard, and we have enough to eat and clothes,' and we were always being told how lucky we were. So I didn't associate my family with [families like those]. And it became obvious to me through the years, and I ended up with a lot of alcoholics in my life, and realized that there's dysfunction. My mother grew up in a very violent alcoholic home. Her dad was a violent alcoholic and she just brought the -ism into my house."

She repeats her belief that her mother married her biological father to escape her family of origin. "And my father—his parents were from England, and there was no emotion shown at all in his house growing up. There was ridicule. . . . I think they just brought their garbage with them, you know, and none of their issues got dealt with, and it's like it will continue." She does not—yet—make any conscious connection between her parents' use of marriage as an escape and her tentative recognition that she did the same thing. Nor can she yet really empathize with her father's own experiences of having been humiliated by his parents. But if her past record is any predictor, she soon will.

They talk about the adults with whom she was close as a child, and Rachel addresses for the first time the implications of some of her early attachments—to older people whom she has up till now subsumed under the catchall "friends." (With every interview, with each advance in her ability to stand on her own two feet, she defines friendship more clearly. She increasingly separates friendship from dependency, from sexuality, from nurturing, and from the other aspects of connectedness that may or may not be part of any given relationship. And when she looks back next year on what she said today, she will probably see it differently still.)

So now she says that she really "tried to attach to a lot of adults. I didn't socialize with kids my age at all. . . . I had a cousin who was older that I started discussing my problems with right before I left the house. And after that, it was always counselors, social workers, anybody older. Except for real authority figures. I couldn't deal with doctors at all—psychiatrists—I would shut them right out." (Here in miniature is her struggle to balance relationship and control.)

As she stops talking about her family, her fluency returns. She begins to fill in some holes in her story—some deliberate ones from years ago, and others that are just the result of passing time. She says now that she's known she was gay ever since high school, when she met the mysterious person whose departure precipitated her flight and marriage. "There was a woman at that school, a counselor who really overstepped her boundaries. And I thought that we were going to spend the rest of our lives together and we were supposed to. And when she left, I was devastated." She met her husband two weeks later, "and it went on from there." (With this revelation, the parsimony of her descriptions of her husband and her marriage first begin to make some sense. She swept two big issues—her sexuality and her dependency—"under the carpet," as she puts it, with her precipitous marriage. But she did discuss them with her husband-to-be. "It didn't bother him, and I guess I was doing what I needed to do to be taken care of.")

Since her divorce, she's made relationships with women, causing strain in the family again. In fact, Rachel's parents got along better with George than with her for a while. But the crisis was a turning point in her relationship with her parents. Rachel learned about Al-Anon and the concept of dysfunctional families. "It really brings on a better relationship with them." She wishes that her mother would change, "and I'm having a real hard time accepting the fact that I can't do it for her. My dad I'm not real concerned about. . . . I'm really glad that I can now not feel that he's that important. I love him. But I'm not going to change him. And I really don't like him. My mom I feel sorry for. That's a difficult relationship. There's good parts when she's okay, but when she's got a lot of anger, whatever, misplaced or displaced, there's no talking to her; then I have to remove myself. It's hard." But Danny (now eight) and her mother have a good relationship. "He can see [what goes on], he can talk about it, he can say things—which are things that I couldn't do."

Rachel says as little about the end of her marriage as she said about the rest of it. She's much more interested in the two relationships that followed it. Unlike her sketchy rendering of George eight years ago, these are detailed, intricate, intimate portraits, and Rachel demonstrates that her level of contemporaneous (as opposed to retrospective) emotional awareness has developed greatly.

Her first lover, Ginny, had alcohol problems in which Rachel got overinvolved, and she couldn't disentangle herself. But they remain close friends, even though the romantic relationship came to grief. They made up to each other for some of the growing they had missed out on earlier. "We know how much we've grown. If it wasn't for the other, neither one of us would be where we were today. So it's an important relationship for me." Rachel's relationship with Ginny enhances for her the awareness of change that has always supported her in hard times.

Characteristically, Rachel uses her Ginny-narrative to work out a new and expanded view of her own contributions to relationship troubles. "I think I have a problem with trust. And at times when Ginny's not open and warm, or when she has an issue or a problem and she tries to close me out, I feel uncomfortable." She tends to get controlling, trying to "make" her relationship with Ginny be certain ways. She wishes she didn't depend on her relationships so much. But old habits die hard. (Also, Rachel is still just learning to distinguish between the ways that depending on relationships is fulfilling and constructive, and the ways that it isn't. For the first time she is thinking explicitly *about* the losses and disappointments that are intrinsic to connections instead of trying to finesse them, control them, or deny them, as she always has before.) She learned to stick up for herself when their relationship was ending—"I had to. . . . It was like sink or swim"—and that was good. She came out of it with a clearer vision of an important issue than she has ever managed before: that her relationships influence too much how she feels about herself.

She took that awareness into her relationship with Marie, who is now her partner. (Here too an early narrative serves as foundation for a later one.) It gives her a perspective that she hasn't had before, and a certain realism. "I missed a lot in my childhood," she says. "And at first I didn't want to admit that. I feel that I made a choice to be lesbian. I think that it was in me, but that somewhere along the line I made that choice. . . . She helps me heal through her mothering, her nurturing. . . . I think friendship came later." Rachel feels that Marie really loves herself, and she finds that very attractive—Marie knows where she's going and what she wants. Rachel likes Marie's independence. There have been complicated times, and they both have painful feelings about the past. But now "we understand each other's histories and what the past can do to us. Or has done to us."

Her statement that she feels no ambivalence about the relationship evokes the old absolute teenage Rachel; but in a couple of years, if she runs true to form, she'll take a more balanced view. She does admit that trust issues from the past still get in the way. "It's not that I don't trust Marie per se," Rachel says. "It's that I don't trust me." She worries all the time that she isn't doing things right, so when a disagreement comes up and Marie wants to remove herself instead of fighting, Rachel hangs on desperately, even if it means fighting more. "It's a real abandonment issue," she says, recognizing this fully at last. But having recognized it, she's learning how to cope—and anyway, she says, it seldom gets to that point anymore. When Rachel is upset with herself, she can seek some distance while she pulls herself together, instead of having to cling to (and fight with) Marie. The capacity to negotiate distance is getting stronger and more reliable every day.

For the first time, she feels that she has both independence and closeness in the same relationship. "Independence is a new one for me in this relationship because it's so close," she says. "It's something I'm afraid of, yet I strive for it. [Marie] has it, and I want it. . . . I go to school full time and she works ten hours a day. That, to me, is independence right now." It's her own wishes and feelings that interfere with her independence, she specifies, not Marie's; sometimes she still gets very needy. But her new awareness of "right now"—as distinct from all the other times in her life—gives her yet another welcome layer of flexibility. Things change, and that is what Rachel knows above all.

How does she see her life changing? Rachel has finally learned to anticipate: now she can look for change in the future, as well as in the past. So she answers for the first time a question that has always stymied her before.

"Well," she says, "I think that I'll have more friendships. I think that the trusting, you know, will start to come and I think I'll be better able to [let people be] themselves without becoming totally affected by what they have to say about me. Their impressions or feelings at any given moment won't really affect how I feel about myself. That's my goal, you know—to not let other people completely influence the way I feel about myself. I see that as a progression now."

RACHEL'S STORY IS a chronicle of the complicated struggle between autonomy, dependence, and connection that haunts human lives. Despite her bravado, mastery comes slowly to Rachel. She makes mistakes along the way, and in some of them she courts real disaster. But once she knows what she wants—the demanding and elusive combination of reliable relationships and charge of her own life—she never falters in her pursuit, or in her faith in the miracle of change.

Rachel's family called itself "close," but no real intimacy was possible within it, and no intimacy at all was permitted outside. Her parents loved Rachel greatly and did their best for her, but their own experiences had left them unreflective and isolated people. In blaming her troubles at school on the other kids' meanness, for example, they were passing on to her their own helplessness about relationship. Their binary assumptions— either you're family or you're not (a very awkward proposition for a child with one adoptive parent); that you succeed or you don't; that it's your fault or someone else's—left no room for the delicate adjustments that make true intimacy possible. Relationship came at such a high cost in autonomy in Rachel's family that for a while Rachel despairs of both. But in time she begins to see that other equations are possible, and her intelligence and creativity come into their own.

She goes after her new goals wholeheartedly. But she hasn't much experience with how good relationships work, and like most teens she tends first to idealize and then to feel shattered or outraged when her lofty expectations are disappointed. Until she realizes that she is driven by a fear of being left, she is easily seduced into dependent or defensive relationships that can't stand up to the intensity of her need. But she perseveres in her efforts to balance togetherness and self-sufficiency; she openly uses her own retrospective and prospective narratives to do the necessary psychological work, and her increasing skills both reflect her perseverance and encourage it.

It would be a mistake to judge Rachel's competence on the decisions she makes as a teenager, or on their outcomes. Adolescents are notorious for seeing only one end of a stick. What *is* significant—and consistent—about Rachel is her conviction that she can influence her life in ever better ways. After her vision of agency, Rachel rejects the victim role.

Reflectiveness comes hard. But having seen that change can happen, she has an abiding and hopeful sense of its possibilities. For a while she sees herself only retrospectively; this is one of the reasons she miscalculates as often as she does. But she *does* see herself retrospectively, and years of after-the-fact reflection teach her to anticipate feelings, and to see herself in "real time."

At first Rachel takes very little responsibility for her own life. But as she notices in retrospect her own complicity in what happens to her, she begins to approach things differently. For Rachel, responsibility is an outgrowth of her sense of agency and the newly motivated reflectiveness that comes with it. Her awareness of what she contributed to her hospitalization, for instance, and her perception of the defensive aspects of her marriage, are reflective reframings *and* admissions of responsibility.

Empathy is kin to reflection, and as Rachel learns to reflect, to pay attention to her own thoughts and feelings, she starts to notice other people's. She constructs a much more complex picture of her family than has ever been possible before. As she begins to acknowledge how painful her withdrawals were to them, she looks for ways to reduce the strain caused by her need for independence.

Rachel's adolescent disregard for Murphy's Law is very disconcerting to the adults in her life. It's a long time before she can tolerate their "disappointment" without feeling diminished, unimportant, and unappreciated. Still, when the tensions subside, she goes back and repairs disrupted ties, testing—always testing—her fear that her growing autonomy will destroy the relationship. As she gets to know herself better, she grasps that the problem is less autonomy per se than her own extreme sensitivity to criticism. Caring less about what "they" think, as she eventually realizes, actually makes for a better relationship.

Rachel is weaving a web of relationships now. She considers herself as Danny's mother, as her parents' child; she thinks about her childhood in parallel with her son's. She still has a lot of work to do on this. For a long time, investigation of her family feelings lags way behind the rest of her emotional development. She doesn't feel safe enough to tackle her anger at her parents' controllingness and their emotional isolation from her; instead, she tries to please them and clings to old platitudes about "always being there." As they struggle over her plan to marry, her decision to divorce, her involvement in a lesbian relationship, Rachel learns how to do what she needs to do and still protect her ties with her parents. But although the overt battles subside, underlying problems remain. Even as she criticizes her parents for their failure to talk about *their* difficult feelings, she is avoiding her own.

So the rage at her father that boils up in the final interviews has been clamoring for her attention for years. It has had to wait until Rachel can handle it; that's how she does things. We can't know now whether this anger is an upsurge of ordinary ambivalence toward a difficult parent that Rachel is finally feeling safe enough to feel, or whether it belongs to the "other" father who really did threaten and abandon her, or whether the Somer house was a much scarier place than anyone admitted. We don't know whether Rachel will settle down and make peace with her father, or on what terms. But the late rage at her father is not the static rage of the contrast-group kids. Rachel is not maintaining the status quo, but taking risks; she's not avoiding self-awareness, but tolerating ever more intense feelings.

Similarly, we can't predict how her sexuality will ultimately settle out. For all her early talk about independence and taking charge, she's learned that this is a hard road and that it involves much more than just making decisions. It takes her a while to realize how much she still wants nurturing and validation, and how intensely she looks for them from older people—especially women. When a person is as hungry for relationship as Rachel is, it's hard to sort out relational needs from sexual ones. She says directly that she made a "choice" to be lesbian as a response to what she had missed in her childhood. Certainly her lesbian identity is an important part of her narrative now, and it may continue to be. On the other hand, as she gets more competent to fulfill more of her own needs, she becomes correspondingly less needful of relationships that are based in a parental sort of nurturance. She may feel free to make a different choice later. But it doesn't really matter what sexual choice she makes. What does matter is that she's growing in autonomy and in connection, that her relationships are improving steadily, that she knows more and more about what she wants in a partner, and that she is learning how to get it. Wherever she ends up, she is enjoying the trip.

6

Sandy

You Can Work with It

SANDY CARLSON WAS FOURTEEN WHEN SHE came to the Children's Center. She had cut both her wrists with a razor blade.

ABOUT A YEAR AND A HALF before her admission, Sandy's parents separated. Her father, an advertising representative who travels a great deal, moved out of the house, and Sandy and her two older brothers remained with their mother, a clerk at the town Water Department. Sandy was in eighth grade at the time. She had always been a very good and hardworking student, but now her grades began to slip, and at school she seemed so depressed that one of her teachers called home to find out what was wrong. Sandy was referred for weekly guidance sessions, and she made it through a difficult school year and an apparently uneventful summer.

That fall, however, her parents sought family counseling. For a while, her mother's fiancé Henry and his four children had been living with the family. Sandy's two brothers were behaving very aggressively, and Sandy wasn't getting along with her mother. The counselor asked Sandy directly about suicidal thoughts, and she admitted to having taken a quantity of her mother's sleeping pills after an argument the previous summer. Sandy was referred to an individual therapist, but she didn't like the person and quit after the second session. And the family therapy fizzled out too, when the parents decided that Mr. Carlson would move back home to stay with the children while Mrs. Carlson went to live with Henry. They thought that things would settle down with the father's stronger disciplinary presence. Sandy seemed to be happier with this arrangement, and by everyone's report, including her own, she did better for the first few months of her ninth-grade year.

Two days before her father was about to leave on a business/ pleasure trip with his girlfriend, Sandy and her boyfriend Paul broke up. The evening before the scheduled departure, Sandy slashed both her wrists. Her oldest brother saw what she had done and called Mr. Carlson, who took her to the emergency service that referred her to High Valley.

SANDY'S PARENTS WERE intelligent, attractive, and well-meaning people, but the High Valley staff wondered if a quality of self-preoccupation that they shared might have been a problem for their children. Mr. Carlson kept a lot of distance; he worked long hours and traveled a great deal. He had had some extreme financial ups and downs. Mrs. Carlson was an angry woman with a history of severe mood disorder in her family and in her own life. It was she who had initiated the separation from her husband, but when she changed her mind about it later and he refused to come back, she got very depressed. Sandy made herself available to her mother during that time, but when Mrs. Carlson began to cheer up—once she met Henry, who eventually became her second husband—she spent less time with the children than ever before.

Mr. Carlson was angry too. Always "smoldering about something" was how he described himself, and when his limit was reached he would explode, sometimes into real violence. He took a sardonic and intellectual approach to things, and had little tolerance for what he called "weakness." Children, he said once, were "just things to support" until they became little adults. He felt like an observer of life rather than a participant, he said, and had never enjoyed anything or been close to anyone. He criticized his own explosive anger with a perfectionist's scorn, and his take on himself was that he kept people away so that they wouldn't end up hating him. He had married Mrs. Carlson when she became pregnant with their older son. From the beginning they had argued constantly, and there were occasional physical fights. He kept away—first in the Army and then on business trips—as much as he could.

Until Sandy was ten, her parents said, she was a "perfect child"—beautiful, good, athletic, talented, bright, competent. She did well at everything. But when she became "more interested in boys than in books," her relationship with her mother grew increasingly hostile. She took to wearing makeup and hanging out with tough older kids. Her parents noted that she had always needed a lot of validation from other people to feel good about herself, and that she was very careful to conform to the mores of the kids she spent time with. She wanted to grow up very fast, and her mother wanted her to slow down.

But it wasn't only hormones. Family history revealed that there had been other stresses on the Carlson family the year Sandy turned ten. Mrs. Carlson's much-loved father died that year, and so did an aunt and uncle. Mrs. Carlson's mother became depressed over her husband's death and died not long afterward; Mrs. Carlson was once again devastated. Only a little more than a year after her mother's death came the separation from her husband. At the time of Sandy's admission to the Center, Mrs. Carlson had just become engaged to Henry.

Mr. Carlson was the disciplinarian in the family. He believed that Sandy saw him as her "white knight." He had been sure that she would feel much better once he moved back into the house, and was devastated at her wrist-slashing. When Sandy got to the Center she could say little to explain herself beyond "I get depressed," which she described as "feeling nothing at all." At first she expressed concern and puzzlement, and settled comfortably into the therapeutic program on the unit. As her discharge date neared, however, she became very angry, anxious, and withdrawn.

Sandy's great strengths were immediately noted—her high intelligence, her social skills, her impulse control, and her frustration tolerance—but the staff also noticed that when emotional stress became too intense, these strengths were not available to her. When real anger was present, especially with any threat of violence, Sandy tended to dissociate. That is, she lost her awareness of herself and the "real world" she was living in.

DSM-IV (the fourth edition of the diagnostic and statistical manual of the American Psychiatric Association), the standard American handbook of psychiatric diagnosis, calls dissociation "a disruption in the usually integrated functions of consciousness, memory, identity, or perception of the environment."[1] Daydreaming and "zoning out" are common and harmless forms of dissociation; sleep is a universal, more profound, and necessary form; trance is a less common occurrence; an extreme and controversial dissociative manifestation is the one called multiple personality disorder. Trauma may impose dissociation. Drugs can induce it, and they are often used deliberately for exactly that purpose. But dissociation can also be a response to overwhelming stress or anxiety, and that is what it was for Sandy, who tended to "turn off" to threatening feelings and to lose awareness of them. (Her father's explosive outbursts, of which he was seldom later aware, had been diagnosed years before as dissociative phenomena.)

Sandy seemed to be afraid of her own thoughts and feelings; as she put it, she "didn't want to think" about things. The staff wondered why she was so anxious. Had the "perfect" child been a very compliant one who had had too little help from her folks in handling emotional distress? Her mother alternated between depression and engrossing private interests, and Mr. Carlson was seldom home. Living arrangements were constantly shifting, and the staff wondered whether Sandy had any stable people in her life at all. Since the Carlsons did not have coverage for a long hospitalization, the team recommended that Sandy be referred to a residential school. They felt that this would foster a constructive separation from her mother, help her maximize her considerable intellectual potential, and perhaps put her in contact with some more attentive and available adults. But Sandy was shocked and infuriated by this plan, and felt betrayed by all who were involved with it. She remained on the unit for six weeks, objecting vehemently and steadily until the day she left, and getting angrier all the time.

The First Interview

Sandy's first comment to the interviewer is that she gets along with only one of her parents, and she lives with only one. So, she said, on the sentence-completion tests about her parents, she crossed out the word "parents" and replaced it with "father." Her mother is "a bitch. . . . She's just always a bitch. I don't know, I can't describe it. . . . Little jabs here and there." This opening theme—who are her parents?—is a real and important one for Sandy. Ten years later, at twenty-five, she will still be pondering the disconcerting comings and goings of her parents in her life.

But from this dramatic opening, things go downhill. Sandy is not interested in making her interviewer's life easy. Most of her answers are dismissive "I don't know"s; the rest are short and cryptic. How has it been since her father moved back? "Good," says Sandy. Why did she try to kill herself? "I don't know," says Sandy. "That's why I'm here, because I don't know why." You still don't know? asks the interviewer. "It doesn't bother me," says Sandy. "They're the ones who want to have the question answered. I don't really care."

The interviewer tries again. What was going on with you? "Nothing particular." Did you feel upset? "No, I was depressed." Do you know about what? "No, I just get depressed." What's it like when you're depressed? "I don't know. I just sit down. I don't talk to no one. If anyone talks to me I get really mad at them. I don't know. I can't describe it." The interviewer tries some strategic flattery: Well, you're doing a good job right now. But Sandy rejects this ploy. "That's not even *half* describing it," she says, perhaps sarcastically.

The interviewer takes another tack. Maybe those questions, like why you tried to kill yourself, are not really *your* questions. Maybe you're not interested in finding out?

"I don't want to think about it," Sandy says. "But people keep bringing it back up. I don't know the answers to the questions. I don't even want to think about it. I don't even ask myself why I tried to do it, because I'm not gonna think about it." She does say that she's angry at being told what to do in the hospital. She doesn't mind when her father asks her to do something, but here it's different. She doesn't know these people. "When my father tells me what to do, I usually do it." And when your mother tells you? "I don't listen to my mother!" says Sandy. (Thinking about nothing, not thinking, are very important themes for Sandy. So is the question of who gets to run her show, which she is at that very moment acting out with the interviewer.)

The interviewer tries to talk about Sandy's leaving the hospital for boarding school, but Sandy rejects this plan as a judgment on her ability to take care of herself.

So everything is okay and could be solved at home?

"Nothing has to be solved."

And it's other people who think things are wrong?

"Yah," says Sandy. "Everything's fine with me."

The interviewer suggests that maybe everybody has some things that aren't fine, even if they're not in a hospital. Sandy agrees with this, and in a nice piece of psychological karate uses it against the interviewer, suggesting that her problems are more like those of people *out* of the hospital than those of people who are in. So they don't get very far. All Sandy will say is that if she were out, she'd just ignore her problems, not even think about them. They'd go away.

But . . . says the interviewer. What about that afternoon?

"Well, I just got depressed," says Sandy. "I don't know why I get depressed. I always get depressed. I have no idea why I get depressed, so it might not even be about problems. . . . It might be about my mother. I have no idea why I get depressed."

This, too, seems like a potential lead, and the interviewer asks *how* the depression might be about her mother. "I don't know," says Sandy. "They could be about anybody. I could just be depressed for any reason."

The interviewer starts over. Have you ever asked yourself the question: *Why* am I depressed?

Sandy sticks to her guns: it's not her, it's the hospital. "I don't know why I'm depressed, but I just seem to be getting more and more depressed since I've been here. This place depresses me. It's screwing me up."

But now, as they laboriously—*very* laboriously—pursue this line of thought, it becomes clear that Sandy resents being discharged so soon. "This place hasn't been any help to me. I've only been here a little over a month and I'm leaving in less than two weeks. It ain't done nothing for me. . . . I don't have any problems, but I guess they think that I do. And if I do, less than two months ain't gonna do anything for me."

When *other* people talk about what her problems might be, the interviewer asks, does that help her see things more clearly? No, Sandy says definitely. People think they know what she thinks, and put words in her mouth. But if they're thinking about her, "it should be what *I* tell them, not what they assume. . . . Well, *I* think you are thinking—whatever." The interviewer suggests that that might be scary. This is exactly the kind of assumption Sandy's objecting to, and she pulls back immediately. "They can't read my mind, 'cause they're always wrong." (Sandy can't express her own feelings, but she gets very angry when anyone tries to help her out. This theme of mind-reading, of having words put in her mouth, is a huge one for Sandy, and gets larger and more encompassing over the years.)

They turn to her other interests. What did she like to do before she came into the hospital? Draw, says Sandy. What? asks the interviewer. Landscapes? People?

No, says Sandy. I just draw whatever comes to my mind.

What's that, usually?

I don't know, says Sandy—but this time the rebuff is perfunctory. She actually goes on to talk about her drawings for a few minutes with a bit of animation. Before she left for the hospital she was working on a pencil sketch of "a good old guy, he had wrinkles all over his face."

The other thing that she likes to do is hang out with her friends. Well, not exactly her *friends*—the group of kids she hangs out with. (Another theme: What makes someone a friend, as opposed to just someone you hang out with?) But she's seen only three of them since she's been here, and only once. The rest all think she's in Florida. She doesn't want them to know that she's at High Valley. "It's a mental institution. They'll think I'm crazy." She agreed to come thinking that she'd be here for only thirty days, and that they didn't have any little white rooms. "I didn't like the idea of the quiet room at all. They told me they didn't have one—my father told me they didn't have one. But they do. . . . I didn't know the doors would be locked. I didn't know anything about this place. . . . I just hate everything." What do you do when you hate something? asks the interviewer. "I don't know," says Sandy.

But she does know that when she had a fight with another girl, things changed after she brought it up at unit meeting. She was told that her attitude would keep her from getting anything out of the hospital, so she decided to change it. (This is not the usual response at the Center, but it shows up quite often among the resilient kids.) The other girls became friendlier, and once they were being nice to her, she reciprocated. "I'm not nice to people who are not nice to me."

The interviewer uses this new context to try again to get Sandy to say more about her feelings. How does Sandy get anger out of her system? There's nothing she can do about getting angry here, she says, so she doesn't. "I have it all boxed up inside of me. I'm not gonna get mad here, because I don't feel like getting put in four points. . . . I don't feel like getting locked up and tied down." (Being helpless terrifies and enrages Sandy. Another huge theme.)

Now that she's talking a tiny bit, they go on to the subject of school. Sandy contemptuously dismisses the one at High Valley as a "kindergarten," but she says about her school at home that although she's been told that she has the intelligence to do well, she doesn't. What do you think about that? asks the interviewer. "I don't know," Sandy says yet again. "I could . . . I would if I could, but I don't. . . . I don't know. . . . I try."

But she hates all of her subjects except art, and she hates hanging around kids her own age. All of her friends are older. Her best friend is seventeen, one of the few people who know that Sandy's here. She's really nice and Sandy misses her. But when the interviewer asks if they give each other advice, Sandy firmly says no. "I never want to ask anybody. I figure things out for myself. . . . I don't know how. I just think about them till I know what to do."

It turns out that Sandy is not doing too well about figuring things out at the moment. "Whatever—I don't know. I can't even think about what I'm thinking about right now. I don't know what to ask people for advice." She feels that she's being forced to go to boarding school, and because of this she can't ask people about it. (She seems to mean that she's too angry to talk to other people. Sandy absolutely hates being told what to do, and she keeps as far away as she can from anyone who tries to boss her around. Another theme is her problem "thinking about what she's thinking," and the struggle to regain access to experiences that she's lost out of fear or rage.)

They begin to talk about her family. Her mother's about to get married again, and Sandy will have a stepsister. That's okay, except that she doesn't get along with her mother. She gets along with one brother and her father, but the other brother not so well. "He's conceited," says Sandy. "I don't know—I just don't get along with him. He's too much like my mother."

She doesn't think she wants a family of her own. There are some little kids at the Center. "They're just little, always screaming, running around, crying. I just don't like little kids. I haven't for a long time, probably since I was a little kid." She laughs. "I don't know. I used to babysit—maybe that's why I stopped. That's why I stopped, because I hate them so much. Drives me crazy." (This is the very beginning of an important theme that Sandy can't yet put into words. In time she will recognize that she has learned to see feelings as the kind of weakness that earns her father's contempt. Small children's uninhibited expression of what they feel reminds her of her own feelings and makes her very uncomfortable—anxious and angry and "crazy.")

Sandy has trouble focusing even on *past* feelings. The interviewer asks her what her nicest experience was. "I don't know," she says. "I have no idea. I don't know. Lots of things happened in the past, I can't even remember half of them. My memory's gone, I can't remember anything anymore, since I've been in here." Well then, a moment when she really enjoyed life? This time Sandy has something to say.

"Well, like whenever I was with my grandfather, on my mother's side of the family. He died. He's real nice. He was real nice." He died four or five years ago, and "I've been to a lot of funerals lately," Sandy goes on. A real lot of relatives—she doesn't even know how many. One of her favorite uncles died; also an aunt, her grandfather, her grandmother, and her great-grandmother, all in the past four years.

How do you feel now, talking about it? asks the interviewer.

I don't like talking about it, Sandy says. But she keeps remembering.

They talk about the breakup with her boyfriend. He was snubbing her. She misses him, but she doesn't want to get back together. It was probably really hard on him too, suggests the interviewer. "He wouldn't talk to me," says Sandy. "I don't know."

So the first interview ends on what is, for the moment, Sandy's characteristic note.

The Second Interview

When Sandy comes back for her second interview a year later, she's sixteen and happily ensconced at boarding school—but not the one the hospital tried to send her to. She and the interviewer have an animated discussion about the school, its reputation, how it works. The only "I don't know" this time is an explicit response to a new piece of information from the interviewer: "No, I didn't know that."

She loves the school, the freedom, the people; she feels she fits in. Discipline is adjudicated by a board of teachers and students, and she likes that better than the public-school approach, where "if you do something wrong, there's just one person who says, 'You're out of the school.'" (Authoritarianism drives Sandy nuts, and this is her first experience with a different approach to governance. From here on, her narratives will include not only her resentment of control, but also an active search for alternatives.)

And she has lots of friends. This school isn't as "cliquey" as her old one, and "most people like most people." There are different groups, but "they're not like enemies. . . . They don't hate each other."

It's like a community, the interviewer suggests, and Sandy agrees. They talk about how a community works: it's informal, it's not snobby, everyone gets along with everyone else, there's a lot of tolerance for different opinions. Her whole experience there has gotten Sandy interested in politics.

She explains that it was her new stepfather who found this school for her. He had gone there himself. She was dead set against going to the one the hospital was pushing, but Henry thought she might like this one, and she does. She feels much more confident. "I was self-conscious last year, and, like, if someone looked at me, you know, I'd feel they were thinking something bad about me. And I'm not that way anymore."

When she talks about her problems of last year, the "I don't knows" creep back a bit, but she can say much more now than she could then. "I was having a lot of trouble with my mother. We weren't even speaking to each other. And the fact that my parents had gotten divorced. And things like that. And I had been going out with this guy for two years, and he had broken up two days before I came here, and that was one of the big factors. And I didn't really admit to that, because I thought it was stupid, you know, over a boy." She still doesn't know why it happened; he never gave her an explanation. But now he's trying to go out with her again, and she just says no. She doesn't want him to think that she still wants to go out with him, or that he screwed up her head. "It would have made him think that he had power over my mind." She laughs. (Here again is her preoccupation about people having power over her mind. But her narrative now includes the possibility of some control over the situation.)

She still misses Paul a lot. She thinks she'll always miss him, even though she has a new boyfriend now. "People always wondered why I liked him so much. . . . It was like a death, my first love," she goes on. "First time, you think, 'Wow, this is gonna last forever!' And when it doesn't, you know, it's total crash, you know, your whole ego is shot and everything." She's knows it wouldn't work to try it again; she's changed too much, and he never will. "'Hoodlum' is a bad word, but it describes him perfectly. A hoodlum, a juvenile delinquent. And he's sixteen, and you know, I think he's going to be that way all his life. . . . I'd never realized it until after—that he, you know, put up a front, and he had to put up a front to be tough."

Once she couldn't tell a front from what was really there, Sandy goes on, but now she can tell if there's something behind it. She makes a finer distinction still: "He's a very nice person behind it, but . . . I think he's going to be doing it all his life. He has to be tougher than anybody else. His whole family's like that."

The interviewer is intrigued by this conundrum of the fronts. (Resilient kids manage to engage responsive adults in a variety of ways. One of Sandy's ways is philosophical speculation.) Who did you love when you say you couldn't look behind it? Did you love the person, did you love the front, or did you love the person that you felt was behind it?

Both, really, says Sandy. "It was weird, 'cause at moments sometimes I'd be with him and there would be other people around and he'd be like really trying to act macho, and it totally turned me off. But then, times when he'd be acting like himself, and *that* would totally turn me off. It was like—both. It was confusing. I was confused a lot when I was going out with him, because he confused me. He just changed so quickly."

They talk about her new boyfriend, and the jealousy of the old one. Old boyfriend knows she broke up with a couple of other guys, and thinks that was because she really still wants to go out with him. So now he thinks she'll break up with her new guy for the same reason, and is very jealous that she hasn't. New boyfriend, Eric, "is really possessive. And that was fine until, like, until about two weeks ago, when I started feeling suffocated. You know, like I'm only sixteen, I can't . . . It makes me worry, because I know we'll end up breaking up sometime, and then I feel that I'm going to be doing to him what Paul did to me, and that makes me worried. Because I don't want to do that."

He's doing better about it now, she says. She's helping him little by little to be less dependent, so that he doesn't feel so rejected when she wants to hang out with her friends, or stay at school over the weekend. "I'll do it really gradually, so it won't hurt him. . . . Because I've been hurt before, and I know what it's like and I just—I couldn't do it to anybody else." (Reflection, responsibility, relationships, agency—Sandy has a lot of psychological skill when she can focus. The problem is that sometimes she can't.)

They go back to how she felt when Paul broke up with her. "I got extremely depressed. Extremely. I couldn't concentrate. When people talked to me, I mean, I didn't even hear them. . . . Sounds like *Romeo and Juliet*, but—" She laughs.

Were you serious when you slashed your wrists? the interviewer asks.

"Yah," Sandy says, "I was, really. It was like, 'What is the sense of living? I don't want to live anymore.'" They digress to a brief discussion of God and life after death, which Sandy acknowledges that she hasn't figured out yet. It's a mystery.

Her parents' divorce became final on her birthday, and it hit her hard. Half the day she was with her father, and half with her mother. "They had been separated for I don't know how long. I was used to having them apart, so it didn't really hit me earlier. And then it hit me again. . . . I got depressed. Depressed, uh, that was one of my problems. It still is. I get depressed, but not as much as I used to. But I'd be totally out of it, couldn't concentrate on like anything. Did really bad in school, you know, people were really worried and everything."

They try to talk about this some more, but Sandy still can't focus on it well or explain it to someone else. The interviewer wants to know if the hospital helped her while she was here. "I don't really think it did. Because I got really dependent on it. . . . It was like another world; it's still another world. And then they told me that I was going to be leaving, and I was glad. But then the day came that I was leaving—I didn't want to leave."

The interviewer asks what her worst experience at the Center was. "[A friend] got really violent, and they had to seclude him. And it took like seven full-grown, huge men. . . . They got him down on the ground and put his legs behind him and his arms behind his back and gave him a shot. And then they took me out. They made me go back to my unit, but I could hear him scream. . . . It just got me depressed that people have to . . . be forced into doing things. But I realize, you know, he was getting violent. He was a really strong, . . . big guy, and he could have totally destroyed the whole unit. It was for the protection of everyone, but . . . I couldn't accept that. . . . It shocked me."

What happens when *she* gets mad?

She gets pretty violent, Sandy says. Not toward human beings. "But, you know, I've broken chairs. My whole family's like that. I mean, like my brother, who's huge—just, like, this gorilla." She describes her brother's rampages. He throws vacuum cleaners and grills; he's put his fist through the dining room wall.

Sandy is having some trouble here. She isn't really scared of Tom, she says. She knows he wouldn't hurt her. He did once, but he was only fourteen, and "I like went off my feet and flew." She laughs nervously. (Sandy gets confused when very angry feelings come too close; this is an example of emotional stress interfering with narrative coherence.) She talks about other fears and angers, but still in an unfocused way, and it's not clear whom she's talking about.

But soon she settles down and starts to delineate her own anger. Unfairness makes her mad, she says. She gets angry about little things and forgets about them, but after awhile they pile up. "It's not like temper tantrums, it's just like—violence. My father told me to clean my room. That's like an ordinary thing for a father to say—'Clean your room.' And I got quite upset, and I went in, and I totally—it looked like a tornado had gone through my room when I was done. And then I just walked out." She laughs. "But I guess it was a buildup of a lot of things."

Like what?

"One day my mother said that I was a tough little street punk, and that I—She called me all sorts of names, and said that I had to stay in the house because she didn't want me out on the street, and things like that. And that's what got me really mad, and I left the house." Sandy and her mother didn't speak to each other again for a long time. Her mother was having problems with her brother, too, and that's when the parents decided that her father would move back in.

The interviewer asks what she thinks was behind all the fighting. "I think the first time was because I blamed the divorce, the separation, totally on her. . . . I took my father's side. I always accused her, which is—You know, it wasn't the very right thing to do. It was a totally wrong thing to do. It hurt her feelings, and I think that's what did it. . . . And that's what my temper's like." (Sandy is increasingly displaying her capacity for reflection, reframing, and responsibility, and using them in the interest of repairing and protecting relationships that are important to her. Earlier in the interview, she mentioned her new awareness that there was more than one way to look at things, and in this next passage she shows that she's been acting upon it.)

"I talked to my mother about it. . . . I've heard her side of it. And I've done the same thing with my father. And then I put them both together. . . . It wasn't all my mother's fault—it wasn't all my father's fault. They just, you know, grew to not be able to live together anymore."

The interviewer comments that that's a really hard piece of work, to put those pieces together. Yah, says Sandy. "But I had to, because I couldn't stand fighting with my mother. 'Cause then if I got in a fight with my father and I was in a fight with my mother, I'd feel like totally alone, and I didn't want that. I wanted to be friends. . . . Me and my mother used to be very close; we are now. And I knew that we could be that way again. I wanted it, so I sat there and figured it out, and I did." School is changing her a lot. She looks at both sides now, more than she used to. Being able to do that makes her feel more grown up. (She's doing a lot of rethinking here. The enemy mother whose name Sandy had crossed off the sentence-completion form is now recalled as someone with whom she used to be close, and those recollections will begin to pile up. The favored father is now someone whose rough spots Sandy can acknowledge. Allegiances are shifting, and Sandy is watching them. She doesn't want to be alone; she wants support; she wants to maintain the connections she needs. And she is actively striving to increase her reflective and analytic skills.)

But when the interviewer asks her if this has changed how she sees herself, she backs off again. (It's still easier for her to look outside than inside, and that shows in the next few passages, both in the sparseness of her commentary and in the lessening of her usual coherence.) "Well, I don't know. I don't really think about what I am or how I am. I'm me. . . . If I change, I change. It'll happen. If I don't, you know, it won't. I don't think about the situation. [People] have to accept me as I am."

And who are you? How would you say who you are?

That's a very hard question, says Sandy. She thinks for a

while. (This question is indeed a hard one for her, and one of her very important narrative themes. But the way she handles the issue this year is different from the way she did last year, when she kept saying that she couldn't think about what she was thinking about.)

"It's a mind boggler. I consider myself, like, a generous person—I don't just jump to conclusions—and pretty together sometimes. There are times when some people think, and I think, you know, 'Maybe I'm going crazy.' Everybody goes through that once in a while. . . . I've put myself together in the past year."

The interviewer asks how therapy helped. Sandy says that she isn't going to therapy anymore.

"I couldn't talk about myself. It opened me up more. I can talk about myself now. I couldn't before. It made me realize a lot of things about me that I . . . thought I could never change." (Here, in particular, some confusion can be discerned, but Sandy is correctly recognizing that she couldn't talk about herself then, whereas she can now. And now that she knows she can, she, like Rachel, focuses on the possibility of change.)

The interviewer asks if there's anything else they should talk about. Anything important for us to know? Not really, says Sandy.

Have you conquered everything that's important in your life? Sandy laughs. "Yeah."

They make plans to meet next year. The interviewer tells her how nice it is that she's found the right school.

"Yah," says Sandy. "I'm really glad I found that school."

The Third Interview

Sandy is not quite eighteen when she comes back a year and a half later and reports some heavy goings-on with her father. She got busted for smoking pot in her dorm. She didn't think it was a big deal, and neither did the school, but her father cut up rough about it.

"He was just like totally shocked that his perfect daughter smoked pot, or so he thought, so we sort of split apart. . . . We didn't talk to each other for about a year, and I started living with my mother and I went away to the country and worked on a farm there for a summer. But we're still not really talking, because he's weird." (Her father's shock at his "perfect" daughter's behavior gives credence to the staff's belief that her parents had a pressing need for Sandy to be "perfect," and that this was a strain on her.) That was hard for her at first, but now she thinks he's being immature. He's newly remarried, and sort of disconnected.

After she got busted, she says, "I called him and he said, 'Well, everybody gets a fresh chance, and just don't do it again.' And then he went home. And I guess him and his wife talked about it, and they sort of worked themselves up into thinking that it was a really terrible thing." Her father threatened severe punishment, and Sandy pointed out that she was already being punished at school, and that two punishments for one thing wasn't fair. "*You* sent me away to school," she told him. "And so now I am the responsibility of the school, and they punish me and not you." Her father insisted, and when a friend who lived on a farm invited Sandy to come visit, and her mother offered to pay for the ticket, she went. Her father couldn't do anything about it, because her mother had custody. And he got really mad.

She had some trouble with her mother too, but now Sandy is seeing that familiar situation differently. "I guess I have always had trouble with people who try to discipline me. . . . She told me to do things, and I hate authority. She didn't *ask* me to do them. . . . She would say, 'Do it!' And I hate that. Because I basically think that people who do that are pulling power trips on other people, so I always just don't do it unless she *asks*. And that sort of started us fighting, and then I did everything possible to go against everything she said I should do. I mean, it was sort of bad, but—it's just—it just happens when people tell me to do things. I don't do it purposely, but it just happens that somehow I go against what they say, unless they ask me politely." (Here is Sandy's familiar antiauthoritarian theme, but now she sees her own contribution to the struggles she gets into. "It just happens" may not rate a ten on the responsibility scale, but the important thing is that Sandy is thinking for the first time about her own rage when she feels controlled, and she's not blanking out.)

And this is true with her father too, she goes on. "You can't ask questions with my father. . . . He sort of makes us do things out of fear. . . . I don't really like that either, so it made me rebel against him too. And then my mother finally figured out that I am the kind of person that you don't tell what to do, and she sort of caught on." Now they are both more reasonable, and they get on very well.

They've both changed. Sandy says she's more sure of herself than she was. "I was really sheltered. . . . And I was also really scared, because I was real scared of my father. I didn't really realize that until a couple of months ago—that I was raised by my father purely on fear, you know. Like, 'You do something, or else!' . . . My mother said the same thing. I was talking to her about that, and she said she lived twenty years of fear with him."

She talks about her father's great physical strength, and how he looks when he's angry. "Even if he doesn't get violent, when he's mad, just the air around him seems violent. . . . Like, all his muscles tense up and like his eyes are steel blue, like a very mean-looking person. He was a boxer, and he used to get into a lot of fights when he was a kid."

The interviewer asks what happens when her father does get violent.

"I got spanked when I was a kid, and that was like the worst thing in the world that could possibly happen to me. But he got violent with my mother. Not a lot—not like he was a compulsive wife-beater or anything. But he did. When they got into terrible fights, he hit her, which is really bad." She goes on to describe an episode when her father threw her brother across the room. "He just picked him up like he was a little doll. . . . It just sort of terrifies you."

Sandy calls her father, tries to keep in touch with him. She has her driver's license now, and she used to go and visit him from time to time, but recently he told her that she should call first. She thinks that's weird, but perhaps he "doesn't like to be caught by surprise." She can see that he is being careful about everything he says. "He couldn't let anything slip out that wasn't supposed to, and if I catch him unaware—that can't happen. He has to be protected at all times, and one way of being protected is not dropping in when he doesn't expect it. Dropping in when he knows—then he can be all ready, you know?" And, she thinks, his wife doesn't like to be reminded about anything that happened before she came along. Her father has told her brothers this. One brother goes along with it and the other ignores it; she's the one who fights back. It's a difficult situation.

But, Sandy goes on, "I seem to get myself into these situations with my parents. . . . I know I didn't *totally* get myself into this. . . . I am a lot like him, which is one of the reasons—the things I don't like about him is a lot what I have. Like I like to get everything I want. I am not physically terrifying, . . . but a lot of ways I'm like him. Like one thing is keeping that front up." (Here, too, Sandy is a little less fluent than usual as she acknowledges openly for the first time a resemblance to her rageful and sometimes violent father. The theme of her responsibility for her angry responses to being controlled has deepened to include not only what she *is* responsible for, but also what she may *not* be.)

The interviewer asks her about the front.

"I have to be strong," Sandy says. Her father is very into not letting anybody see his emotions—you can't show any weakness. She picked that up from him, but she's slowly getting rid of it, because it's bad in relationships. She would like to be different, to find it easier to show feelings. It's hard for her to trust people, so she doesn't have many close friends. And she's very competitive—always wants to be ahead of everybody and be the best.

What happens when you're not?

"I get really depressed. Not depressed, but just down on myself." (This is a distinction that Sandy could not always make.) "I was never really popular," she goes on, "but I think that's because I was so different from everybody I went to school with. I guess I just totally thought different from them or something. I go back there and it's just like so funny."

She gives a careful retrospective analysis of her attempt to be popular in her public school by imitating the people she wanted to be accepted by—the *cool* people—even if that meant smoking and rebelling and not doing your schoolwork. Now she thinks it was sort of stupid to get F's in school as the price of having friends. She had a hard time getting back into the swing of things, once she decided that she didn't want to be bad anymore. But she did it, and she's doing some work in oral history now, which is really interesting. Everyone, she says, has their own point of view.

She's becoming more aware of *her* own point of view. Newspapers used to bore her, but now she reads them. She's spending more time with the family of her current boyfriend, Jacob, and comparing it with hers. "Sitting around the dinner table, we never talked about politics, we never talked about anything." But *his* parents are interested in the world and they talk about psychology and politics and all kinds of things. Her parents talk only about what their friends are doing. "I was sheltered," Sandy says again. "I had no idea what was going on. And it sort of bums me out." Lots of learning at Jacob's house—even her vocabulary has improved—and at school, too.

Sandy has moved out of her dorm, and is living as a boarder in a private house. She's very happy with Jacob and she enjoys the independence of her new digs, but she finds it a little lonely sometimes. She broke up with Eric when he started pressing to marry her. She was just sixteen, and "I was changing and he wasn't." As she had predicted, she had to break up with him, and she felt very guilty about it.

How did you experience the guilt? asks the interviewer.

"It was just depressing," Sandy says. She'd feel guilty when he would cry on the phone, and then get depressed because she did—"because being guilty is a weakness, and I can't feel weak. And so I would get mad at myself for that. And also, feeling guilty—that has always been a big problem of mine." She struggles fruitlessly for a while, trying to sort out her guilty feelings from her feelings *about* guilt. (Once feelings have fallen into the darkness subsumed under *depressing,* they become less visible to Sandy. But more of her feelings are remaining available to her longer now, and she's even sometimes able to retrieve some that have already fallen into the void.)

When did you start feeling guilty?

Sandy says that it's very weird for her to think back. "Because I think of it as a weakness. A big weakness, you know, like a *ma-*

jor weakness in my life. And it's really hard to think about because I can't think of the reasons why now." (The dissociated feelings back then, and the very intense "depression" that resulted in her hospitalization, are still not easily available to her. She can't think about them well, and she can't talk about them well.) She knows there was a lot going on. All the stuff in the family and her parents' divorce—she didn't want to think that had so much of an impact on her, Sandy says, but she guesses that it did. But really the main thing was the breakup with Paul.

"Three days later I tried to kill myself. And I think back to it now and think how stupid it was. Which is another reason why I don't like to feel weak—because that sort of put the idea in my head somehow that being in love is a weakness, which is really bad when it comes to relationships. Because it's like you have to protect yourself against falling in love—because if you fall in love, you know the same thing is going to happen and you are going to get hurt all over again. And I have been trying to get that whole idea out of my head. . . . It's coming between me and Jacob."

Jacob is a sensitive, smart, cultured guy. He's not a limited person who is going to try to own her; he can let her do what she wants. She never thought she'd go out with someone like that.

Why not? the interviewer wants to know.

"Because before, I wanted cool," says Sandy. "People who are smart aren't cool. And people who are sensitive aren't cool, and people who are compassionate and understanding aren't cool. And so I always assumed that I would go out with people who wore leather jackets and all that stuff, and he is totally different. And I am a lot happier with someone like him. It is a little more like myself. A real person—not one of the fronts I put up, but what I am really like, even though I am not cultured. He's smart,

smart, and by my definitions of the past, he would be the most uncool person around, you know. But like about coolness, he doesn't care about that."

Jacob's family also has money, and that's another issue for Sandy.

"We went through a time when I was like between six and eight, when we had close to no money. My father's company went bankrupt, and my mother was on unemployment, and that was basically how we got our food, you know, and I had like one pair of pants and that has made me always want to be rich. . . . I have always been sort of jealous of rich people, because they haven't had to know what it was like to get teased in school because you are not wearing Levi's in the fourth grade."

She tries to dissect her feelings about Jacob's family's money. He's not spoiled, she says, because although he has had anything he wants, he doesn't want much. He's rich, but he doesn't care. She's jealous of how naive he is about it. "He says, 'I don't really need money.' Like we get in little arguments about it, because I say I wish I had this, or I wish I had a car. . . . He says, 'Money is not important or anything,' and I say, 'You don't know what it's like *not* to have money,' and he says, 'I could give all my money away right now and it wouldn't matter.' . . . He seems really sincere about it, [but] that's because he's always had it. He doesn't know what it's like not to have it. I've never been like poverty-stricken out in the streets, with no money at all, but . . ."

From there, they move onto the things that aren't going well. Sandy's worried about getting into college. She was shocked when she found that her SAT scores were only a little above average. She resents the idea that a person could be turned down by a college just for SAT scores. It's humiliating. And she's getting over a lot of things from before that she now realizes are influencing the way she is now.

Like what?

Like my father, says Sandy. "My mother is sensitive and she's smart and she's really caring. And I guess I'm like her on the inside. But I'm like my father too, and it seems like they are battling each other. . . . I mean, I am so different from the people at my school. . . . [My parents] seem more conservative, tightlaced, not as open, and they weren't as open with us about our feelings or anything. I can't remember my mother ever sitting down and having a really serious open talk with me until now. . . . I don't remember ever learning anything from my parents, because they were so—It had to be right. They were so worried about being the right kind of parents. They were trying so hard—and then they weren't doing the right thing."

But she is seeing them very differently now. "I think it's hard for my mother. . . . She's—I hate to say this about my mother, but she's sheltered too. Grew up in a sheltered life, sheltered childhood, you know, she got married at eighteen, and she didn't really do anything for twenty years except to try to make it with my father, try to make it work, and raise kids. . . . She is just starting to live, really, I think, since she married Henry."

She's never seen her father read a paper. "Henry seems to know about everything, and I can sit down and talk about physics, my physics class, with Henry. Henry is a much better father than my father ever was. Which is sort of sad."

Since it hasn't come up, the interviewer goes back to Sandy's hospitalization: Why do you think you ended up here, and what did it do for you?

"Why I ended up here was, well, because it felt like everything was collapsing around me. My parents. My family. My school. Because I had always been so good at school and now I was doing bad, and . . . that boyfriend of mine, and—I don't know. Just—I guess I felt that my world was basically collapsing around me and I had to get out of it, so I ended up here. . . . It made it so I didn't want to kill myself. I think that is what it did for me."

The interviewer asks if she was serious about that. She's not sure. "It seemed like such an easy way out, but I could have just been doing it to get the attention—to say, look, that this is my last resort, maybe I will do it. But maybe it was like a warning to everybody from myself. I don't really know if I really had the courage to do it. But I think if I did, I mean I probably would have. I mean, I wouldn't have tried, I would have *done* it, because usually I do what I want to do. . . . I don't think I got that much out of the hospital. Except that I didn't want to kill myself anymore, which I guess is a lot. Also, they were the ones who told my parents, 'She needs to be away from the house.'"

She had hated the discharge plans at first, and the special unit-like school she thought that they had in mind. But her boarding school was more important to her than the hospitalization. The important things happened after she left.

The interviewer asks if there's anything important that they should cover.

Yes, Sandy says, there is one thing that happened last fall. "I put myself into another hospital. Because I was doing a lot of drugs, and doing downers, and it was just another form of escape. . . . I wasn't addicted, but . . . I liked it so much, and it was so good when I was on Valiums, that I didn't want not to take them. I was only there for two weeks or something. I checked myself out. I was really depressed and I was crying all the time, and it was during that time that I put myself in. And once [the drugs] had all worn off or whatever, I realized that I didn't really need to be in there. And I didn't; it was just like I sort of straightened myself out by myself. . . . It was more like I had to help myself and I couldn't have done it at home. Because I really have a lot of trouble living at home."

So you were depressed? asks the interviewer.

"Yah, or I think I was just bored. I get that way. I just get so bored with everything. . . . I started doing these downers, because it was something else to do, and I just got too into it." (Sandy makes her first connection here between boredom and the peculiar emptiness she calls "depression," and on that note the session ends.)

The Fourth Interview

Sandy is eighteen. She's about to set off for her first year in college. The big deal in her life besides graduation is that she's broken up with Jacob. "We just didn't get along anymore. . . . I couldn't deal with him, actually, so I figured that I might as well break up with him before he gets really hurt. So I did." She describes how Jacob has been screwed up by his very strange family.

The interviewer comments that just last year she had described that family in glowing terms, and that the very things she admired most about them—their intensity and their intellectual preoccupations—are now the things she thinks are weird. What happened? (Much of this interview deals with Sandy's new ways of seeing old things and relationships—her boyfriends, her parents, her ideas. The interviewer points out repeatedly that she has made rapid about-faces in many areas, and so she appears to have done. But these are more than capricious changes of mind. She has found a much wider perspective on her past experiences, and in that expanded context she judges experiences, and acts upon them, differently.)

At first it was all so new and so different and so exciting, Sandy says. But then it got to be really repetitive and a bit too much. The father had no time for his kids, he was so busy with work—but still he had all these plans about how his children should be. All Jacob does is rebel against his parents. "His whole life is trying to figure out who he is, and that's what he does all day. He tries to figure out who he is, and I kept saying to him, 'You know, if you don't spend so much time trying to figure out who you are, and do other things, you'll finally figure out who you are just by doing everything else.'"

Still, she admits, Jacob's family helped her a lot. They were so opposite to what she was used to that it gave her a whole new viewpoint from which to assess her own family and find a comfortable medium. "My parents don't put pressure on us, like with college applications [the way Jacob's did]. My parents just said, you know, 'Are you going to college?' and 'You can deal with it.' . . . My family was like, 'Do what you want.' . . . It makes you feel more independent. . . . I did it for myself, not for my family, and Jacob thought that if *he* did it, it would be for his family and not for himself."

The interviewer reminds Sandy again that she had described her parents much less positively last time. "I think I probably thought just they didn't care," Sandy says. "But they did. They just figured I'd do it myself." She can tell that they care by their delight in her accomplishments. On the other hand, she goes on to speculate, if she'd been living at home they'd have been after her about homework, and she would have rebelled.

What caused her to break off the relationship with Jacob?

What got to her, Sandy says, is that he was so preoccupied with the pressure he was under that he could never even push it aside. He couldn't forget about it, the way she could. "I used to get really mad about it, and I'd just be like, you know, 'You can't let your whole life be run by your family. You have to like break away from them.' And he couldn't. And that used to get me so mad. . . . Which is really bad. And finally we just decided that it was better for both of us." She's the little girl with the little curl, she says—when she's bad, she's horrid.

The interviewer comments that she sounds contemptuous of Jacob's need to "find himself." Yet that isn't an unusual thing for an adolescent to want to do. What is she thinking about it?

"Well," Sandy says, "I'm pretty sure of myself. I don't know if I've found my true self or anything, but I don't sit in my room for hours and say, 'Okay, what am I and who am I and what am I going to be?' . . . After lots of experience and stuff, I'll finally be someone. . . . I think it's like everything altogether. You create what you like and want to do, and then stuff that happens around you, that you have no control over, influences from the outside. That helps with it."

On balance, do you think you have more or less control?

"More control," Sandy says without hesitation. Her college applications—she decided not to look at places that were either "all peace and love" or rigidly academic. She wanted a school where she could go to classes and do three or four hours of homework a day and still have lots of time for friends and fun.

Her new boyfriend is sort of in between Jacob and Paul—not a spoiled rich brat, but not a hood either. Once more, the interviewer comments that her views here have changed drastically. Does that reflect a change in her?

Sandy says that she was taken with Jacob's whole way of life, particularly the sense that he had a future. Most of the people she grew up with had no future—they'd be working in gas stations all their lives, hanging out on street corners. But now she thinks that "you can't intellectualize everything. You have to have a little bit of both in you to be stable."

She's very excited about starting college. She wants a career, because that's how you can be independent. "If I do have a husband or something, you know, and have kids, it won't be till later—it'll be after I've made myself into something." Her parents never had careers, "and that always really bothered me too, . . . because they're both really, really smart people. And I think it's a waste of a life." And she still wants to have plenty of money. It was very painful not having it as a kid. "But it's not like the top on the list. I'd say it's about third." She giggles. She's interested in the sciences. Those are good fields for women.

She knows she'll have to discipline herself. But college won't be her first time away from home, and she's gotten some of her wild partying out of her system. She's more moderate than she was in the ninth grade, when she was drinking a lot—she doesn't like the feeling of losing control, and she doesn't want hangovers. She smokes some hash. But no more downers, ever at all. They're not worth it.

"I loved them—they were great. They made you feel like you were fine, totally carefree, nothing ever could be wrong. And so you do a little more, and then after a while it's just like you totally crash and everything's awful."

They talk some more about self-discipline. In high school, her goals helped to keep her focused. She wanted to get into a good college. Now she wants to get into an excellent graduate program. And she knows now that her friends won't forget her if she stays in to work sometimes, when it's important.

Sandy says that she's getting along fine with her family now —as long as she isn't living with them. When she is, they start telling her what to do, and she's been away from home for so long that she just can't have people telling her what to do. "I do the opposite." Now that her mother doesn't try to boss her anymore, they get along great; they talk on the phone a lot and have supper together. But if they have to stand each other for more than eight hours at a time, it doesn't work.

She moves on to her father. When *he* tells her to do something, she's learned to go along. She'll say sure. "But I won't do it. I'll just agree with him." He's totally different from her. They have fights about politics, for instance, so Sandy keeps things superficial to avoid arguments. "I don't want to get in an argument with him, because we're both so stubborn that we just won't talk to each other for a year."

But she doesn't think her new opinions are a reaction against his. It's more that she used to share his ideas, because he was great—he was everything to her. But her views widened at school. "So we don't get along in that way, and he has this way of—You say something and he'll twist your words into saying, 'Well you just said exactly what I said.' . . . He's really good with it. He's done it all my life. . . . It gets really confusing." She wishes that just once in a while she could win—beat her father at his own game. "I will, someday."

The interviewer asks her about her change in focus from art to science. She says that she likes the creative stuff too. But she likes science. She's very good at photography, and very interested in it, "because it's a really logical kind of art. . . . You can't change what's on the negative, but you can work with it. You can make it lighter or darker or take out the—make it contrastier, or make it really have no contrast at all. . . . I mean you can work with it, but you can't change what's there. And I like that."

Sandy talks some about her mother. She's incredibly moody. She makes everything awful around her when she's in a bad mood, which is pretty bad. "She's really, really sensitive and sweet. . . . But then when she gets in a bad mood, everything goes. I mean . . . the whole house feels like it's trembling." Sandy can do the same thing. "I can regret it after, and say 'I'm really, really sorry.' You know, 'I didn't mean to do that.' But when I'm in a bad mood, I don't care. . . . And I hate that. I hate that part of me."

But Sandy doesn't think she's as selfish as her mother. "If I get in a bad mood and I know I'm going to get in a bad mood, it turns into a depression before I can start being really nasty to people. Like, I try to make myself really stop, and she doesn't even try." (Here's a clear statement of how Sandy uses "depression" to handle anger, and why.)

The Follow-Up Interviews

When Sandy comes back at twenty-five, she reports that her life hasn't shaped up exactly as she expected. She dropped out of college to get married—a surprise to her, and a decision that's left her with one important goal yet unmet. She's delighted with her marriage and happy with her husband, but she's still not certain what she wants to do with herself. For the time being, she's working in an administrative job. Her relationships with her parents are satisfactory, although the one with her mother is much richer than the one with her father. And after many years of important but transient friendships, she is just beginning to luxuriate in the pleasures of a long and close relationship with a best friend. The big issue for Sandy now is the conflict between her wish to connect with other people and her complete unwillingness to be told what to do. She can take a stance of comfortable tolerance toward her parents—as long as she's sure that she's going to make her own decisions. And that's pretty much how she feels about the rest of the world.

Sandy and her mother were at swords' points when Sandy was admitted to High Valley all those years ago, but when she looks back on their early times together, she remembers some very good ones. Her mother was her playmate and companion, and the person into whose bed she would climb when she woke up in the middle of the night and couldn't get back to sleep.

She was scared of her father, though. He wasn't around much, but when he was, he was "very disciplinary." He was pure parent, not the companion her mother was, and his will had to be obeyed immediately. Her mother made it easy to be close, and was loving and nice. But Sandy doesn't remember her father ever telling them that he loved them. "You couldn't get close to my father. I think that he didn't know how to express any kind of feelings. . . . He didn't show any love, so I thought maybe he didn't want us to show *him* any love, you know?"

She sees both of them in herself. "I think my mother has really helped me a lot, because she has made it possible for me to be an emotional person," Sandy says. "My father—I have his strength I think, and I have his stubbornness. . . . I feel my father's strictness coming out in me when kids get around me." And she sees that her parents reflect the web of relationships out of which they came, just as she does. Her mother's parents were very loving and warm, and her father's parents were not. "It's funny, people are so much like their parents."

Still, Sandy thinks now, she didn't rely on her mother long for emotional support. She supposes that she must have gone to her mother for comfort when she was little, but she doesn't remember it. More than anything, she remembers talking to her stuffed animals. "I had a lot of stuffed animals," she adds with a touch of wryness. Maybe she'd go to her mother after a fight with her brother. But if she was upset with her *mother,* it was definitely the stuffed animals. When she skinned her knee playing, she learned quickly to put peroxide on it herself and go back out. Sandy remembers only one illness from her childhood, but that wasn't an occasion for parental caretaking either. She was left with a babysitter when she got the flu, so that the family could go and visit a great-aunt who was moving to a smaller apartment and distributing her household goods.

But since the bad times in her teens, they've all gotten along fine. Sandy has lots of contact with her mother. She talks to her father weekly for fifteen minutes, and sees him about four times a year. They live very near him. But her father tends to block them out, Sandy says. He's very caught up in his life with his second wife. Sandy loves her. "She is a great person, but it's almost like he didn't have a life before her, there was nothing there, a black hole, so that kind of annoys me." (This is quite a laid-back statement of what must be a painful situation. Sandy may not yet be altogether comfortable with anger, and her next comment—about what she learned from her childhood experiences —supports that supposition.)

"I would say that no matter how much I disagreed with the way they did things, . . . it turned out to be okay. As much as I hated them when I was a teenager, I would probably handle everything that they did the same way. Surprise!"

Friendship is one of Sandy's pieces of unfinished business. Since her boarding school days, she's found friendships exciting and satisfying. But they haven't always endured as Sandy moved on in her life. Just as Pete had to convince himself that he was safe enough and tough enough before he could relax into steady friendships, so Sandy had to convince herself that she was her own boss before she could concentrate on maintaining long-term connections.

"It's not that I don't keep friends for long," she says, "but I've moved around. . . . I really don't keep in touch with people. I just kind of get caught up in my life." Now, for the first time, she is nurturing a friendship that goes back many years. She and her best friend Luce went to high school together, and they were roommates in college until Sandy left. Now they're back in the same town. "She's the one person I have [kept up with], so I'm almost proud to have held on to her, you know?"

Sandy and Luce talk about everything—almost. "Except my husband. I really don't discuss anything about my husband really with anybody. If my husband and I are having problems, we deal with them—I don't let people know about it. But anything else. And she knows my family."

Sandy values having someone with whom she can look back. "The things that are most meaningful are when we talk about the past. . . . And it makes me feel like I don't completely abandon everybody in my life the minute I move away from them, because I really do tend to do that."

Her marriage to Ed? That's "great, definitely great," Sandy says. "We have a very good relationship, a very open relationship." But the terms are clear: if she wants to do something, she does it. "I am a very independent person, very hard to—I've had people try to tie me down and tell me what to do type thing. 'No, you really can't go out with your friends tonight.' And I don't take kindly to that at all, and neither does he. So we kind of let each other breathe, which is nice."

What kind of feelings come up? "Oh, every feeling, every emotion. I mean, we're best friends. But there are times we are definitely opposites, and there's no doubt about it. He and I like completely different things, have different attitudes, have different opinions about a lot of things, so there are times when everything is smooth running, but there are times there are definitely conflicts. But I think that's healthy—I think that's good."

What does she like about the relationship? "He's got a great sense of humor," she says. "Wacky. Everything. He's a hard worker. He's got that work ethic that I like. I don't know—everything. And he's a good person to be with. I am never bored when I'm with him. He definitely keeps me entertained."

They do a lot together. "I cook a lot. He will hang around with me when I cook. He's not the best cook in the world, but . . .

he keeps me company. . . . There's a large garage area behind the house, and he has a ham radio set up back there. I'll go out and hang out with him when he's working out there. It's interesting. We do a lot."

Sandy's number-one personal problem is the fact that she hasn't finished her college degree. "It's important to him that I go back to school, because it's important to me. But he doesn't care. Either way, he'll love me no matter what. But he knows that it's really, really important to me, so he really wants me to."

She tries to support him, too—he has an old injury that is getting worse over time, and this depresses him. "I just try to encourage him and let him know that he can't stop living. I've seen people be injured and let it completely affect their lives, so they won't do anything—they're scared to do anything. . . . If he wants to go out dirt-bike riding, it's going to kill him and he's going to be in a lot of pain for three days. But he's not going to be scared of it, and he's going to do it, because he enjoys it. And he'll just face the consequences later." (This is Sandy's manifesto in a nutshell; she offers it to Ed as a gift of love.)

Characteristically, Sandy says that closeness in marriage means more to her than being together. It also means that "we can let each other do our own thing. . . . He goes camping in the winter. There is absolutely no way I am going to go camping in the winter! And so he'll say, 'Gee, I really want to go camping,' or 'I want to do something,' and I say, 'Go ahead.' And I have a lot of girlfriends who say, 'How can you let him go away without you?' and, you know, 'You don't know what he's doing.' And of course *I* think closeness is trusting each other enough to let each other do whatever we want."

She describes her current techniques of fighting. "I'll put things off. The laundry is sitting there and needs to be folded and I say, 'Oh God, I'll fold it tomorrow.' . . . He'll say, 'You're just going to let it *sit* there?' . . . I'll say, 'Yah, you're right, it's sitting there, and I'm going to do it tomorrow!' And he'll laugh, because I always say I am going to do something tomorrow—Scarlett O'Hara, I'll think about it tomorrow. And he'll complain about it for a while. And then, depending on my mood, if I'm feeling rambunctious and like no one is going to tell me what to do, I won't do it, just to prove a point. If I don't feel like listening to him complain about me not cleaning, I will just clean."

Does she think that's a good way to handle it? Yes, says Sandy. If she cleaned every time he wanted her to, she'd be cleaning twenty-four hours a day. She goes on: "Normally I just keep my mouth shut, because I've found that that's the best way. Every once in a while I'll just argue back, and once I get into that mood I'm the type of person who always has to get the last word, and it really annoys him. So I've learned to just let it pass. . . . I'll make my point that I think he's wrong about something, but I won't stand up for myself to the point where we're in a rip-roaring fight."

Independence is very important to her, Sandy says. "Doing what I want, being able to . . . Independence really means I will do what I damn well please. . . . He may be upset by it and it may really bother him—but it's my life, you know?

"The minute somebody starts infringing on my independence, the hair on the back of my neck stands up. And as open-minded as he tries to be, people are what they come from. And *his* background is, his mother sat home with the kids and didn't work and had dinner on the table every day by five o'clock. . . . He's trying to break that stereotype, the typical thinking that I should be home with my apron on. I like to cook, but not when I'm told to."

How has her relationship with Ed affected Sandy's feelings about herself?

"It's good," she says. "Since I met him, I've become a lot more self-confident. He's done nothing but good for me, I'd say. There are no negatives. He has taught me to keep my cool. I used to be a lot more of a hothead. He's done really well for me."

They begin to sum up. The interviewer inquires into Sandy's wishes for the future. She's been feeling the lack of close friends. "I have other girlfriends, but am really not that close to anybody. Luce is the closest person. . . . Because I don't keep friendships that well. I'm sort of hoping that Luce will move to my area, so we can be together, be closer, hang around, you know." She'd like a big house in the country, lots of animals; wants to get her college degree and go on for a Master's, maybe, in economics or business. "I don't know. Be happy."

Do *you* have any questions? the interviewer finally asks her.

Yah, Sandy says. "You know what I would love? . . . At some point, maybe when the study comes out—I probably wouldn't understand a word of it anyway—I'd love to know what I was like."

SANDY WAS DIFFERENT from many of the kids at High Valley. She didn't have a long history of obvious psychiatric disturbance. She wasn't a behavior problem; all she did was infuriate her parents occasionally. She had never been in trouble; in fact she had a history of success, and had accomplished handily just about everything anyone had asked of her. Even the suicide gesture for which she was admitted looked like a reaction to her parents' separation. But the glittering surface hid a shaky infrastructure.

Ideally, children learn to handle feelings in a process like inoculation. When they have empathic and attentive caregivers who feed them before they get *too* hungry, hold them before they get *too* scared, calm them before they get *too* angry, they get to grapple with feelings in manageable quanta that stretch, but do not overwhelm, their developing capacity to "keep it together." There is plenty of room for error in this process. No parents are always available, attentive, and empathic, and there's no reason that they should be; children need lots of opportunities—within reason—to handle the ordinary demands of life on their own.

But the demands of Sandy's life were not ordinary, and she had to handle them on her own to an extraordinary degree. Sandy's parents did the best they could for her, and in time she comes to appreciate this; but they were too preoccupied with keeping their own precarious emotional balance to have much attention to spare for their daughter's. The string of accomplishments with which Sandy courted her parents' approval could not protect her from a family whirlpool that sometimes threatened to drag her under.

Sandy's parents didn't notice much about her emotional states—a full-blown depression had to be pointed out to them by a teacher; a suicide attempt went unnoticed for months. In fact, it was often Sandy who helped her parents handle their feelings, rather than the other way around. When Mrs. Carlson was depressed, Sandy made herself available for company and comfort—but for her own comfort she turned to stuffed animals. She protected her labile father's equilibrium by suppressing any feelings that might bring up the ones he couldn't tolerate—weakness, anger, even love. Mr. Carlson's idea that Sandy's troubles would vanish when he moved back into the house reflected a sincere wish that she might feel better, and may have relieved *his* anxiety. But it did little for hers, and it distracted her parents from her need for help. They abandoned the attempt at family work, and they did not encourage Sandy to persevere in therapy after the revelation of her first suicidal gesture. The family turmoil went underground again until Sandy made it visible in blood.

In a calmer family, Sandy might have been able to tolerate her emotional solitude, but the atmosphere at the Carlsons' was unusually intense—Mr. Carlson described the household as a "seething pit." The parents argued and fought, sometimes physically. Mr. Carlson got enraged; Mrs. Carlson got extremely depressed. One of Sandy's brothers shared his father's disposition to violence, and turned it occasionally on her. On the other hand, Sandy might have been able to manage the intensity if someone had been around to help her cope—or even to make sure that she was allowed to cope in her own way. But there wasn't any such someone around, and Sandy's parents' way of keeping emotional intensity down to levels that they could comfortably handle was to control rigorously what Sandy was allowed to express. As long as she was docile, successful, and undemanding, she was the golden girl. But her distress when things became too much for her was interpreted as insurrection, and was strictly suppressed by authorities desperate to maintain their own status quo.

So by the time Sandy came to High Valley, she was wild with rage at the relentless and intrusive control by which her parents kept themselves together. Her fury terrified her, but her skills for handling it were overwhelmed by the war with her mother, her father's rigid authoritarianism, the impending divorce and remarriages, the on-again off-again parenting at home. Experience had taught her that anger was dangerous; but when it threatened to get the better of her, all she knew to do was to shut it down—by drinking, by zoning out, and above all by what she called "depression," the emptiness of thinking and feeling nothing. By her own testimony later, her suicide attempts had two components:

they were a way out of an intolerable situation, and they were a warning. The warning at last was heard.

At first, Sandy shows little interest in her situation. "I don't know" is all she says; depression, to her, is "feeling nothing." Did she lack insight as completely as she seemed to? Or did she have more self-knowledge than she was willing to share? Her later understanding of herself suggests that both were true. Sandy was very angry and very untrusting, and not given to easy confidences. She actively made choices—to speak or not to speak, for example—for what she believed was her own protection. But something else was going on too.

When something had to give, Sandy turned to techniques that dampen awareness of emotion. Some were deliberate, like her alcohol and drug use, but when even those failed, episodes of involuntary dissociation protected her from the impact of her terrifying fury. Those were the times when she didn't hear when people spoke to her. Although like all the resilient kids Sandy struggled very hard for active control most of the time, when things got too threatening she turned her awareness away until there was "nothing" there but "depression." (This is a sort of reverse of the process that her father described: he ignored anger as long as he could, and when that was no longer possible he exploded into a blind rage that he later couldn't remember.) Sandy makes it absolutely clear as she gets older that "depression" is her way of handling anger, and that she has chosen it actively in preference to her father's technique—that is, she gets depressed "before I can start being really nasty to people." But it isn't a good way. The emptiness makes her feel dead and it makes her want to die. It also perpetuates her problem by keeping her from getting to know her feelings and eventually learning to deal with them.

So Sandy's task is to become able to feel what she feels without blowing her fuses—without "a disruption in the usually integrated functions of consciousness," as DSM-IV puts it. She has to install new heavy-duty wiring that can carry a full emotional current without shorting out, and then identify and label all the circuits. Her story is about how she makes the repairs.

ALTHOUGH SANDY'S SILENCE at first is partly a decision to keep her own counsel, the emptiness of her first interview reflects more than just willpower. The interviewer's questions feel so overwhelming that she can hardly sit there while they're being discussed. "I don't even want to think about it," she says. "I'm not gonna think about it." This is her initial narrative. Subsequent ones deal with learning to ask her own questions, and coming to know herself. Every new insight into emptiness or feelings or "fronts" she explores first in narrative, and then in action.

Sandy can't stand High Valley; it terrifies her. She is fighting for her life against psychological domination, and the hospital pushes every button she's got. "I feel controlled in here, and there's nothing I can do about it." Even talking to people is a loaded issue. The hospital team tries hard to listen, but Sandy's vision of having her words twisted, of being overpowered and silenced, colors her experience of her hospitalization profoundly. She is appalled at the idea of being sent away to school, imagining endless years of infantilization and control of the sort she perceives at High Valley. "I'm like a little two-year-old," she says sardonically. "I can't take care of myself." Many distraught kids feel at least some comfort in the structure of the place, but for Sandy there's no comfort at all. The intrinsic authoritarianism of High Valley is a recapitulation of what tortures her at home. She feels totally helpless in its grip, and then furious and despairing. Still, she surveys the situation and does the best she can. She can't get out, but she can control her behavior, thus keeping herself out of her most dreaded situation of all, the quintessence of helplessness: getting "locked up and tied down." And she can decide who she will and won't talk to.

Sandy has an indomitable streak. She hates being controlled by other people, but when self-determination is impossible, she falls back on self-control (unusual at the Children's Center) to keep herself as autonomous as she can. This major theme—being her own boss—will occupy her narratives for ten years. Her self-control isn't perfect, especially about anger, and that's why she's scared. And her choices aren't always the wisest. But she is no passive endurer. In fact, passive endurance is Sandy's idea of hell. *She's* going to call her own shots. And she does, even in her oppositional first interview.

Still, it's also true that at first she won't or can't talk about how she feels. "Whatever—I don't know. I can't even think about what I'm thinking about right now." When the rage surfaces it has to be blocked out; she can't let herself look at it.

Once she's at the new school, though, Sandy starts to change. By the second interview, she's resembling the old "perfect" Sandy of her youth, but this time she's not building on sand. The things she loves about the place are making clear to her exactly what the problems were at home. Her old narratives begin to expand. Sandy's fear of her own anger comes partly from her identification with her furious father, but it also has to do with the way rage blanks everything else out of her awareness. It scares her into oblivion: "I'd be totally out of it, couldn't concentrate on like anything." But now, for the first time ever, she's free of the need to comply.

She's less angry now, vivacious and thoughtful, very different from the blank furious creature of a year ago. She's interested in "fronts"—a theme that she revisits repeatedly over the years as she learns to tolerate emotional experience and recognizes the limits of her parents' ability to do the same. She pays close attention to her own limits, too.

Sandy soon recognizes the narrowness of her father's thinking, and correctly connects it with his rigidity and the code of "strength" that he unrealistically promulgates. She works on a more tolerant narrative, seeking out complicated debates, relishing the power of different points of view. When her new perspective gains her a more useful analysis of her parents' marriage, it's a dazzling validation for Sandy of a whole new style of thought.

In this context, she starts—confusedly at first—delineating her own anger. She carefully circles around the huge question at the heart of her "depression." How dangerous *are* feelings? Who controls them? Is "restraining" them the only way to keep them from doing harm? With the capacity to reflect comes for the first time the capacity to take responsibility for her rage.

This is scary work. Sandy wants company, and she makes up with her mother. But not compliantly this time. And suddenly the two of them are on much better terms. Her new reflectiveness has helped her to make a real improvement in an important relationship—for the first time since she was ten, there is some warmth in her family life—and that gains her a new sense of efficacy as well as her mother's support.

By the third interview, Sandy is focusing more closely on *her* experiences of feelings—it's not just the way her father gets angry that causes her trouble, but the way she herself feels his rage: *the air around him seems violent.* This shocking and painful image illuminates for her both her father's limits in containing his feelings and her own possible reasons for blanking out. Because now that she's blanking out less, she can really see her father. She spots his anxiety about other people, and reframes his hurtful request that she not drop in on him unexpectedly as an aspect of his need for a "front," not a rejection of her. She also recognizes similar dynamics in herself. She worries that they are not good for relationships—and in this way she is *not* like her father, who by his own admission prefers to avoid other people. Sandy feels her parents battling it out inside her, and she starts to analyze: How do you keep from hurting other people, or getting hurt yourself?

Now Sandy is thinking again, and bringing her considerable intelligence to bear on these questions. Before, she says, "I was sheltered." She doesn't use this word in a positive sense. It seems to be a metaphor for her dissociation: *I had no idea what was going on.* Now she wants to know what's going on, in herself and elsewhere.

A year out of the hospital, Sandy is so bright and so interested and so engaged in her life that it's tempting to dismiss her problems as trivial, and her suicide attempt as an overreaction that could have been managed at home. But Sandy did not end up at High Valley by fluke or by mistake, nor has she made a miraculous recovery by age sixteen. She is still living with the fire hazard of her faulty wiring, and she still, to use her father's metaphor, smolders sometimes. When that happens, when explosion threatens, the circuit breaker trips and she shuts down. The summer after her first year at boarding school, when she goes back to live at home for the summer, the pressure starts to mount again, and she turns to drugs to blank herself out.

But this time she notices what's going on, and it gives her an important new insight. She sees how the "depression" and the "escape" are related, and having recognized that the emptiness is more dangerous even than rage, she girds herself to struggle against it. Sandy experiences the struggle as an inner battle between her two parents, in which her mother's too-vulnerable connectedness and her father's too-rigid perfectionism eventually mitigate each other. Sandy ends up feeling not like an unstructured heap of their disparate parts, but like a stable and trustworthy amalgam of the aspects of her parents that *she* has chosen as worthwhile. She has access now both to her mother's capacity for emotion and to her father's strength and stubbornness. This is satisfying. She can tolerate her weaknesses because she's learned to trust her strengths.

Sandy's first priority has been to make certain that she's her own boss. "It's *my* life!" is her battle cry. But now she feels secure enough to begin to look for connection. She chooses a husband who offers her a whole new kind of relationship. He's a combination of "cool" and "classy" that transcends her stereotypes and intrigues and satisfies her. "He's very smart," Sandy says, "but he can't recite Shakespeare." ("Neither can I," she adds dryly.) He can deal with "weakness" when he has to. *And* he can deal with Sandy. If her willfulness annoys him occasionally, he can stand it. He doesn't try to stop it. He doesn't even particularly resent it. He lets her breathe. She can put down her dukes and be with him without feeling like an occupied country.

But childhood wounds seldom heal completely. The old blankness cost Sandy something, and this haunts her, even now that it no longer threatens her life. Even the revival of an old friendship hasn't filled in all the gaps, and her last words to her interviewer have a ring of poignant truth: *You know what I would love? At some point, maybe when the study comes out, I'd love to know what I was like.*

7 | *Billy*

It All Worked Out Fairly Well

BILLY MAYOR WAS NOT QUITE TWELVE WHEN HE came to High Valley. In the preceding weeks he had gone after his mother twice with a knife and once with a kettle of boiling water. He was admitted after a fourth violent outburst.

WHEN THE TROUBLES BEGAN, Billy was living with his mother, a court stenographer, and his brother Kenny, who was six. His father, a skilled carpenter, was no longer living with the family. One evening Mrs. Mayor refused to drive Billy to a scout meeting with a load of posters he was supposed to deliver. He stormed into the kitchen swinging a belt. She took it away, and she hit him with it after Billy smashed a television set on the floor. As the battle escalated, Billy threw a lamp at her, screaming, "Call the police!"

There had been other episodes like this, but usually Billy was compliant, well-mannered, and, his mother said, "as sweet as can be." Mrs. Mayor didn't call the police this time either, but she did report the fight to a community child guidance clinic, and the clinic referred her to High Valley. Billy was admitted the next day.

The family had been unstable since Mr. Mayor got laid off from his long-time job. He couldn't find work anywhere near home, and he finally had to take a temporary job, and temporary lodging, about eight hours away. While he was living there, he had an affair. He told his wife about it. She demanded a separation at first, but then they decided to try again, and the whole family moved to the Midwest, where Mr. Mayor had lined up a good job.

The new start they were hoping for lasted only six weeks. Mr. Mayor got involved again with a woman, and when his wife learned about it she packed up the kids and moved back east— this time to the city where most of her family lived. Her widowed mother moved in with her. It was the kids' second new home in two months.

Soon Billy's father, without explanation, dropped the sporadic phone contact he had been keeping with his sons. By the time divorce proceedings began to approach finalization, Mrs. Mayer had lost track of exactly where her husband was.

Billy started to complain of feeling ill in the mornings. At first he just played hooky or refused outright to go to school. He stayed home all day, avoiding other children. He argued a lot with his mother and picked on Kenny, for whom he often babysat. Then the violent outbursts began. Billy always felt bad about them afterward and would try to make up by doing something especially nice for his mother, but they continued until the final crisis that brought him to High Valley.

BILLY WAS AN UNPLANNED CHILD, Mrs. Mayor told the hospital staff, but she had welcomed him because she was lonely and wanted "something to fill the time." He had developed normally. He wasn't much of a talker, so that you didn't always know what he was feeling, but he was "a nice kid who tried to be helpful." She had been preoccupied with finding a job since the move back east, and she hadn't been paying much attention to the boys, or to the loss that the impending divorce represented to them. In fact, when Billy got angry at her and expressed a wish to live with his father, she sometimes retaliated by taunting him with his father's abandonment.

The Children's Center evaluation team noted that Mrs. Mayor had few connections outside her family. Her main attachment was to her own mother, who wielded great influence in the new household. She was the only one who could intervene effectively in domestic battles. But she couldn't fill the need for practical support that Mr. Mayor's absence had created.

On the unit, Billy was well liked and generally well behaved. Unlike many of the kids, he was content to be there, recognizing that he needed a "vacation" from his mother. He got on well with the other kids, though he didn't actively seek them out. He did seek out one-to-one contact with his favorite staffers, and seemed to form attachments to them, but he said little about the problems at home. His team thought he was intelligent but very immature, and insufficiently able to control his aggression and talk about his feelings.

They also thought he had an overstimulating and too-close relationship with his mother. Mr. Mayor had been an important buffer between them, and after he moved away, Mrs. Mayor had turned to Billy for support (cooking, shopping, and babysitting) and companionship. This confused and enraged Billy at the same time that it flattered him, and it kept him very close to home, making it hard for him to consolidate friendships at his brand-new school. The team recommended that he remain at the Center until he had enough control over his temper to behave acceptably at home, and that Mrs. Mayor work with her therapist on filling her needs for nurturance elsewhere, so that she could give Billy the room that adolescents need.

When Billy left High Valley four months later, he was considerably less volatile. But the staff felt that he still didn't tolerate frustration easily, and that he was young for his age socially and sexually. There were concerns, too, about whether Billy's mother would allow him to grow away from her, or whether she would go on depending too much on him for her own security.

The First Interview

Billy comes for his first interview on his last day at High Valley, about a week after his twelfth birthday. He and the interviewer start out with some small talk about sports, but when the interviewer starts to focus on Billy's feelings, Billy responds with an array of distancing techniques—jokes, yawns, diversions—and the interview settles down to a protracted struggle over what he will and won't talk about.

You've been here for a while now, the interviewer says.

A hundred and nineteen days, Billy agrees. But who's counting? They laugh over this. (As it turns out, though, it wasn't really a joke. Dates preoccupy Billy, who is always tracking the length of his father's absence. Time and precision are serious narrative lines for him.)

After a lot of pressure, Billy says that his time on the unit has been like "a nightmare—well, a dream." (The dream/nightmare theme appears frequently in the interchanges between Billy and the interviewer. Billy's tendency is to accentuate the positive, especially things he can do something about. The interviewer tends to look on the darker side.) At the interviewer's request, he elaborates. The nightmare was a "riot" on the unit, when a bunch of kids "barricaded themselves in one room, right? And they're smokin' and everything. Smoking marijuana and all that stuff. Cigarettes and everything. They were painting on the room. So they broke the window out, right? And Security had to come and everything. The Fire Department. They threw mattresses out, and they jumped out the window. Each kid was jumping out the window." They got caught, though, and taken into state custody.

Why do you think it happened? asks the interviewer.

"I don't know," says Billy. "They were probably just mad at the staff." He won't speculate further, just repeats "I don't know," and fends the interviewer off with yes-and-no answers and loud yawns.

As the yawns get more intrusive, the interviewer tries the road not taken.

What's the dream, the good part of being here?

"Well, it helps," Billy says, and shuts down again.

With long wooing, he relaxes enough to volunteer that he was uptight about some problems he was having at home. He was keeping anger and hate inside. He feels great now. But when the interviewer asks what he was so angry about, he falls back on "I don't know"s and facile agreements.

This goes on for a while. Billy doesn't filibuster the way Pete does when cornered. He gives brief answers, then stops. The interviewer introduces the subject of friends, but that doesn't go anywhere either. He used to have friends, Billy says, but then they moved.

They go over the history of the family's moves, but Billy won't talk about the family itself. He stonewalls until the interviewer goes back to the subject of Billy's lost friends. How do you think they've changed? asks the interviewer. "Probably gotten older," says Billy.

That's a fair statement, says the interviewer, and Billy laughs. This diffuses the tension of the struggle between them. It also effectively changes the subject, because the topic of family is abandoned while they talk about how *Billy* has changed. He's matured, he says. The interviewer keeps trying to get him to elaborate, and finally Billy says in a bored voice, "I became smarter—I don't rip off 7-Elevens anymore." (Finally they've found something that Billy will talk about. In fact, it becomes clear that macho risk-taking is what Billy *wants* to talk about —and think about—to keep his mind off what's going on at home.)

Billy stole models. Well, one model. He never got caught. He describes other larcenous techniques, like walking in with an empty Coke can, putting it into the refrigerator, and walking out with a full one.

How did you think of that? asks the interviewer.

Billy laughs. "Easy. I saw somebody else do it."

He must've told you about it.

"I followed him," Billy says. It was a friend's big brother, an older guy of twenty-five or twenty-six. The friend had told Billy what his brother was doing, and Billy decided to follow him to see how he was doing it. (He used to follow his father around, too, he comments later.)

The conversation limps along. Billy's friends steal things too. Bicycles. With chain cutters. Then they file the serial number off and paint them and sell them. But Billy doesn't do that. He thinks a bike is too easy to get caught with—you could get nailed with the goods.

And then?

"You'd get arrested."

And then?

"Probably go to court."

And then?

"Maybe Juvenile Hall."

Whatever, the risk isn't worth it. The other kids pressure him. "Well, we made almost a hundred bucks last week," they'd say. "So, we'll keep getting 'em, we'll keep doing it. We haven't been caught yet." Billy mimics their conspiratorial voices. (One of his talents is a flair for dramatic storytelling, and he makes good use of it as a distraction when need be. But it is very effective in engaging adults. It also gives him pleasure, and sometimes he can be seduced into saying something just for the fun of describing it. Tales of skill, guile, and courage under fire are a major narrative theme for Billy.)

But even under duress Billy never participates in the bike-stealing ring—the only one of his group who doesn't. That takes some guts, says the interviewer.

Billy is quiet for a minute, and when he responds, for the first time there's no subtext of struggle. "They understood how I felt because, like . . ." He hesitates. "One kid, he was with our group for a while, then he left, right? He moves somewhere else, right, and was caught, um, stealing this other kid's bike, and got knifed." The kid didn't die, but still it was terrible. Billy doesn't want to be involved in anything like that.

They try talking about school. Billy's doing well. His favorite subject is recess. He and the interviewer share a laugh. Or gym. Or spelling. Why spelling? Because it's the last subject of the day.

The interviewer realizes that Billy is putting him on—and that he's not really talking about school. He casts around for a new topic and again Billy reengages a bit on the subject of lost friends. He and the neighborhood guys aren't all in the same school, so when they want to get together they have to cruise around until they spot each other. He also acknowledges that when he started having trouble at home, he also began having trouble at school. He started to flunk.

What do you think was the problem that got you to flunk?

"I don't know. I just had too much on my mind, I guess."

What was on your mind when you were in school?

"What had happened the night before at home or—what was going on at home." ("What was going on at home" is one of Billy's two central themes. The other is learning how to do what he needs to do—his passion for mastery.)

The interviewer invites him to say more. Maybe it's time to talk a little bit about that, he says. Because it really is an important part of your life, and this interview is about me getting to know what's important to you. Even if it's hard, maybe you could try to tell me a little bit about some of the problems. Billy responds briefly to this more empathic approach.

"I was beginning to get a very bad temper. Right now I get violent and . . ."

What did you do when you got violent?

"Yell, scream." Throw things, too.

What made you so mad?

"I don't know," says Billy.

There must've been something that got to you.

"No," says Billy. "Nothing that I could think of."

It just came out of the blue?

"Yah." He sounds mystified.

The interviewer approaches the issue more concretely. Do you remember any time when you really got mad at someone?

"Yah," Billy says. "Most of the time I hit my mother."

Did she do something before you got mad that got you mad?

"No."

Never?

Well . . . Billy hesitates. "She'd say no to me."

No to what?

"Like one time I asked her to drop me somewhere, right? Drop off these posters for the Boy Scouts? Um. She said no, and I got mad. That was the night before I came here."

An awkward series of exchanges ensues. The shrink at the community clinic was too tall; he gave Billy a stiff neck. Billy is doing better with his doctor here, because they're closer to the same height. He's going back to the old guy when he leaves, but it'll be better because Billy will be going to camp. (Billy has been yawning throughout. It's hard to tell if he's really listening to the questions, or just diffusing tension with his joshing about stiff necks. His capacity for coherence is overwhelmed; he seems to mean not that the doctor will be better because Billy is going to camp, but that *Billy* will be better, because he'll have more to do.) For a while Billy agrees perfunctorily to everything the interviewer suggests, and then he laughs. "Sort of confusing." It isn't clear whether he's referring to himself or the interviewer.

Hm, says the interviewer. What do you do when you're in a situation that's confusing?

"Just try to sort it out."

How do you do that?

"I try to figure out the things that are hard. I try to work them out and make them easier." (This is Billy's other big theme: mastery.)

How do you go about making them easier?

"I talk to my shrink." (At the High Valley Children's Center, a statement like this can mean a lot of things: authentic engagement in psychotherapy; ingratiating compliance; telling-'em-what-they-want-to-hear. Billy doesn't give it much weight.) The interviewer can't draw Billy out beyond an indifferent "Yah" or two, so he finally gives up and asks about Billy's brother.

Kenny is seven now, and he's a real headache sometimes. "Yells, screams, pulls my hair, yanks at my ears, screams in them. Everything possible that can make you aggravated. . . . I used to pull *his* hair, but now he's got a wiffle. I've no hair to pull unless I use a pair of tweezers. Like, his hair's only about a quarter of an inch thick."

Why is that? asks the interviewer

"It's a *wiffle!*" Billy says. "Zzzzz! Shaved all his *hair off!*" The last two words are a loud whisper. "It's just about—it's like an SOS pad."

The interviewer laughs at the drama, and they're safely away from the brother and onto Billy's own hair. He's in a struggle with his mother and brother about it. They want him to chop it off, but he wants it long. When the style was for long hair, Billy says, he wanted his short. "So I wore it short. People used to make fun of me, but I said, 'Be myself,' 'cause I don't like long hair. Now I'm wearing long hair when the hair is short." He laughs. He doesn't care. He'll do what he wants.

Billy's grandmother is seventy-two: "Words of wisdom from the elders," Billy says, lowering his voice melodramatically. He laughs, but there's real feeling there. He details the way he cajoles her into lending him money. She's the only one who supports his right to have his hair the way he wants it. But he'll get it trimmed, not cut. That should make everybody happy.

They talk about power dynamics in the family. Billy's mother makes the decisions at home, Billy says, but his grandmother influences them. When the two of them disagree, the grandmother usually wins. She can talk his mother out of things. Like persuading her to get a cheaper car than the one she had been thinking about. (This is a theme too. Billy is a man of action, even at twelve; he's looking for ways to make things turn out the way he wants. He can see that his grandmother's persuasive techniques work better than his mother's, and this interests him.)

The interviewer wants to talk about what it's like when Billy's mother tells him what to do, says no to him. Billy heaves a loud sigh, but the interviewer presses on. Does she try to talk you out of things, or does she just tell you no?

She just tells me no, Billy says. Like, she moved his brother into his room. What a pain in the neck! Now he can't have girls over to study anymore. (This is all very histrionic and full of disgust.)

To Billy's delight, the interviewer takes the bait. He asks about the girls. Billy says gleefully that he has a girlfriend—most boys do, he adds. (Another theme. Billy is being held too close in a predominantly female household, and he is looking hard for ways to define himself as a man.) They go bike riding together.

By now, Billy is completely the boss of the interview. He's into joke mode; when the interviewer isn't following, he just laughs quietly to himself. He responds to some questions about his goals, but neither consistently nor coherently, and it isn't clear if he's even really attending. Maybe he'll become a childcare worker. Go to the beach, to ice cream places, on trips. Maybe go to college and get a Ph.D. and be a veterinarian. He likes animals—hey, he likes his brother!

The interviewer asks why they moved away from their old home.

His father had a new job, Billy says, but then his parents broke up "'cause it wasn't—it just wasn't going good." He hasn't seen his father since last year, doesn't know where he is. But it's all right. When the interviewer expresses doubt, Billy says that it *is* all right, not to hear them fighting. They'd been fighting for a long time. (This is a classic example of optimistic reframing.)

What was that like for you, when you heard them fighting?

"I didn't like it, but there was nothin' I could do about it."

Did it get very loud?

"Yah."

Physical too?

"I don't know. I just turned my stereo up over it so I couldn't hear it."

That's hard, though. To hear parents yell at each other.

"Yah." (Long pause.)

For a whole year you haven't seen your father?

"Right." (Long pause.)

Do you ever miss him?

"No." (Long pause.)

Suddenly there was a big change in the family, the interviewer says. It wasn't just you who had problems. A real breakup of parents is always really hard.

"Yah," says Billy. He seems to get dreamy and absent. The interviewer asks what he's thinking, and Billy comes back with a start. He laughs, yawns, denies any thoughts.

Well, says the interviewer, the last question I have is: When you think back, what's the thought that makes you happiest?

"When I was back home," Billy says wistfully, "playin' football with my friends."

And what's the thing when you look back that was hardest?

"Hearin' my parents fight." (This is a big piece of the "what was going on at home" theme, and there will be many negotiations over the years about how Billy expands this narrative. He concentrates on the relief of no longer hearing his parents fight; the interviewer wants to concentrate on the pain of loss. It takes them a long time to work this out. But in the struggle, and in the narrative, Billy clearly demonstrates his own very effective style of playing from strength and moving on from there. He also demonstrates how something that might not on the surface appear conducive to resilience—that is, ignoring certain feelings—may be obscuring a truly resilient process underneath.)

They're winding down now, and the interviewer asks if Billy has any questions. He has lots, about the upcoming family interview; but while the interviewer is answering them, Billy gets ever more anxious and restless. Finally the interviewer wishes him well till next year. "Next week, isn't it?" Billy asks. No, the interviewer says. I won't be at the family meeting next week. But we'll meet again next year. Okay?

Okay, says Billy.

The Second Interview

When Billy comes back a year later, he's just thirteen, going into eighth grade. He and the interviewer look back on the day Billy left the Center. "I remember the exact time that I left High Valley," says Billy. "Exactly when I walked out the door." He comments that precision is important to him. "It makes it easier to remember stuff." Place stuff, too, like getting back and forth to the hospital—which was easy, even though he's never taken the train before.

What's happened over the past year?

Well, Billy says, "I went to school, I joined the Community Youth Guild, I started taking the drums. And that's really it." The family moved to a new apartment near their old one. "Because it was a better apartment," says Billy. "Plus, the other one—the price was going up." Billy is very aware of the rents on the several apartments he's lived in lately. He also knows that the new apartment is smaller than the old—he's sharing a room permanently with the demon brother. And his friends are now two miles farther away. But he says cheerfully enough that he can still see them. He rides his bike back and forth and tracks the mileage on the odometer. He clocks his speed, too, going down hills. (Billy's attitude toward the new apartment is another skillful piece of the optimistic reframing that is characteristic of the resilient kids.)

How fast were you going?

"I did forty-five. One time I did sixty."

Sixty miles per hour on a *bicycle?*

"Yeah," says Billy. "I was really ripping. Oh *yeah,* it was a big hill! I was coming down the hill practically straight down. My feet started to sweat, my hands started sweating. It was fun, though! I had a little trouble stopping . . ." I can imagine, interrupts the interviewer. Billy laughs. "But I skidded on a patch of dirt."

You have courage, it sounds like, the interviewer says.

"No," says Billy, "I ain't got no brains." But he did make it down the hill. "It usually takes me five minutes to go down. I made it down that hill in two seconds. *ZOOM!!!* . . . I wasn't even pedaling fast. I mean, I was pedaling at a normal pace, but I was really moving!"

Billy expands on his story—it's a dramatic and exciting one, with lots of tension and suspense. The climax is the revelation that the brakes were out. When he slows down, the interviewer asks: But were you scared at all?

"No," says Billy. "I was petrified at the end, 'cause I saw my life flash before my eyes."

How did you feel then?

"I began to get nervous."

And then did you shake or . . .

"No!" Billy says again. It was his cool head and good management that saved him. "'Cause if I shook, I'd be dead. 'Cause my hands wouldn't do anything. . . . It suddenly hit me, that I was going sixty miles an hour, I had no brakes. It's like going over a bridge at a hundred and twenty with no brakes, and there's a tollbooth at the end."

That's very scary. How long did it take you to get over it?

"Five minutes," says Billy.

Yet again the interviewer asks Billy if he got scared. Again Billy doesn't bite. Instead he reveals something important about his subjective experience of life. It's not fear, he says, it's excitement. He likes it.

What other feelings do you feel? the interviewer asks.

"Sadness sometimes," Billy says. "Like when I see my report card." He's doing pretty well in school. Not in Theater Arts, but that's because he doesn't understand it, and it's not a major subject.

They talk about friendships. Billy has a friend he does stuff with. They play baseball. But they're not together all the time. A best friend is "somebody you can trust and talk to and that type of stuff." Billy can do that with his friend Cal. But the first chance he gets, he deflects the interviewer away from friends and back to his bike, which was a birthday present from his mother.

The interviewer seizes his opportunity. How are things going with her?

Billy dismisses the question with an airy "Good, good." The interviewer keeps trying, but Billy keeps his counsel. The interviewer finally says directly: Can you say a little more? Like a couple more sentences?

"Like what?" Billy says, and snickers. After even more pressure, he gives a muddled overview of life at home: In a nutshell, it's fine.

You *never* fight? *Never??*

No, says Billy, and then takes it back. "Well, I can't say *never*. Everybody fights sometimes." He tells a confusing story about how his mother always gets her own way and Billy can never win.

The interviewer asks for an example, and Billy's coherence returns as he analyzes the politics of garbage disposal in the Mayor family. His mother tells him to take out the garbage. He hates that. It's disgusting. Smells, flies, ugh. So he doesn't do it. He tells his brother to do it. But while Billy and Kenny and their mother are arguing over who's actually going to pick up the bag, "my grandmother says, 'Never mind!' And she takes it out and does it herself." (This is the important part of the story to Billy—his grandmother's good sense in keeping out of power struggles and just doing what has to be done. But it's a hard conversation to follow. Billy is joking around, snickering occasionally, not paying much attention, and concentrating on directing the discussion. Once he has successfully evaded the subject of his battles with his mother, they turn their attention to his victories over Ken.)

Now Billy tells a long and complicated tale about handcuffing his brother to a tree and losing the key and leaving him there all night. There's a lot of internal inconsistency in this story, and it's not clear how much of it is being made up on the fly. In fact, Billy rather shamefacedly takes back the all-night part, and when the interviewer presses him about some other details, he changes the subject completely: Your calendar is wrong, he accuses. "It says the fourth, but it's the twenty-sixth."

This time the interviewer doesn't get sidetracked. He wants to stick with the handcuff story. But Billy foils him yet again, taking him literally and talking not about Kenny but about the cuffs themselves: "Bought 'em in the Army-Navy Store. It was good. I could buy a real billy club too."

What would you use that for?

"If he wakes me up in the morning—*BOP!*"

Kenny is a pain, Billy says. Like athlete's foot. They went to a carnival and Billy won a stuffed animal for him in a basketball contest. They're going to go back and trade that one in, and Billy will get him a big teddy bear. (Billy can express his feelings very well, even when he's stubbornly avoiding the "mad, sad, glad" vocabulary of psychospeak.)

His mother is liking him a little more these days, he goes on, because he doesn't bug her the way his brother does. She's working hard; he leaves her some peace. The interviewer asks how his hospitalization has affected his family life. Billy doesn't know. They go back over the usual ground. Why was Billy at High Valley?

"Well, I had a bad temper."

What did you do?

"Well, I threatened my mother."

Do you remember what you did exactly?

"No. I know I threatened her, that's for sure."

And then, when you left here, did that still occur?

"No."

Not at all?

"No."

How do you explain that change?

"I don't know."

Try, says the interviewer. I mean, you had something, and then suddenly you didn't have it any more?

"Right, right," says Billy. "One morning I had it, and the other morning I didn't." He yawns.

Billy is giving the interviewer the business again. This time the interviewer sees it and comes on tough. Do you have any understanding of why you might have threatened her?

"No," says Billy. "Nope, not whatsoever."

Did you ever try to understand it?

"Yeah," says Billy, "but it—I don't know."

Now the conversation is very labored indeed, mostly questions and extremely long pauses. Billy won't, or can't, talk about this; he sounds baffled. When the interviewer gives up and changes the subject to Billy's activities, Billy becomes more animated. He talks about groups he's joined, shooting pool, participating in stuff. (This is partly diversion from the threats to his mother, but also he really *is* participating in stuff, and he's pleased. It's important. When he left the hospital, his social isolation had been everyone's biggest worry.)

The interviewer tries the topic of family again. Billy goes right back to yawns, pauses, sighs. He doesn't know where his father is; he calls once in a while, but Billy hasn't seen him in three years.

What's that like?

It doesn't make any difference to him, Billy says, *except* when his father calls early in the morning and wakes him up. "It's like driving this spike through my head, 'cause I'm still groggy and everything." His father asks what he's doing; Billy tells him. It gets on his nerves. "When I'm going to sleep, he talks to me, and when I wake up he's stiiiilll talking!"

Do you miss him?

"Once in a while. Not very often, though."

The interviewer says that three years is a long time, but Billy says he's gotten used to it. He was already used to not seeing his father much, because he was away on jobs a lot.

The interviewer suggests that it must have been hard in the beginning, and Billy agrees. But his parents used to fight a lot, mostly when he was in bed. He'd just roll over and ignore it.

Did it scare you?

"No. . . . I mean, like it's none of my business." The interviewer asks if he thinks his behavior had anything to do with it, and Billy says no.

They look back again to the hospitalization. What helped the most?

"I don't know," Billy says. "Just being away from my mother for a while." They'd been getting on each other's nerves. He liked the people and the staff. He was only in the quiet room twice. He doesn't remember what for, and it was only for a little while.

What was it like to be there? the interviewer asks, and Billy says with a private little keep-away laugh that he doesn't know, he fell asleep. And he left the hospital with the most privileges possible.

What's it like to be back?

"Not any different than it was when I left."

It's a place that doesn't change much, the interviewer says.

"Right," says Billy. "The people do. I can only say if they didn't change, it's got to be something going on here. A conspiracy."

What kind of conspiracy?

"Suck everybody dry. . . . With the insurance fees and all of the doctors' fees and all that stuff." It's expensive, says the interviewer. "Yeah," says Billy, laughing softly. "Very." (It's not clear exactly what Billy means about the change part. His concern seems to be with whether High Valley is worth what it costs. This develops into a big theme later.)

You're not sure whether the hospital helped you enough?

"Oh, yeah, it did for me, but for some people it didn't. Some people, they went to a residential school, which doesn't . . . I mean, to me it doesn't seem like it helped them that much."

Why not?

"I don't know. It just seems like they didn't do enough. They should have been able to help the person more." He yawns. "More than they did." (It's possible that Billy is harboring some wishes that he himself might have been sent to a residential school, where he could have continued his "vacation" from his mother. This thread is not followed up, however.) The interviewer remarks on Billy's yawning. Billy says that he's tired.

"It took me, you know, an hour and twenty minutes to get over here." But this visit was worth it, because this time *they're* paying *him*. He'd come from twice as far for that money, even if he had to walk. But he wouldn't have to—he'd take his bike.

He suckers the interviewer again, this time into a discussion about buying snow tires for his bike with the money he's getting for the interview, and from there he segues into tales of high-speed chases across ice and snow. He's back in joke-and-snicker mode.

The interviewer asks Billy if he's interested in girls.

"Yeah," says Billy. "What boy isn't?"

I ask everyone that, the interviewer says defensively, and *Gotcha!* the trap snaps shut.

"Oh," Billy says. "Girls too?"

Well, *girls*, the interviewer says. I ask *them* if they're interested in boys. While he's getting his foot out of his mouth, Billy goes off on a riff: "Interested in boys, yeah, that could get embarrassing. . . . Whaaaaaat do you think I *AMMMMMMMM?!?!*" He laughs. He does have a girlfriend. He took her out for dinner and she ate so much he could barely pay the bill. But he didn't mind. Petty cash.

He declines to raise any subjects of his own, and the interviewer asks him what he does when he gets mad about something.

"Ummmm, maybe just go outside, relax." (This discovery that he can diminish the pressure of rage by "going out" turns out to be a transformative one for Billy, and it gets more important as the years pass. He elaborates it in narrative, and builds upon it in ever more sophisticated ways. When he knows he can escape if he has to, he can handle relationships with confidence.)

Does it go away then?

Yah.

But that sounds different from before, when you were here, or just before you came here. When you got mad you did things, right?

Yah.

Like you threw things, or you'd do something like . . .

"Yeah, I threw my little brother before . . ."

They're talking over each other now. Billy is telling a tale about how he tosses his brother around. The interviewer is trying to learn whether he could have stopped himself or not. Billy is giving him the runaround, snickering and teasing. He says no, he couldn't have helped it.

What do you think it was that made you do it?

Gotcha again! "The devil made me do it!" Billy crows. This time he lures the interviewer into a discussion of religion that consists mostly of scatological derivations of the word "pew."

Gamely the interviewer presses on. If Billy can control himself now when he gets angry, he says, that's a big step. What happened? This is still Billy's unfavoritest subject. He struggles with all the "feeling" talk for a while, but finally he says simply, "I think I just kept trying hard to change and I did." He hasn't had any temper problems in the last year at all.

Never?

"No."

What problems *does* he have at the moment?

"Getting home," says Billy. He starts talking about train tickets. The interviewer asks if he's happy with himself.

"Yeah," Billy says. "Yeah, I'm happy with myself."

That's a really big move, says the interviewer, because you weren't happy last year about the problems, about the family problems. You were kind of depressed about them.

But Billy is watching the tape recorder. "There's a light flashing on that thing."

I know, says the weary interviewer. We're going to be finished in a second.

The transcriber notes that the tape was turned over, but the other side is blank.

The Third Interview

The next year Billy is fourteen. He's just been accepted at an excellent and highly selective technical high school. He wanted to go there, he applied on his own initiative, and he is very, very pleased with himself. "I took a test. It surprised me—I was smarter than I thought."

That's fantastic! says the interviewer.

Billy thinks so too. "I didn't even think I was going to get in. I thought I would try. My mother was shocked when I got the notice I was accepted. She almost had a heart attack."

Really! She didn't think you would get accepted?

"Nope, she didn't even think I had a chance."

Why did you do it, if you didn't think you had a chance, and your mother didn't think you had a chance?

"I wanted to try." (A huge theme.) He figured he did pretty good.

In fact he's been doing pretty good for a while. He caught up by "hard studying." When he has to do something he doesn't like, he just puts his mind to it, to get it over quickly.

Do you ever give in? asks the interviewer. Do you ever say, 'I don't want to—I won't do it'?

Once in a while, Billy says. Last week. "The teacher put a whole lot of compositions on the board, right? I think like he put three- or four-page compositions on the board, and I was going to do it that night and I put my mind to it and I sat down and I couldn't think of it, so I just said forget it, I would do it tomorrow."

Did you do it tomorrow?

"Nope. I haven't done it yet. I'm probably going to do it this weekend. Because I want to get all my work done for the term so I can just relax."

What if you don't do it? Then you can't relax?

"Well, no, I just keep doing it until I get it done with." He wants "to graduate and everything. . . . I don't want to be kept back."

Is there a danger that you could be kept back?

"Well, not really, but I just don't want to be."

The new school is going to be harder and stricter, Billy says, because he's going to have to compete with people just to stay in. But that's where he wants to go. "They give you like two diplomas at the end, one is for graduating high school and one is for putting in twelve hundred hours of a certain course, like computer programming. I can go as a junior programmer, which is a regular programmer. I can go right to work after that, and that means like $250 a week."

He likes computers—they give you information. "I figure everything is going to be computerized someday, right? So I figure I might as well help it and program computers." In the meantime, though, he's hanging loose at home. He's getting along better with Kenny. The interviewer reminds him of the way things used to be, and Billy tells another handcuff story. "I hand-cuffed him to a chair over my friend's house and the key was broken or something and we couldn't get him off the chair, be-cause the handcuffs were on and we had to use a screwdriver and everything to pry the handcuffs, the whole thing. Handcuffs are expensive. They're like seven dollars."

Were you scared? the interviewer wants to know.

Yah, says Billy. "I was hoping my friend's mother wouldn't come home and see him sitting there handcuffed to her new chair." (Last year's episode was a tale of power and control; this time it's a narrow escape from an anxious situation. When this theme comes up again later, it's in yet a third context: keeping the people you love close to you.)

He's okay about his brother now. They do things together. Kenny knows when to lay off. Billy's glad he's older. He has more freedom. But he also still has to babysit sometimes.

How do you feel then, when you have to do something you don't want to do?

"I just do it. I just do because I figure I am doing my mother a favor so she can go out and stuff." (This attitude of pragmatic cooperation is becoming increasingly typical of Billy.)

How do you *feel* about it, though?

Okay—Kenny can do whatever he wants; all Billy has to do is be around.

What about your mother and you? How are things going there?

Oh, they're okay, he says. They're better than they were.

Looking back now, what do you think was wrong?

"Well, we just didn't get along too good." A pause. "I don't know—every time we would be together, we would get on each other's nerves and fight and stuff." She used to ask him to do things and he wouldn't want to, or would forget, and she'd start to yell and scream and they'd start to fight. The interviewer asks what Billy thinks is responsible for the change. "I don't know," he says. "We've both gotten older. . . . I can control myself more. . . . Sometimes when I get mad, I just go out on my bike and ride around for a while. Or listen to my radio or something, up in my room. . . . I used to stand out there and keep yelling and fighting and everything."

You couldn't leave the situation?

"Yah," says Billy.

When you get mad, do you get very mad?

"Not anymore."

Give me an example of when you got very mad.

Billy does; this is the first time he's been able to talk about it. "Well, I smashed my brother's head against the wall and I sort of cracked the plaster. And one time I put my fist through the wall."

What got you so mad then?

"I don't know. I can't remember anymore. It was three years ago."

Before you came to the Center? Were those the two incidents that actually led to your coming here? Looking back, do you think it was the right decision? Why?

The interviewer fires a barrage of questions, one after the other, without waiting for an answer. Billy is saying "Yah, yah," throughout. When the interviewer slows down, Billy says only: "Well, I figure I needed help at the time."

Did you think that back then, too?

"No."

What *did* you think back then?

"I figured my mother was making a mistake and there was something wrong with her."

What did the hospital do for you?

"Not much, but it taught me how to control myself more."

How so? What do you think made the difference?

"Well, I had to learn to talk stuff out with my mother instead of just yelling at her." The family therapy sessions were helpful, except when his brother was jumping all over the place. "He is a little nut sometimes," Billy adds, with what sounds suspiciously like affection.

The interviewer tries to get Billy to articulate exactly what was helpful. All Billy will say is that "we could just talk to each other better in the family meetings than we could at home." But he does remark—and this time it sounds like he means it—that it helped on the unit to talk his problems out with his doctor, who would sit there nodding his head. That told Billy that he was listening. "Sometimes I felt that my mother wasn't." She would fall asleep, and Billy would wake her, and then she would get mad.

What did you think when your mother would fall asleep?

"I would think she was tired from work." (It's hard for Billy to talk about this. He goes on trying—harder than he's ever tried before—but he's awkward. The gist seems to be that sometimes he wanted to hang out with his mother and talk to her. But she would get mad if he tried to keep her awake, so he'd watch TV while she slept.)

Not that he thinks the hospital was perfect. You should have been able to earn a key to the front door, so you weren't locked in. Also, Billy says (perhaps reflecting the difficult enmeshment with his mother), there wasn't enough privacy. Kids should have their own rooms.

The interviewer asks Billy about his times in the quiet room. Billy brushed him off last year, but this time he answers. Once he had to go because he didn't want to go to a family meeting. The other time he forgot to control his temper.

Did it help?

"Not really," says Billy. "It just gave me time to cool down, but that was it."

Well, that's an important change, that you're able to put the lid on things when you need to. What about your father?

"It's okay. I think it's better now than it was before."

How was it before?

"Well, it used to be okay—we used to do a lot of stuff, like we used to go camping and stuff. But like there was always something missing. My father would always go to different states to work and stuff, so he was hardly ever there, so most of the time, for a couple of years, it was just me and my mother and brother anyway. So . . ."

How old were you when he started working in other states? Until you were eight, you were always together? What do you remember back then?

Another barrage. Billy heaves a long sigh. "Well, we used to go camping and everything." (He's not happy about it, but he'll talk a bit now about missing his father without the denial or bravado of the previous years.) People were getting laid off, he says; his father had to move around. He was too far away to come home on weekends, although they talked on the phone. Billy can remember missing him. He felt sort of lonely. And bored, because they weren't going camping anymore. He figured that his mother missed his father too, but he didn't ask. He figured she'd talk when she wanted to. He worried about her sometimes, but he didn't see her much. She worked nights, and he was usually in bed when she came home. (This is a much more developed version of the "what was going on at home" theme, and it covers a wider range of feelings and circumstances than before. It also displays once again Billy's unsentimental empathy.)

He won't talk yet about what he wanted from his mother, though. All he'll say is that everything was fine. Usually he'd wait up for her, and make her dinner when she got home. But then his father's comings and goings began. Eventually they split for good; they just couldn't get along anymore. Billy didn't like moving, but his mother wanted to be closer to her family. Billy has no contact at all with his father now.

The interviewer asks why there's no contact. It's his father's decision, Billy says.

Would you want more?

I don't care, Billy says.

He gets briefly distracted by the blinking light on the tape recorder. When the tape has been turned over, he goes on. He talks to his best friend, Cal. But "I like to handle my problems myself. I guess I like being independent and that kind of stuff. . . . I don't have to depend on anybody. I do things myself." He thinks he might have turned out that way because when his father first left, "my mother would be at work and everything, and I didn't have a father. I would just solve it myself. Decide which I should do." Now he likes to be alone. He plays with his dog, goes for walks, rides his bike.

What about your mother? Are there a lot of things that you keep inside of yourself there?

"Yah," says Billy. "Nobody tells their mother everything."

Why do you think that's important to you?

"I don't know, I just sort of—I don't like depending on my mother for anything. I don't know, there's just something about me."

Billy doesn't have any questions of his own. They go over a few administrative details, and they say goodbye.

The Fourth Interview

Billy is fifteen now, a freshman in his new school. He's been working—first on a delivery truck, now in a grocery store. History is his favorite subject. "It's like things from the past—you can tell they're happening now and they happened like a couple of years ago. And stuff like that." He had a history teacher last year that he liked. That guy made them work, even in eighth grade, which is supposed to be a mess-around year. But it was good.

The interviewer wants to know what friendships are like in high school. Different, Billy says. In grammar school, friends were closer. In high school, it's like every man for himself, so there's no one to help. There's also less room for pranks. (He details some ingenious examples in his old vaudeville style.)

Did you get into real trouble?

"No, the teachers, they're all—now they're all hard-core steady guys. Teachers back then—they didn't really care, as long as you did your work."

Have you done any of that stuff in high school?

Uh-uh, Billy says. He'd get kicked out.

Do you miss the old days?

Yah, Billy says, as the spate of questions runs down. Yes, he misses them a little. "It was unbelievable how much fun we really had, when you look back on it." Now he works after school, and he's got too many bosses in his job. When he can't stand it, he goes on break. "I mean yesterday—just forget it. And I left." He doesn't get into trouble, though. The other kid he works with does all the work. Billy returns the favor for his buddy when *he* needs it.

He doesn't mind his tight schedule. "I mind doing the homework, but I don't mind working. It's sort of nice to have money in my pocket—that's the only way I look at it. It's the only way you can. It's not an easy job. It's not fun." But then he adds, characteristically, "Sometimes it is."

What's fun?

"Playing football and stuff when we're supposed to be stocking the aisles, right? Throwing cans and stuff back and forth, stacking up cans and throwing stuff, throwing cans of tuna fish at them, playing shuffleboard in the aisles and stuff. Or I'll be sitting in the back room drinking Coke when we're supposed to be working. It's not bad. I mean on Tuesdays, when there's no bosses around, that's when it's fun."

Uh-huh. What do you do then?

Whatever they want. Work gets done, but not quite so much as when the bosses are there. There were fewer bosses on the delivery job. That was more fun, but the pay was the pits.

What's the story at home? the interviewer asks.

"Well, I'm hardly home at all now. I'm either out with friends or working or at school or something. All I do is come home and sleep."

He doesn't see his family much. They aren't generally home all together.

Is that how he wants it? the interviewer asks.

Sort of, says Billy. "There are never any problems when we're not all together. Plus, I'm more relaxed when I'm not home." (One of Billy's biggest jobs has been to learn to manage distance and closeness in his relationships, because that's how he keeps from getting too angry. Now he is actively thinking about that process and how it works for him.)

What happens at home, when you are together?

"Nuthin.'"

It sounds like you prefer being by yourself?

"Well, I prefer being out."

There's a long pause. The interviewer tries again to get Billy to think about what it's like when he and his mother and brother are together. Another long pause.

"Well, when we're all together, my mother is usually asleep on the couch. My brother is sort of in his whiny mood. I'm sort of just, 'Leave me alone, I'm tired, I've worked all afternoon.'" Do they fight? "No," says Billy. He goes up to his room. Otherwise Kenny would aggravate him, and they *would* fight. Billy would punch him out. Kenny would cry and wake their mother up, and she'd yell at Billy. So it's just safer for him to go upstairs.

She yells at Kenny a lot less than at him. That's not fair, says the interviewer. "I know," says Billy. "That's probably another reason why I'm hardly ever at home." If he complains to his mother, she just says, "Oh, he's my baby."

"So I say, 'Fine.' And I leave, and I usually go out."

That must be really hard on you.

"You get used to it after a while."

Kind of, says the interviewer. I understand that you're *trying* to get used to it. But I think it's hard to have your mother favor another. (Billy yawns.) Do you ever get mad about it?

Yah, Billy says. "That's usually when I go up and lock myself in my room and watch TV. . . . I'd rather be in a room away from everybody than putting up with the aggravation of listening to them." (This whole discussion is punctuated with very long pauses and yawns. The interviewer really tries to get Billy to talk about feelings of rivalry toward Ken; but as they continue, things get more confused until it becomes apparent to both of them that they're talking at cross-purposes. When they finally step back from the skirmish, Billy returns to the subject *he* has been thinking about—being alone and not depending on anybody—a theme that will explode into new importance as he approaches adulthood.)

"From what I heard, that's a good way to be. . . . From what I've learned, I am the only one I can depend on. So . . ."

What does it mean, to depend on?

"Like if you need them for something."

So you try not to need anymore?

"Yah."

Do you depend on your mom at all?

Not much, Billy says. He gets his food at work. He earns his own money. He gives his mother some for room and board. The rest he keeps. He has his own phone and he pays his own phone bill. "The easiest way to get things done is to do it yourself, right? So that way you don't have to depend on anyone else to do things for you."

What would happen if you started depending on people?

"I don't know."

Try to think. What could happen?

"I just think it won't get done. Because I'd wind up getting stuck doing it myself anyways." The interviewer asks for an example. (Characteristically, when Billy is asked what would happen if he started depending on people, he doesn't talk about feelings—worries that they might fail him, or that he might be hurt or abandoned or engulfed. His example is practical. But it says a lot.)

"Say, when I went home I had to cook my own dinner and stuff. My mother is supposed to do that, right? So, I usually get stuck doing that. My own laundry. If I was depending on her doing laundry, she was just forgetting about it." A pause.

So you always do your own laundry?

"Yah."

Does your brother do his own laundry?

"No." But Billy didn't do his laundry when he was ten, either. He just started doing it this past year.

He's become much more independent, the interviewer acknowledges. Does his father have anything to do with his feeling that he has to rely on himself?

"I don't know," says Billy. "I haven't spoken to him in a while."

They get into a real struggle this time. The interviewer wants Billy to see a connection between his need for independence and his father's disappearance. Billy isn't having it. The interviewer asks why Billy has no contact with him. Billy repeats what he's said before: "That is by his choice." The interview begins to sound like an interrogation, but Billy holds his own. He becomes less forthcoming, but even under pressure he doesn't lose his temper or even disengage completely. After a very long pause, the interviewer concedes defeat and agrees to change the subject. But he still can't quite let it go.

It sounds like that is a hard area—that you never get in touch.

The struggle resumes briefly, and Billy is the one who breaks it definitively by reframing his father's absence into a positive: "I sort of like it that way, because I make my own rules."

He keeps out of trouble now. His temper isn't as bad as it used to be. He doesn't fight with his brother so much. He hasn't had an outburst in a year and a half. (He's yawning.) The interviewer asks him what he does to control his anger.

"I don't know," says Billy. "Nothing makes me mad anymore." He tries not to let things bother him. Sometimes he has to work at it—he'll relax, he'll listen to the radio. He and his best friend go out, and they don't go home until they've made sure they've had some fun, even if it takes till four in the morning. He tells a wild tale about a rainy night and a cracked catalytic converter.

But it was fine, he concludes. They kept the car from blowing up, and a good time—eventually—was had by all. They talk about things; they cheer each other up when they're depressed. The interviewer asks if Billy's friend understands him.

"Yah," says Billy, "and I understand him better than he understands himself sometimes. . . . Like I can put myself in his place and he can put himself in mine, and things like that."

Do you see the world exactly the same way? Do you see it through his eyes? Or do you see it through your eyes?

"I see it through his eyes," Billy says.

How do you know?

"I don't know—just—I can tell. Like sometimes it won't be my exact thinking, but I can see where he's coming from."

Plans for the future? "I don't know," Billy says. "Basically, graduate high school. Maybe go on to college. That's about it. Because I don't like looking too far into the future. I just like living it like one day at a time."

The interviewer asks if Billy has any questions, and as usual Billy hasn't. The interviewer says that they can stop. But Billy's been watching the tape recorder again. "Boy," he says, "we didn't use the whole tape this time."

Almost, says the interviewer. Why? Last time we used it all the way?

"Yah," Billy says, "because at the end, the light kept flashing."

That's right, you have a good memory.

"Maybe it's a longer tape."

You may be right, says the interviewer. Do you think we haven't covered something that we should have covered?

"We covered everything," says Billy.

Sure?

Billy's sure.

The Follow-Up Interviews

When Billy comes back at twenty-three, he's got a job—he's a policeman—a wife, a family. He's got friends who are dear to him, and he's grappling in a mood of tolerant competence with the complexities of adult life. For instance, that he and his father have come to the end of the road. "I lived with him for a little while out West. But we didn't get along, because he had a whole new family and everything. So it just didn't work out. That's when I moved back here." He's had no contact with his father in eight years. His mother and brother don't hear from him either. His mother wanted Billy to invite his father to his wedding, but Billy said, "The hell with him." His father doesn't even know that Billy has a child. But Billy and his mother talk a lot. He worries about her, and wishes that she would tell him more about her health. She just says, "Oh, I'm fine." But aside from that, things between them are good.

Part of the work of the adult interviews is to look back on childhood, and Billy applies himself to the task. "Oh, it was good when I was younger, because we used to go on vacations and everything together and did a lot of traveling. I was always closer to my father though, until they split up. Yah, I don't know, maybe it's the oldest son being closer to his father, I don't know. I resented my mother for the divorce for a long time."

He speaks for the first time of the pleasures of being with his mother when he was very small—and of his resentment of his brother, a subject previously taboo. "He's a baby, he needs this, he needs that—you know. You're older, you can take care of yourself. That type of stuff—which is true, you know, but I didn't look at it like that at the time. I was like, '*You* had this little monster, and now you're taking him, making him better than me.'"

But that was then. Now he offers a new dimension of his relationship with Kenny. "When my father went on the road, I had to take care of my brother a lot, because she started working part time at night. So it's like I was basically the father, because I took care of my brother, did everything for him, cooked and everything for him and . . ."

You were awfully young for so much responsibility, the new interviewer comments. About eight, right? Billy agrees. He thinks he took too much on himself, things little kids shouldn't have to worry about. "How my parents were doing, and things like that. . . . Making sure there was always enough stuff in the house, as far as food, my brother had whatever we needed, you know, all things like that. . . . Keeping track, making sure that my mother had enough, was making everything meet. Which really didn't have anything to do with me.

"I resented my brother more because he was little. I had to take care of him—I couldn't go out with my friends and all that stuff. Which rubbed off onto my father being away, you know, not at home where he should be. Because at that time . . . it was regular families. It's not like it is now—what is it, like 75 percent of the people are divorced or separated." (When Billy does finally talk about his resentment of Kenny, he portrays it as something far more complex than the competitive struggle the first interviewer imagined.)

Billy understands now that his mother hadn't forced his father out. There wasn't any work, and his father had to go where the jobs were. But he still doesn't find it easy to talk about his father, whom he sees as strict and abusive and not very able to listen. He gets uncharacteristically confused a few times, too, going back and forth between an adult vision of his childhood and a much earlier one. Along with the good times, there were rough ones. When his father got angry with the boys he used a belt,

Billy says, and once he punched Billy in the face and gave him a black eye.

But a few minutes later he contradicts himself: punishment was never much more than a few spankings. "'Cause after the first couple of times you learn, you know?" He doesn't notice the discrepancy, or recall that his father's very severe discipline had been a source of struggle between the Mayor parents. (This is a loss of narrative coherence.) And a minute later he approaches the subject a new way, this time thinking about his toddler stepson, Nick: "There's times with my little boy that I turn around and he just said something and I want to beat that child, and I just, you know—well, he needs a spanking or something, and I just can't even bring myself to. I might yell at him, but that's about it."

Billy isn't sure now whether his greater sense of closeness to his father was because they had fun together or because it was a way of keeping out of the way of beatings. His mother was closer to his brother. "I think that happens a lot, though, when you have two kids. One's closer to one parent than it is to the other."

How did he get attention when it wasn't forthcoming? asks the interviewer. Billy recenters himself, and soon he's on a roll. "We had this one closet that had a lock on it so the kids couldn't get in it. Well, my mother went in the closet for something and I didn't see her in there—or maybe I *did* see her in there—but she had always said to make sure all the doors are closed. 'Close them up.' So I went by and closed the door. Locked her in the closet for like four and a half, five hours. . . . I couldn't open it, because I was too short, so Dad comes home from work and Mom's locked in the closet." He laughs. "You know, it's not *my* fault I was short!"

He doesn't blame her now for being upset. Looking back, in fact, he thinks she did a good job. "Now I can see what she was going through. But still . . . It makes me think, you know—to work harder at my marriage, just trying to make things work right. Because I couldn't put a kid through what I went through. No matter how bad it got. . . . I didn't want to get married at first, because I didn't want it to wind up the way it wound up with my parents. I still think deep down that that bothers me every once in awhile, because I keep a lot of stuff in. . . . I don't want to discuss anything in front of the kid, because I figure it's not right to fight in front of the children . . ."

When the interviewer asks if there are parts of his childhood experience that set him back in his development, Billy shows again his gift for optimistic reframing. "Not really," he says. "It wasn't really any *setbacks.* I mean, there were when I was young, but everything seemed to work out fairly well."

Is there something particular that you've learned from the way you were raised? One thing that you've learned above all?

"Yah," says Billy. "You really have to *listen* to what the kids are saying, you know, and try to figure out what the overall effect is. What's going on at the time, what's going on around you, as well as the situation at hand. Because you can't take everything at face value. . . . I can't just take one side over the other, you know. I try to sort things out."

They move on to Billy's other relationships, which Billy gets a kick out of describing. His old jokiness comes through briefly when he claims a (nonexistent) girlfriend as his main romantic relationship. But he's serious when he talks about his best friend Ken.

Billy and Ken have been working together off and on for almost four years. They are "basically brothers," he says, closer in some ways than Billy and his real brother, who is also named Ken. "We can communicate, you know? I don't know what it is, but we're both there for each other when we need it. Like if something's bothering me, I can call him up—'If you want to talk, stop by.' You know, stuff like that. And it's the same thing him with me. If we need each other, the other one's always there." They can talk about just about anything—relationships, the job.

When Billy and Donna were fighting over his work hours, he took the problem to Ken. And he reciprocates when Ken needs support with one of his complicated girlfriend scenarios. "I told him what I thought, you know. I told him I can't tell him what to do—but I can give him an outlook on it that he might not have thought of. He does the same thing for me."

They've shared dangerous experiences that he can't talk to Donna about. "One night I had this junkie with a gun up to my head and he was going to blow my brains out, and it was definitely a stressful moment, and I went over to Kenny's house and we had a couple of drinks after that, and we were just talking and it was unbelievable." Ken wasn't there when it happened, but Billy knew he would understand. "Just letting me talk, and listening. Because, you know, my wife doesn't understand half the stuff that we go through at work. One time I had a guy who was on something, I think he was on heroin. He had a gun and was trying to throw a newborn baby out an eighteenth-floor window. And he was determined to throw that baby out the window. And me and my partner took him down, you know. . . . I just can't bring it home. If I told her half the stuff that went on—I've been stabbed once. I couldn't tell her everything, or she'd be a nervous wreck all the time."

Billy and Ken have differences but no disagreements, Billy says. "We haven't had any conflicts, probably because we rely on each other so heavily." Donna and Ken don't get along, but Billy thinks that's more her issue than Kenny's; she's jealous sometimes of their closeness, and she fears that Ken will lure Billy back to his old single-guy habits. Billy can't convince her that it isn't like that.

After they dispose of the mythical girlfriend, Billy tells the interviewer about his relationship with his wife. They've known each other five years and have been married seven months. The relationship "comes and goes," Billy says. Donna seems like a totally different person since they got married, and Billy's buddies think that's just the way of it. But there are lots of things he likes about her. "She's easy to talk to and she's usually pretty cheerful. She's kind of pleasant. She's good with the kid, for the most part. You should see them—they fight! Other than that, she's okay." They talk about all kinds of things, from bills to work to schedules to what's going on with Nick in school. They share some personal worries. It's a problem that sometimes they don't see each other for several days at a time, because of the way their work schedules conflict. But there are little things that make the relationship special. The way she cooks dinner, or his bringing her a card when he comes home from work.

Donna's right that he has some mixed feelings about not being single and running wild with his friends anymore, Billy says. The things you give up for a family. And the guys at work give him a hard time sometimes. But that's just the way it is; he feels 100 percent committed to the relationship.

Do they understand each other? Up to a point, Billy says. "She doesn't really understand what I go through at work. But yet, I don't understand everything that she's gone through in the past, and all this stuff. Because she's been married before, so there's a lot that she's been through that I don't— But other than that, there's not much."

To Billy, closeness in his marriage means "just being together.

She's there whether she's there or not, you know? Just—she's part of me."

Billy and Donna *do* have disagreements. "My friends, her friends, my hours at work. Let me see. Her spending too much. Typical." She wanted to get rid of the old car. "I said, 'Look, it's almost paid for!' . . . But she wants to go out and buy a new convertible or something, you know, and she said, 'Well, we can afford it.' And I'm like, 'Yah, but I'm tired of just affording everything.' I'd like to start, you know, saving. Because we're trying to pay for a house now. Well, we're paying for the house. But between mortgage payments and everything else, it's just getting to be a lot, and I'm tired of working overtime. I want to just settle for what— . . . I told her, when her car's paid off, then we'll discuss it. Until then, leave me alone."

That's how the fight ended. Billy says he's not going to bother discussing it until the time comes. "And then when I sit down and I look at the books—if we can afford it, then we'll get one. But if we can't, we won't."

Sometimes he wishes he'd handled an argument differently. He likes to wait until things have calmed down to talk, and he'll leave. But she wants to talk about it right then, and that's hard for him.

When she's upset with him, she ignores him. "She'll lock herself in the bedroom and just not say a word." It blows over in time. Once in a while she yells, but usually she keeps it to herself. Billy thinks he's assertive with her about work things, but if she gives him a sad look and says, "But honey, *pleeeease?*" he gives in. Like going to Disney World on the Fourth of July to see the fireworks . . .

And suddenly the twelve-year-old raconteur is back. "You know how many people were in Epcot??? A hundred and sixty thousand people! Crammed into Epcot!! And she wanted to go to this *one specific spot*. Because, she said, she's only five foot two, and she said, 'I can see them from there.' And we're standing right in the middle of *a hundred and sixty thousand people!* She was determined to go. 'Okay, we'll go!' I could really care less about fireworks, you know, and she wanted to go, and it was our honeymoon, so I figured I better give in."

He contemplates the dependency balance between them. "I am independent from her, but it's like, she's also independent and she doesn't rely on me for much. She does, but she doesn't. It still seems like she's got a lot of dependency for her parents. . . . I guess it's a matter of time."

How does Billy's relationship with Donna affect the way he feels about himself?

"It really doesn't," Billy says. "I mean, there's times when I look at her and look at the baby, you know, that I feel good. But other than that, it's comfortable, you know?"

Do you see your friendships changing in the future? This is the interviewer's last question.

Not unless I move, says Billy. He's a conservative guy, and he keeps his old friends. But one of Billy's oldest friends moved out to California and they haven't seen each other for years. On that open-ended note, the last interview ends.

BILLY'S INTERVIEWS MAKE a good contrast with the others. He's a very bright guy, but he's not into thinking for the fun of it. He doesn't contemplate his feelings for pleasure; he's indifferent to intellectual abstractions; and he doesn't bring to bear on himself the kind of analytic powers that Pete, Rachel, and Sandy enjoy developing. His background is different from theirs, and his goals and ambitions are different. What he *does* care about is doing well the things that seem good to him to do, and living well in the way that seems good to him to live. He's a practical man and he's interested in practical things. He's also proof positive that reflection, relatedness, and a vital and constructive sense of agency are not about speechifying; they are not the exclusive birthright of an elite and educated few, and they have nothing to do with the gift of gab. They are ways of processing experience, and they bear fruit in action at least as fundamentally as in words. Billy practices them as hard as anyone, and develops them as thoroughly. He just talks about it less.

Billy's way is action, and his interviews illustrate this wonderfully. Time after time, he seizes control of the process and takes it where *he* wants it to go. The other three rely on verbal camouflage when the going gets rough, but Billy takes the offensive. Very pleasantly, most of the time, but also very effectively.

The dynamic of control between Billy and his interviewers is perhaps the most fascinating aspect of his narrative, which displays in microcosm exactly the techniques that he eventually uses to such good effect in the real world. The other three kids give beautiful descriptions of their search for mastery, but Billy demonstrates his.

His first interview is a killer; twenty-five years later, the interviewer still groans when he thinks about it. Billy does *not* want to talk about this stuff, and when Billy doesn't want to talk about something, by golly they talk about something else. He drops some clues, perhaps inadvertently, that he is concerned about what adults can and can't give kids. But mostly he jokes around, he yawns, he watches the clock.

That doesn't mean that no psychological work is going on. Billy's reluctant comment that his one hundred and nineteen (but who's counting?) days at the Center have been "a nightmare—well, a dream" applies equally to the home life that brought him there and that he won't speak about directly. Which was the dream and which was the nightmare? Billy has lost his father—a nightmare. But he no longer has to cover his ears at night to keep out the sound of his parents' fights, so his dreams are a bit less troubled. He has an intimacy with his mother that most children only fantasize about: he has replaced her spouse as her most valued partner. But it's the wrong kind of intimacy, and that dream turns out to be a nightmare after all. Even as a boy, Billy is very aware of such complex equilibria. He seems to know by instinct that dreams and nightmares are two sides of one coin, and he struggles with the interviewer most doggedly when one half of an ambivalence is being addressed at the expense of the other.

And he always wins the struggles. For a long time, he will only talk about what *he* wants to talk about. He's never mean or nasty about it; he offers quite a lot of friendliness to buffer his intransigence. And in his way, on his own terms, he opens himself. He may refuse to talk *directly* about sadness or loneliness, but the bravado in his sagas certainly bespeaks the vulnerability underneath.

He doesn't complain about missing his father, but he describes following older guys around to learn from them. He doesn't analyze his own behavior, but he carefully explains his qualms about the bike thieves. He doesn't fuss about hurt feelings, but he joyously recounts his surprise acceptance at a very prestigious school. He can withstand a lot of pressure. The interviewer appreciates this and acknowledges it to Billy, though the acknowledgment turns somewhat rueful when he's the one whose pressure Billy has decided to withstand.

Furthermore, though Billy may be reticent, he is not without insight. He knows that there's a connection between his troubles at home and his trouble at school. Concerns about "what was going on at home" are very common in kids with unexpected school problems, but not all of them see this as clearly as Billy does, and few take responsibility for it so economically.

His description (when he finally gives it) of the episode that landed him in the hospital is a good one. It's concrete, but it concisely delineates a complicated emotional dilemma. His mother says she wants him to go out and be with friends, but she refuses his age-appropriate request for help in fulfilling his responsibilities to them. Yes, she's been working all day. But, we learn, so has Billy—he's been taking care of her other son and doing the shopping, to say nothing of waiting up for her and cooking her supper. This labyrinthine situation has temporarily overwhelmed him. But sorting things out is Billy's fundamental approach to the world, and he knows it.

His greatest pleasure is in the growth of mastery and autonomy. This is a major strength, but it also makes Billy vulnerable to exploitation. He will eventually make clear that his anger at his mother's authoritarianism is more than simple resentment at being frustrated. He is engaged in a mighty struggle against a double bind. He's shouldered several of his mother's adult burdens. Yet when it's convenient, she dismisses him as if he were no more than an importunate child. It's not fair, and the unfairness drives his macho aggression and his preoccupation with rights and responsibilities. Billy refuses to be infantilized—worse, feminized. When the interviewer focuses too one-sidedly on his vulnerability, Billy redresses the balance with displays of manly competence.

And he *is* competent. He looks for the bright side, he does his damnedest to cope, and he doesn't want his efforts undermined, dismissed, or patronized. If he doesn't bemoan his father's absence, it's because he concentrates on the things he can do something about, rather than the ones he can't. He's very much an agent; he relies on his own resources, and he tries not to wish for what he can't have. He doesn't speak his longing directly, but it shows in other ways, including the wistful question to the interviewer who wishes him well till next year: "Next *week,* isn't it?"

Billy is much more participatory in his later interviews, which is both good news and bad news for his long-suffering interviewer. The "subject" is now willing to participate in a dialogue, but it is not quite the dialogue that the interviewer has in mind. The interviewer wants to *talk* about how you handle feelings; Billy wants to *show* how he does it—with courage, skill, and nerves of steel. His pleasure in excitement and in mastering danger are such important themes for him that he builds them permanently into his life narrative by choosing the police force for his profession.

Billy never evades responsibility when he thinks back on his time in the hospital ("I threatened my mother. . . . I know I threatened her, that's for sure"), but it takes him a while to get a sense of where his rage comes from. It's a more complicated rage than Pete's or even Sandy's, and Billy hasn't analyzed it. He hasn't thought about the intricate and dangerous seductions to which his father has abandoned him. Only much later does he begin to perceive them—concretely, not abstractly—in the pull he feels between freedom and family, between danger and domesticity, between male companionship and the siren song of the female.

High Valley "feeling talk" is not his style, but he does engage in reflection—in his own way. He acknowledges both his longing for his father and his anger at him in the fantasy (disguised as complaint) about those hours-long phone calls. He suspects rightly that "just being away from my mother for a while" is what helped him the most. It is the anomalous and imprisoning overintimacy with her that has been stoking his rage, and he notices right away that he's much less angry when they're apart.

This reflection rings the bell on his mastery-meter, and "getting out" becomes one of his great organizing principles—the technique that assures him emotional space to deal with complex relationship situations. It appears in ever more refined and abstract forms in his narratives as he learns to adjust distance psychologically as well as physically. This is one of the most elegant examples in our narratives of the way a story—"I needed a vacation from my mother"—can both reflect past experiences and shape future ones.

Another permanent preoccupation of Billy's is how you decide what something is worth. Is stealing bikes or escaping from the Center worth the risk of being handed over to the cops? Is High Valley worth the small fortune it costs? Is freedom worth the effort and responsibility it demands? Above all, is the special closeness with his mother worth the resulting confinement and rage? This theme becomes more and more salient for Billy as he takes on the world as an independent individual, making choices of his own.

The interviewer pushes Billy to talk about his feelings, but Billy has learned that "getting out" is his way to handle emotional pressure. And he demonstrates this in action, as when the interviewer asks him once too often if he's depressed about his father's absence. "Yeah," Billy says. "There's a light flashing on that thing." When people don't give Billy enough room, he makes his own—with jokes, with yawns, with flashing lights, and, when he's absolutely had to, with boiling water or a knife. He is very persistent. But he doesn't need the knives any more.

Billy's optimism in trying for a special school is typical of the resilient kids. So is his willingness to act on his own behalf, despite his mother's vote of no confidence. Perseverance and striving are bread and butter to Billy. If something is going to happen, he figures, you might as well be in there directing it. He doesn't become a programmer after all, but his reasoning stays the same: someone has to keep babies from being thrown out of windows, so it might as well be Billy. (His complex interest in handcuffs takes on yet a new set of overtones in this aspect of his development from assaultive boy to caretaking man. As a policeman, committed to protecting others, he uses them to keep the peace.)

As the years go by, Billy's view of his life as a child takes on more texture and detail. His descriptions of the old days with his mother sometimes sound like a bad marriage in which he functioned as a weary paterfamilias, coming home after a hard day's work to a cranky wife and child. But having learned to get out, Billy takes responsibility for improving the situation himself, without bothering much about what his mother is or isn't doing. His attention is on what *he* has to do, and can do, to change things. He can go to his room, ride his bike, toss around a tunafish football. Eventually he learns to table a tense conversation till things calm down. These skills improve his chances for the future and give him a better perspective on the past.

In his typically laconic fashion, Billy slowly becomes able to talk about his father's disappearance. Yes, he did miss him. But he still maintains the attention to balance that he has had from the beginning. He's not going to weep like an abandoned child. He's going to get a life. He can make his own money, pay for his room and board. He's working hard to handle the central tension of his life: How do you balance conflicting wishes? How do you balance the longing to be a kid—free to play, but helpless—and the desire to be an adult, fettered by responsibilities but self-sufficient? Weeping doesn't help you there.

Billy is less afraid of being "hurt" than Pete or Rachel. But having been trapped by dependency once, he doesn't want it ever to happen again. Paradoxically, it is his self-sufficiency that gives him the sense of safety he needs to get closer to others. Billy tells tersely the story of his final overture to his father—his anger to the fore at last, and unmistakable. But he faces the finality of the loss, gives up on his father once and for all, and comes home. He finishes his high school diploma at night school, and applies to the Police Academy.

In the new context of his marriage, he's motivated for the first time to think back on his early family life. Confident in his independence now, he can remember some nice times with his mother, and even openly acknowledge his longing for her—in his own distinctive style. His story about keeping her locked in a closet all day is yet another iteration of the loneliness that he never complains about, but that once drove him to handcuffs (now part of his everyday equipment) to keep people where he needed them. He's rethinking it all in his determination that his stepson will never suffer what he did. Even his first interviewer couldn't fault the way he talks about feelings now.

Billy's hopes for Nick show him that his resentment of his brother was more than simple competition for their mother's attention. He knows now that he gave his brother the childhood that his father's disappearance stole from him. The rote parental admonition that infuriates so many kids—"You're the oldest, it's your responsibility"—had a sharp edge for Billy, who had to bear too young responsibilities not properly his own. Did he see Kenny the way his father had seen him—as someone to control and to escape from? It shouldn't have been like that, Billy thinks now. "I brought too much on myself." He's come to the same conclusion that his team had reached at High Valley ten years before. Like Pete, he is taking more responsibility than is strictly warranted. He did not "bring" those responsibilities upon himself; they were imposed on him. But also like Pete, Billy would rather feel like an agent than a helpless pawn, even retrospectively. And his mysterious rage at Kenny now has a human face: his father's.

Typically, Billy ends up reframing the difficulties of his childhood in a positive light. In another context, such an avowal might be seen as denial, or at the very least a Pollyanna-ish view of emotional life. But the resilient kids do tend to make good use of what comes to them. For them, this kind of thinking is truer than not.

Billy's preoccupation with freedom and responsibility isn't likely to go away. The tension between his own macho longings and the needs of the woman in his life causes him some distress, but Billy has been working on this problem since he was twelve, and he does his best to handle it honestly and considerately. Donna feels threatened, as Billy's mother did, by his identification with a male "pack"—she wants him there for her, domesticated, as partner and provider. She doesn't trust him to balance both roles. But although Billy has plenty of mixed feelings about giving up his bachelorhood, he doesn't have regrets. He's committed to his marriage and to his child, and to working out the issues that arise. He knows that in the work schedules that keep him and Donna out of touch for days at a time, he's replicating his early disjunction with his mother. But in his marriage, he knows it to be a problem; it's no longer a necessary technique for avoiding trouble. Characteristically, he tries to be realistic, both about closeness and about distance.

Billy is still cautious about relationships, and he's content for now with a small circle of his own trusted friends and the new connections brought to him by his wife. Like Pete, Rachel, and Sandy—like most people his age—he still has plenty of psychological work to keep him busy. His desire to be a good parent may cause him to reopen some closed areas. And since his drive for mastery remains firm and powerful, and his techniques for maintaining equilibrium under stress seem to be effective and reliable, it's not hard to believe that when he's ready to move on, he'll do just fine.

For now, he's a steady, devoted, and kind-hearted young man with a strong fabric of carefully chosen and maintained relationships, and a complicated life that he tussles with and enjoys. He says in so many words that he doesn't like looking to the future too much; he likes to take life as it comes. So his response to the interviewer's last question is an interesting one. She wants to know how he sees his friendships changing—not Billy's favorite kind of thinking. He doesn't see them changing, he says. But he adds a caveat: "Unless I move." One of his friends did; Billy hasn't seen him in years. But underneath the sadness of that recognition is a happier one that is very characteristic of the resilient men and women of this study: you're always free to move.

8

Seeing in the Dark

A PRIME MOTIVE FOR RESILIENCE STUDIES IS THE wish to build a society optimally hospitable to children. People with solid childhoods behind them can count on resources of confidence, competence, and self-esteem to support them when catastrophe strikes. Less fortunate adults possess at least some accumulated experience and a certain amount of physical strength. But children have few established reserves of experience and skill, nor are they their own masters in the eyes of their parents or the law. They are vulnerable to ill fortune in ways that most adults, even fragile ones, will never be.

Resilience is not an irresistible force that sweeps all obstacles away before it. The thirst for agency, self-awareness, and relationship can do only so much to keep kids from foundering. More is needed—food, safety, medical care, education, new people, new circumstances, new possibilities. A dollop of luck never hurts either. But until we can reliably supply those things, we have to improvise. To the extent that these narratives show a glimmer of the kind of thinking that supports resilience, they help us think about ways to develop it in at-risk children, and so perhaps spare them years of danger, failure, and pain. Even well-functioning teenagers (and their parents) may have an easier time of it if we—those of us who live or work with teenagers, or make policy concerning them—can learn to recognize in "ordinary" adolescent vexatiousness the seeds of critical life skills.

THE HIGH VALLEY NARRATIVES gave us an unexpected chance to deconstruct the *processes* of resilience, which are elusive. At times of capitulation they are by definition little in evidence, and as recovery progresses they increasingly and confusingly resemble the very outcomes they are bringing about. An interest in other people may show up as good relationships later; an interest in mastery may show up as competence. Yet resilience does not lie in either the competence or the relationships; it lies in the *development* of competence or relationship where they did not exist before. It is easy to confound positive outcomes with the processes that produce them, especially when people are studied for resilient qualities after their resilience has become known. For these kids we had narratives dating from the days when they were still in trouble, before a resilient outcome had emerged or was even imaginable. We wanted to know what had helped some of them to better understandings and broader opportunities, and left others mired in self-defeating helplessness and narrowing possibilities.

We thought that this wealth of early data from two comparable but distinct groups of people would give us a chance to untangle the stubborn process/outcome duality, to let us see what differences might emerge between individuals who later turned out to be resilient and those who did not, in narratives that long predated the time when resilience would be established.

Our intention was not to try to distinguish resilient from nonresilient people; our two groups had been distinguished already—not by their narratives but by reliable standardized measures of ego development, social competence, and relational capacity. And more to the point, no such strict division is possible. Resilience is not a static but a dynamic state of affairs, and the ultimate aim of resilience studies is to make the tragic apparent division between "resilient" and "not resilient" less salient rather than more. To that end we seized the unprecedented opportunity offered by the transcripts to observe whether characteristic kinds of thinking could be seen emerging from the stories of people who would later appear resilient.

We are now persuaded that there are such characteristics. Important identifiable themes run consistently through the narratives of the nine resilient High Valley patients—themes that are conspicuously absent from the narratives of the others. The auspicious trio foreshadowed repeatedly in the resilience literature—belief that one can influence one's environment, the ability to handle one's thoughts and feelings, and the capacity to form caring relationships[1]—can be seen very clearly in the narratives of Pete, Rachel, Sandy, and Billy as the stepping stones by which four resilient teenagers escaped their troubles. In these stories, abstract "protective factors" come to visible life. As lightning at dusk briefly illuminates a dark landscape, the light cast by these narratives provides glimpses of developing resilience in its purest form.

Agency and the Quest for Mastery

There's nothing comfortable or predictable in the way the resilient kids go about things. Their belief that they can influence their environment is a dynamic, living force—no placid reservoir of self-confidence, but a raging torrent. They are engaged with it all the time, whether they're bobbing along on the surface, swimming straight ahead, or swept along helter-skelter. Sometimes they come much closer to the falls than they want to admit. The swift current inspires and exhilarates them, but that doesn't mean it's always safe.

There would be less turmoil if the kids didn't respond to changes in their narratives, but they do. They experiment with everything: drugs, weapons; sex, love; work, quitting; law, anarchy; life, death. When their enriched narratives—their expanded explanations—give them ideas, they try them, sometimes very impetuously, and the experiments usually don't turn out as planned. But the kids always learn from them. Pete's flight doesn't free him from his old self, but it proves to him incontrovertibly that he is going to have to come to terms with it. Rachel's headlong rush to marriage and motherhood does not give her the security she craves, but it forces her to learn to tolerate risk. Sandy's declaration of independence does not relieve her empty depression, but it eventually shows her how she oppresses herself. Billy's move to his father's house doesn't give him the relationship he craves, but it clarifies for him the reality of his father's limitations and his own fatherly potential.

And there's purpose behind their rashness. Sandy zigs and zags in her search for self-determination. She tries obedience and rebellion; she finds boyfriends and leaves them; she quits old drugs and tests new ones; she hospitalizes herself and splits; she sets off for college and drops out. But she's very consistent about one thing: as long as she feels like a rat in someone else's maze, she will look for a way out, and she'll keep looking until she finds it. The repetition compulsion, as psychoanalysts call it, is not for her. She's young and impulsive—she's an adolescent— and her decisions show it. On the other hand, she sees where she makes mistakes, and she doesn't often repeat them. Sandy does not bang her head against walls.

Pete, too, throws himself with abandon into a succession of plans, formulating each in his inimitable bold style. The rhetoric of his reckless departure for the West Coast is inflated, but the idea isn't too bad. Pete is trying to learn to see himself through his own eyes. His sense of self has come largely from the way he uses and is used by other people, and he is looking for something more substantial. His odyssey is an extreme version of the year luckier kids take off from college, to "find themselves" in backpacking through distant lands. He comes home at the end of it stronger and wiser.

The contrast-group kids make changes too, but their changes are less purposeful than those of the resilient kids, and they learn less from them. Jeff and Magda do a lot of geographical wandering, but their perspective is not particularly enhanced by it; the experiences they acquire do not widen their insight into themselves or the world they live in. Vick and Charlie avoid exploration in favor of repetition and the familiar—for Vick the series of babies that makes nursing school impossible, and for Charlie the comforts of old friends and drink.

The resilient kids display what psychologists call an *optimistic bias,* a phenomenon closely linked to the drive for mastery. They focus on the upside of whatever they're doing. It's easy to think that Pete is too optimistic much of the time; Rachel, too. It's known, however, that people who view the world that way often show great competence in their lives. Optimistic beliefs about how much we can change our environments not only inspire action, but also soften the inevitable failures and setbacks that accompany any bold course.[2]

The contrast-group kids display plenty of optimism at times, but it's a kind that makes little concession to the demands of reality. Magda's upbeat tone is striking. But the keystone on which she builds her narrative is "Usually I don't even know what I'm going to do tomorrow." And that story influences her as surely as Sandy's and Pete's stories influence them. Magda acts as though tomorrow doesn't matter, and she never harnesses her substantial talents in the service of a goal that might really engage her. Even in adulthood her confidence is grounded not in any experience of accomplishment or enduring interest, but in a job provided by her lover and a set of motivational tapes. She sounds a bit like Pete did when he was fourteen and figuring to be a rock star. But Pete is always working on *something*, and in ten years he learns a lot about working in general. By the time he's twenty-five, he's earned a first-rate college degree and is being paid for expertise that he's gone to some trouble to acquire. Vick says repeatedly as a youngster that she wants to be a nurse, and this is clearly a serious interest. Yet she makes no connection between her professed goals and the need, say, not to get kicked out of science classes just because she doesn't like the teacher. The resilient kids recognize the difference between optimism and daydreaming.

ALL OF THE KIDS ARE IMPULSIVE at times. But the resilient ones also give their lives and problems steady and serious attention. Pete grapples with his two great banes: the terrible vulnerability that he counters with aggression, and the need for admiration to support his wobbly self-esteem. Even while he's floundering around in dead ends—acting school, the Tenderloin—he's putting concentrated effort into the central act of mastery on which, for him, all else depends: developing the physical prowess he needs to feel safe. His narrative conditions his experience. As his strength and confidence grow, he focuses his drive less impulsively into new areas of relationship and accomplishment.

The fine line between planning and impulse is clearest in Pete's changing stories about the theft of his grandfather's gun.

Over the years, he associates that deed with different motivations and different strategies. His view at twenty-five is that he had an innate cunning about making exactly the right kind of trouble to get himself what he needed. This is a bit romanticized, since it overlooks how out of control he was, and how scared. But he is always refining his understanding—a tendency characteristic of the resilient kids, but not of their less successful fellows.

Rachel's ten-year plan for her life is so expansive and ambitious that when she comes a cropper she hits the ground hard. But she, too, acts on steadily expanding narratives. Having recognized that change is possible, she puts herself in the way of it. She makes risky decisions and sometimes she suffers for them, but the direction she's moving in is good. Rachel in her teens protects her son from the fallout of an ill-advised marriage far better than Sandy's or Pete's or Billy's or Magda's much more experienced parents protected them. Once aimless nearly to the point of paralysis, she regroups after every frustration, setback, disappointment, and—yes—failure, and gets back in the saddle again, a better rider.

Then there is Billy. Mastery is Billy's thing, the way strength is Pete's and autonomy is Sandy's and relationship is Rachel's. From stealing Cokes to stacking groceries to listening to his son, whatever Billy does he wants to do well. He bore a lot of responsibility very young, and is more aware than most young people that everything worthwhile has a price. His high-risk highjinks with bicycles and handcuffs are experiments in how that price can be paid, how freedom and connection can coexist. He has a far more pragmatic view of the world than the other three (perhaps because he has never had as much of a financial cushion). The joy of coping is Billy's motive force, and it may well have been his mother's foreclosure on this at home that tipped him over the edge for a while. But as soon as he's his own man again at the age of thirteen, he resumes his methodical effort to get a grip. "I think I just kept trying hard to change, and I did," he says of the new relationship with his mother, and he maintains a quiet conviction that he'll be able to figure out any other problems that happen along.

Not all kids see themselves so clearly as active agents (rather than as objects of other people's actions). While most of the sixteen play dumb occasionally about why they were in the hospital, over time the resilient ones pay a lot of attention to the circumstances of their hospitalizations; there's nothing passive about it. But the protestations of ignorance and helplessness ring all too true from the contrast-group kids. The same with their scenarios of victimization and exculpation. A year after her hospitalization, Vick is still blaming the "old shrink" who "put her" in the hospital. The fact that she had been barraging her parents with questions about suicide still has no meaning for her.

The contrast-group kids experiment less than their resilient fellows, and certainly the stories they tell themselves don't encourage them to formulate plans and persist in them. They don't necessarily experience themselves as completely ineffectual. But they believe that their influence over what happens to them is very limited, and this is the belief they enshrine in their narratives and then act upon. They don't share the optimistic bias either, at least not in the sense of making lemonade out of lemons. While all the resilient kids award a few (a very few) grudging points to the Children's Center, Charlie doesn't. "Nothing, nothing. I lost. I didn't gain. . . . I lost a whole summer. I lost part of my winter; a whole spring. Now it's almost winter again. A whole year. I lost a whole year." When he gets his time back, though, he uses it to get into trouble again, and back on probation.

Charlie in his blank pessimism contrasts somberly with the feisty and combative resilient kids, who blend tales (both veridical and defensive) of deceit, treachery, and intrigue with open interest about their own roles in how it all happened. Even Rachel, the least definite of them all at the beginning, eventually understands her self-mutilation as a way of getting out of her parents' house. If the adult narratives include some optimistic reframings, they are reframings in the service of a stronger sense of empowerment, not of abdication. These people repeatedly portray themselves as taking action and watching the world respond. Theirs is a rough world, an unforgiving world, a dangerous world. But that doesn't stop them from prodding it to see what it does. They pay attention to it and to themselves, and they are ever on the alert to improve their strategies and their tactics.

The resilient kids assume that once they learn the rules of the game, they'll be able to play it. They may choose (or need) to work their way around the rules at times, but that's all the more reason to figure them out—the better to anticipate, the better to cope, the better to survive. Their wild experimentation eventually settles down to serious research, and science develops out of sorcery as they begin to figure out what matters, what helps, what works, and what doesn't.

Their experiments are wonderful examples of how resilience can kick in before it shows—that is, how a resilience process may be operating powerfully underneath exactly the kind of behavior that would most seem to controvert it. Sandy in her enraged rejection of the hospital's discharge recommendation, and Rachel in her intransigent insistence on marriage and motherhood at sixteen, defeat every bit of adult "guidance" that comes their way. They are stubborn, arrogant, heedless, and unappreciative. But underneath the rebellion, they are actively trying to do what they feel they must, and carefully gauging the results. Billy's application to a very selective high school would be applauded by many onlookers as a sign of resilience, but observing adults were aghast at Sandy's and Rachel's plans, and put a lot of pressure on them to give them up.

Among the contrast group, there are few such examples of risky plans systematically carried out against determined opposition or challenge. There's plenty of rebellion, and there's plenty of stubborness, but it's reactive rather than purposeful and not particularly productive in intent—in fact, often there is no intent to it at all. Rory defends his skipping school against the authorities, but he's doing it out of defiance, not out of any conviction that this is a crucial step in his own development. Rachel's early graduation from high school requires prolonged effort in pursuit of a goal that is as important to her as it is appalling to her parents. Unlike their more passive counterparts, the resilient kids devote a lot of energy to making potential control real. So striking is this difference that it is sometimes tempting to wonder whether this might be the trait that ultimately distinguishes resilient people. Human history, however, overflows with examples of desperation giving rise to great feats of energy and drive, from Hillary's final assault on Mount Everest to the successful rescue of the Apollo 13 astronauts. The resilient kids' strivings for mastery, sometimes imprudent but always ingenious, put them at the end of the long line of forebears for whom necessity—sometimes dire necessity—was the mother of invention. From that perspective, the surprising stories are those of the others—the kids who, when desperate, give up. How society's approach to troubled teenagers may stifle their drive for mastery—their willingness to come back and try again—is an important topic that we'll return to at the end of this chapter.

Looking Inward: The Taste for Reflection

Because the concept of resilience has no meaning separate from the context of adversity, and because real adversity produces emotional upheaval, by definition we have to look for early signs of resilience in people who are upset, and whose behavior is likely to reflect this. Resilience and disturbance are conjoined twins, impossible to uncouple. Resilience can easily coexist with "bad" behavior, and often does. And the capacity to reflect is no guarantee of adult judgment; Pete's determined concentration on martial arts at the expense of school considerably frustrates a lot of well-meaning adults. While resilient qualities sometimes appear in forms that rational adults approve of (Sandy's declaration that she's "not gonna get mad, because I don't feel like getting put in four points" is an example), sometimes they don't. And Sandy's success in avoiding the QR is in fact less important than the fact that she was noticing her own thoughts and feelings, and recognizing that she had plenty of control over how they played out. Processes like that can be at work underneath less encouraging behavior, such as the violent outbursts during which Billy begged—or dared—his mother to call the police.

Reflection is more than just noticing what one feels and wanting more or less of it; it's an effort to make sense out of feelings. Reflection is the ability to think *about* one's thought processes.[3] "When I get out of this place, I'm gonna keep this place out of my mind!" Sandy vows. Well, maybe she will and maybe she won't—keeping things out of our minds is not always easy. But despite the counterexample set at home, Sandy is *interested* in her mind and what it does. She's treating this as a choice. A decision not to think about High Valley is very different from the unwitting and automatic inattention of the contrast-group kids. In spite of her early denials, Sandy *does* think about what she's thinking, and she also thinks about ways to think more productively.

That is where reflectiveness is linked to the drive for mastery. The resilient kids suspect early that the inner world requires as much skill as the external environment; they look for the rocks that shipwrecked them before, the better to steer clear. In that search, and sometimes just out of curiosity, they are willing to look inward.

They observe what goes on in their heads, and their observations accurately show them the conflicting pulls of emotional life. They know themselves as complex. Pete states this most explicitly in the extended metaphor of his various "sides," but they all do it, both in the moment and in their development over time. They recognize that others are complex, too. This can be a hard truth to accept, as Rory's struggle shows. But having recognized it, they grapple with it, ending up with a rueful acknowledgment of the merits of the computerized stepfather, or of the need to sedate and seclude a dangerously violent friend.

The perceptions of the contrast group are flatter and in some ways more complacent. Even as an adult, the very intelligent Jeff has not imagined a context for his relationship with his mother that is larger than his romantic child's ideal of perfect unconditional love, the "just open kabloom that should have been there." Magda seems sometimes to find a malicious relish in facile judgments: "Fat people . . . really bug me because, you know, I always know that they could be skinny if they really tried." How much the tendency to reductionism is a matter of ability and how much a matter of preference isn't clear. Jeff, who thinks about these things, wishes openly and earnestly that emotional life could be simpler. At seventeen, he has a clear wish for the future: "to be able to be free from worry and really be happy." As an adult, he says several times that he wishes he could forget his past. "I wish I could change something and sort of forget it. . . . I wish, you know, I wish [for] just simple memories, like reading stories. That would be a little bit easier." It would take a heart of stone not to be moved by a wish like that. But it can never come true. Emotional life *isn't* simple, and as long as he clings to the wish that it might be, Jeff is denying himself the chance to come to terms with his own reality.

DESPITE HER VOW TO KEEP HIGH VALLEY out of her mind, the minute Sandy is out she starts thinking about "that place" with a vengeance, trying to make sense of the whole horrible business. Vick, however, is still shutting her eyes long after the actual discomfort of the hospitalization is over. The year after her discharge, she insists that she remembers nothing about her time at the Center. "I don't remember anything. I don't want to. . . . I just don't want to remember, so I blocked it out."

Magda blocks things out without even being aware of it. "I just forget about it, and then I don't care," she says, and she does indeed act on this narrative. But the determined unawareness that she relies on for protection from "caring" keeps her from rethinking or revising her thoughts and feelings—either now or at some later time when a broader perspective might have become possible. We don't learn much from the things we refuse to notice.

Pete also tries to control his thoughts and emotions. "Lobotomy"—surgical excision of three-quarters of his "wildness"—is his chilling image for containing his rage. But his conviction as a very young person that the quarter that remains must be protected and nurtured is just as striking. He knows that people can't do without large chunks of their emotional equipment. Even before he's confident of his own strength, he's blunt and direct with himself about his feelings. "Aren't I the evil person?" he quips in the wake of a diabolical revenge fantasy. But when the quiet, animal-loving Vick unexpectedly turns out to share with him a rather nasty taste in what she calls "practical jokes," she handles it very differently. "The assistant principal of the junior high lives down the street, and when I walked my grandmother's dog I saved the dog mess and put it in a paper bag and set it on fire and left it on his doorstep and rang the doorbell. He came out and he stepped on it, and got dog mess all over his feet and spread it all over his rug." There's a concept worthy of Pete, all right, but unlike him, Vick acts on it. And it's only the "joke" that amuses her—she doesn't see her own hostility, let alone laugh at herself for it.

All of the kids sometimes feel overwhelmed by the intensity of the fury that their lives have evoked. But the resilient ones make active efforts to learn to manage it. Sandy talks about it; Billy "gets out." Pete stays angriest longest, and even when he returns as a young adult, his anger is still a formidable force. But he has learned to ride it as a surfer rides a monster wave—deftly at times, more awkwardly at others, but with fewer and fewer wipeouts.

When the resilient kids get scared, they hone their survival skills; they don't waste much effort hoping to escape the rigors of life. The other kids' ineffectualness with their own feelings undermines their practical grasp on the outside world; because they can't reflect, they never learn to handle anxiety well. Jeff expresses a lot of concern about what will happen to him once he is out of the frustrating but sheltered environs of home and school: "High school is sort of nice, actually. Because you have all your sports and all your courses to do and you don't have to support yourself." But the caged raccoon of Vick's fantasy—happy that it doesn't have to search for its own food and water—does not look so lucky to Billy or Pete.

The contrast-group kids have so little interest in inner experience, their own or other people's, that they don't notice much of what goes on around them. Their explanations for what happens in their lives don't expand. They resort repeatedly to a few favorites that don't mature over time. Jeff remains consistent in the conviction that his father's suicide and his mother's inability to express unconditional love are the source of his problems. He may well be right. But the explanation isn't helpful to him in that form; it doesn't offer him any way out. And he doesn't look beyond the generalization to explore explicitly what his parents' failings might have meant to him, or why they should have made such a catastrophic and inexorable difference. Magda in her third interview is still insisting that she was sent to High Valley because she was hanging out with an older guy. Rarely do these kids raise questions about their own motives or reactions, or those of their families or friends. As older adolescents and as adults, their narratives differ most strikingly from those of the resilient former patients in their lack of reference to the significance—sometimes even the existence—of an inner life.

In fact, their later narratives sometimes suggest that capacities they once did possess have withered. Magda knows early on that her embittered father has been obsessively preoccupied with the dangers of relations between the sexes since his wife walked out on him. She can "psychoanalyze" her father, she tells the interviewer: "He won't forget things that happened in the past, and he keeps reliving them. . . . And he doesn't want me to get hurt the same way he did." She knows that he's using that wish to try to control her, and in that attempt she even recognizes a kinship between them: "We're both pigs. . . . We don't want to work hard. . . . We both try to get our own way."

This is good thinking for a fifteen-year-old. But her discernment doesn't deepen as she gets older; it vanishes. By the time she's eighteen, there's nothing left of her interest in psychoanalyzing. Now her own reasons for distrusting marriage are concrete and utterly unpsychological. "Well, oh, the bad points— God, where are you going to go? If he has the car, then you're stuck at home, you know? I just don't want to be married, I don't think." She has nothing else to say about it. Adolescence is a time of great plasticity. But that plasticity can go both ways, and this is why the stakes in the teen years are so very high. It is tragic to see interest evolve into indifference, perception into blindness.

Never is the blindness more dramatic than when the contrast-group kids look back on their days in the hospital and what they themselves were like there. Magda never makes Rachel's leap of insight about changing: "It's hard to see yourself change," Magda says. "You don't, really." Even Jeff, who is fluent in the psychological vernacular, wants little connection with his psychological self, now or then. He used to be less "in touch," he says, adopting the term fashionable at the time for being aware of one's feelings. But then he adds, "I'm not quite sure what I mean by 'I was less in touch,'" and he goes on with a telling elaboration. "Just more in touch and in that way a little more confused. I think about things more now, and it makes me more confused. I'm not sure how to stop that." Jeff says the right things, and he means them very sincerely. But his narrative tells him that the confusion that accompanies real attention to one's feelings is a *bad* thing. It's not just a temporary obstacle on the road to better understanding, but something that shouldn't be there. And he acts on this story by stopping the whole confusing process of reflection, reverting quickly to superficial formulas and relinquishing the search for a more substantive grasp of his own emotional experience.

We don't yet know the whys of these differences. Some resilient people (like Rachel) experience connection with their inner selves as ballast that stabilizes their ships on the unpredictable external seas they sail. Some (like Pete) use reflection as a vital and safe arena for emotional exploration. Some (Billy) may experience reflection as a psychological refuge from the day-to-day chaos in which they live. But Jeff experiences feelings—as opposed to thoughts—as very upsetting and something to be avoided. Inner life has a reality of its own whether we deny it or not, and that reality influences future behavior and action. Along with refuge, reflective people have access to a source of intense emotional vitality—perhaps that encourages the resilient kids as well. For while the inner life can be turbulent too, there is some comfort in the control we have in the privacy of our own minds and in the ways that we think about our thinking.

The Pivotal Place of Relationship

Relationships have not gone well for many of the Children's Center patients, who as a group collected an appalling accumulation of losses, abuses, inconsistencies, rejections, and abandonments. Yet the resilient kids retain an interest in forming new relationships (or reforming old ones) that is apparently boundless, and their skill in relationship grows almost before our eyes as the years pass. Surely this is both a testament to their resilience and a reflection of one of the compelling engines that drives it.

We do not want to minimize the potentially (and frequently) catastrophic effects of adverse socioeconomic conditions such as poverty, violence, and racism. But poor-quality primary relationships also affect children. In fact, the damage caused by certain social conditions may have to do at least in part with the destruction that they wreak on primary relationships. One of our hopes for this study and others like it is that we may find ways to promote *inner* resources by which children can establish the helpful relationships they need to blunt the impact of social stressors, even as the long struggle to prevent and ameliorate social injustice continues.[4]

It is an old axiom in resilience studies that "one good relationship" can help an individual out of despair and into a satisfying life. Account after account turns on a child's discovery of the caring person with whom he or she can really connect, the person who makes all the difference.[5] That scenario is fine, as far as it goes. But it begs its own provocative questions: What determines *which* at-risk children end up with that all-important relationship? Is it the luck of the draw, or is there something systematic at work? And what is so valuable about a relationship, anyway? The narratives of the resilient patients suggest that far more than luck is involved, and they also highlight elements of relationships that may be important for kids' resilient development.

The narratives display their authors engaged in minute and persistent observation of relationships. Often the kids purposefully recruit them, but even when they are not actively courting connection, they are watching and listening. When a sufficiently tempting relationship comes along, they are well positioned to take advantage of it. In this realm, too, they experiment; they devote energy and attention; they learn.

Pete, Rachel, Sandy, and Billy all start out with painfully ambivalent and complicated associations with their parents, but in time they transform most of them into more helpful connections. They pay attention and they work well with the relationships they have to deal with. As Sandy takes on her issues with externally imposed authority, she comes back to reestablish her relationship with her mother on much more satisfactory terms. Pete develops a relatively benign relationship with his father despite his father's manifest limitations, and a strong and positive one with his stepfather. When Rachel finally tackles her anger at her father, she manages to do it without cutting herself off from him. Even Billy handles his father's definitive rejection of him first by making other relationships that work, and then by concentrating on being a good father to his stepson. Leftover unease about old problems may remain, but it does not keep these kids from pursuing the relationships they want for the future.

The contrast-group kids have a much harder time tolerating ambivalent feelings in themselves and others, and accepting the limitations that all people bring to their affiliations. Their relationships start out governed by anger and resentment, and this does not change much. Jeff maintains his animus toward his mother. Magda feels aggrieved by her parents' concerns about her choice of boyfriend years after it has ceased to be a practical issue. Rory stays angry at his father for a very long time; his attitude softens as he begins to show other signs of reflective and connective processes. In general, these people describe fewer reliable relationships than the resilient kids do; their bonds with family and friends, as they tell it, are confusing and impoverished. We don't know whether this is because good relationships were less available to them, or because they did not know how to make use of the ones that came their way. Overtones of estrangement and isolation haunt their stories.

Other people as separate individuals appear to mean little to them. Sometimes they don't attend closely enough to other people really to notice them, and sometimes they attend to them mostly for what they can (and can't) get out of it. They seem not to respond to the depths in other people's characters any more than in their own, and their relationships remain correspondingly shallow. Their stories lack richly developed characters; the rare heroes are interchangeable, and even the villains aren't memorable. People are described in unintegrated and unshaded dualities—good or bad, caring or uncaring, generous or selfish—with little subtlety or detail. Magda at twenty-five says of the man she lives with, "Oh, he's really smart and he's successful and he has money, and he's good looking. That's all." And it is.

But the people in the resilient kids' stories are drawn in impassioned shades of approbation and vilification—there's nothing one-dimensional about *them*. Sandy's portrayal of Jacob and his enigmatic family sparkles, and so does Pete's description of his brilliant but robotic stepfather. The vivid ambivalence of the portraits, far from discrediting them, makes them all the more intriguing. They honor the complexities of real people, they lure the kids toward deeper understandings, and they engage the listener in a way that the more perfunctory narratives do not. Perhaps one occult danger of unreflectiveness is that it lessens a troubled kid's chances of being able to tell the kind of story that will engage a responsive adult.

This is why bromides about "luck" or "access" can never explain fully the way relationships "become available" to some children and not others: the children themselves have something to do with it. Some are more open to the idea. Even when they're feeling moody, rejecting, or dangerous, they notice, they respond, and they give other people something to respond to. It takes an indifferent listener indeed to tune out Pete's tales of murder and mayhem or Billy's accounts of Olympian prowess; the girls' delicate explorations of love and friendship are just as captivating.

So the correlation between "one good relationship" (it doesn't have to be literally *one,* of course) and positive adaptation is another case of how hard it is to separate the processes of resilience from the outcome. The resilient teens don't just stumble onto better relationships than the other kids do; they take themselves to where the action is. Luck may account for the appearance of a Henry or a Herb, but the resilient kids make the resources to take advantage of it. This may be why programs designed with the primary goal of promoting relationships have not always yielded the expected results.[6] The availability of caring adults is only part of the problem; the capacity of troubled kids to make use of them is the rest.

THESE THREE CHARACTERISTICS—agency, looking inward, caring about relationships—of the resilient teens are essential aspects of competence in human social interaction. Whatever other things these kids may want—love, success, even just survival—they concentrate hardest on learning to cope with emotions, desires, and impulses. Their inner focus is not a withdrawal from the world—as Jeff's tends to be, for instance—but an attempt to understand their own roles in connection. In their hunger for relationship they are looking for something more than selfish advantage; Rachel is the most eloquent in her passion for reciprocity, but she isn't alone. These stories suggest that mastery of human emotional and social interaction may be the crucial culmination of all the other aspects of resilience. It allows the kids to find ways of connecting with others; these others then pull them into "healthier contexts,"[7] and give them access to the new satisfactions that they explore as young adults. We exist in a material world, but we live in a relational one.

What Does It All Mean?

The belief in personal agency, the inner focus, and the interest in relationship that are consistently found in resilient people are reflected clearly in the narratives of the nine resilient High Valley patients, where they can be seen in operation, opening the kids up to, and providing motivation for, choices and decisions that help them move steadily toward more promising surroundings and ever more discerning modes of thought.

Psychology has a tradition of models inspired by powerful case studies. From their observations of individuals, Sigmund Freud, Erik Erikson, and Jean Piaget all developed theoretical systems that were only later, and gradually, modified by research. We pay homage to this tradition in offering case material that we believe has the substance to inspire and support important theoretical work. It is broad enough and deep enough to allow us to look beyond individual stories to the common elements among them, and to begin to generalize in new and important directions. And as theoretical fashions change and established models develop, it is an invaluable luxury to possess a repository of primary material against which to assess them.[8] When we took the opportunity that the narratives afforded us, we knew that any questions remaining at the end would motivate a new round of study. The High Valley Resilience Study was itself an approach to unanswered questions from a previous research effort. Our own analysis of these narratives for the original longitudinal project had of necessity been theory-driven. In our responsibility to the hypotheses we were testing, we had had to ignore significant aspects of our subjects' experience, and we were haunted by the conviction that we were missing something meaningful. In this new study, we were no longer testing the ways that we as theorists make sense of *our* world, but could concentrate instead on how our subjects were making sense of *their* worlds. Still, because the resilience study arose out of another piece of research on another subject, we knew that we would not have available to us certain information that we would have striven for had we designed the study from the ground up.

For example, we did not have the data to determine how

much the kids' different outcomes reflected their histories, their backgrounds, or the particular constellations of their individual problems. Some psychiatric disturbances are harder to recover from than others. Chronic or repeated trauma takes a larger toll than an isolated injury; autistic and psychotic conditions confound the capacities to relate and to think, while depression notoriously undermines the sense of agency. By the same token, we do not know how much the greater success of some kids might reflect a greater degree of clinical improvement—the lifting of a depression, say—at the time they were tested and interviewed as young adults.

We are sometimes asked whether more psychotherapy or a longer stay at High Valley (and therefore, by extension, greater financial resources) might account for the differences between the two groups. None of the four resilient patients described here had much psychotherapy before they were admitted to High Valley, and after their discharge all four soon discontinued it—at least until they were much older. There is no evidence that Sandy or Billy ever sought psychotherapy on their own. Pete and Rachel did find therapists as adults, but by that time they were already well along in their quests for better lives and relationships. Likewise Rory, who we hope may now be on a happier path, had no interest in psychotherapy for a very long time. As he began to grapple with his old pain, however, he changed his mind. Here again is the vexing interweaving of process and outcome; but given the timing, it seems likely that the use of psychotherapy by Pete, Rachel, and Rory was less a *cause* of their resilience than a *reflection* of resilience-enabling processes that were already established in them. People who are open to relationship and reflection may find psychotherapy a useful sort of enterprise; others usually do not.

Could the length of stay at High Valley have made the difference? Pete and Rachel were there for about ten months, considerably longer than many kids, but Jeff stayed longer than either of them. Billy remained in the hospital for four months, Sandy for only six weeks. There was no statistical difference in length of stay between the group of resilient patients and the other seven. This doesn't mean that length of stay might not have had an impact. But again, it can't tell us anything about *how* the developments we call "resilience" actually came to pass.

Do our conclusions apply only to highly privileged white adolescents? Clearly not; the kids were all Caucasian, but a third of them came from the lower-middle and working classes, and the resilient group scored lower for social status than the contrast group. As to the issue of race, whether our findings can be replicated in other populations remains to be tested.

So while these are all interesting questions, we focused on a different one: How do people recover, *whatever* the adversity that afflicts them? No diagnosis, however detailed, can tell us anything about the *processes* by which an individual patient arrives at one endpoint or another. It may well be that someday we will identify historical factors or constitutional traits that make recovery easier, but the process of recovery will always still need to be accounted for. This process is what we see in the narratives of the resilient patients.

In fact, the two groups of kids look far more similar than different until well into adolescence. In their early teens, by the accounts of parents, teachers, therapists, courts, and the police, all of the kids were functioning at exceptionally poor levels. They were full of rage and exploding in violent or self-destructive behavior. They were impulsive. They were abusing drugs and alcohol; they had school problems; they were socially isolated or engaged in dangerous relationships. But there were forces operating underneath that common surface in all of them, for good or ill, and by the time these people were in their mid-twenties they were no longer looking so similar. We don't know where the divergent forces came from—whether they were historical, constitutional, interpersonal, structural, pathological, or something altogether different—or what activated or inhibited them. But something made a big difference. *And one way that this difference appears to develop is through an individual's attention to agency, reflection, and relationship.*

That raises more questions. Are resources like these latent in all or most kids? We'd like to think so, and to learn how to bring them out. Are the circumstances of some kids' development such that even qualities that should be universal may have no chance at all to take root? Unhappily, this may well be so—and if it is, we will have to learn how to plant new seeds and help them to grow.

Were the resilient kids simply luckier than the others? In some ways, all of the High Valley kids were lucky. When Pete dissed a classmate, he wasn't knifed on the spot. When Rory ran afoul of the cops, the incident didn't end in a shooting. Magda had a father to live with after her mother walked out. None of them had to deal with a physical deformity or a chronic illness. None were born addicted to drugs. They were all of at least average intelligence. Their parents eventually managed to muster the resources (not necessarily financial) and competence to get them into a safe place before anyone got seriously hurt. Yes, they were lucky.

But in other ways, they were not lucky at all. They lacked the fundamental interpersonal security that vast numbers of parents create for their children even under the harshest imaginable conditions of racism, poverty, war, and catastrophe. If the nine resilient kids had had burdens like those added to the loads they already carried, they might well not have made it. Of course things could have been worse. But still, how many of us would choose to have grown up in their shoes? Pete's family had more money than most of the others', but he got into worse trouble earlier, and stayed in it longer, than any of them. Billy's family had less, but Billy did very well without the supportive resources that were available to Pete, Sandy, Rachel—and Jeff. Contrasts like these can be pulled endlessly from this material. Does the presence of money offset the absence of a parent, or vice versa? Is it better to be intelligent and abused, or slow-witted and not? Beautiful and poor, or plain and wealthy? Talented and black, or inept and white? Abstract comparison of adversities is futile.

But while all of the kids were lucky to have found a safe place before the worst could happen, only some were lucky enough to survive a period of extremely compromised functioning without being hobbled forever by the consequences. The resilient kids overcame the problem of *cumulative continuity*[9]—the tendency of people to continue to function as they have been functioning, in part because the effects of their previous behaviors accumulate, pushing them further in the direction they were already heading. Misfortune, that is, conduces to more misfortune. The resilient kids had something that enabled them to withstand this pressure, and that "something" is something that all kids need.

Fostering Resilience

Watching very young people overcome misfortune and set their lives on new courses is an arresting experience. And every brief glimpse we catch of the internal resources that seem to facilitate such heady successes only raises more questions. We don't yet know how such characteristics come to be. We don't yet know whether they are intrinsic to all children but are destroyed in some.

Neither of our two best explanations of human behavior—parental nurturance and genetic makeup—has provided a satisfactory answer. Nurture was for the most part highly problematic in the lives of these adolescents, and is not likely to have been the foundation of their resilience. On the other hand, to attribute resilience to the genes implies an absolute endowment, an invariant potential or lack of it, that is not at all consistent with observation. A third possibility is that the capacity of some kids to reshape their own environments may enable the expression of strengths that, although present in potential before, had had no room to flourish in chaotic or threatening old settings. As we begin to identify the internal and environmental enablers of resilience, we will have to move on to the question of how to protect and foster them.

The enablers of resilient change as we are understanding them here, the well-established trio of reflection, agency, and relatedness, are not always easy to recognize amid the uproar of teenage behavior. They *can* be seen, however, in the narratives of the resilient High Valley teenagers. In the stories, it is clear that thought is changing for the better, both in content and in structure: broader contexts for the facts and forces that shape kids' lives are developing out of constraining old ones. The stories display how self-knowledge grows, is tested, and is used; how new perspectives trigger new stories; how circumstances are modified for the better; how relationships are sought and kept. The stories of the contrast group change less—or, more ominously, for the worse, as in Magda's abandonment of her early insight. As stories lose explanatory power, they cease to be adaptive guides for the future. Are storytelling skills in an adolescent a sign of psychological robustness? Does awareness of personal change herald greater adaptive capacities?

We now think that the answer to these questions is yes. How, then, can we encourage these vital skills in teenagers?

THE FIRST STEP is to learn to see in the dark—to learn to recognize signs of health even when they are obscured by troubled behavior. Psychologists delineate adolescent "symptoms" with elegant precision, and teachers and police officers recount with lurid relish the latest trespasses of the kids in their care. It's much harder to talk exactly about how a teenager is maturing. Without a systematic picture of the skills and processes that adolescents need to make it through that period of risk and promise, we end up assessing kids on such concrete adult concerns as responsibility, competence, social skills, and judgment. Yet critical or defiant or feckless behavior may hide invaluable resources of relatedness or agency or reflection—gifts that need to be recognized and tended.

Our picture of adolescent kids' balance sheets is not balanced at all. We need to pay more attention to progressive qualities, learn to recognize them even in their most primitive forms, and then hunt for and cultivate them with the same energy, intensity, and precision that we have long brought to the practice of symptom assessment. Otherwise we are nothing more than confused accountants, scrupulously totting up every jot and tittle of the debt of a bankruptcy-threatened client, but ignoring the very assets that might avert such an unhappy eventuality.

Martin Seligman and Mihaly Csikszentmihalyi are founders of the positive psychology movement, which supports the use of psychological tools to expand and develop human strengths. They point out that "working exclusively on personal weakness . . . has rendered science poorly equipped to do effective prevention. We need now to call for massive research on human strength and virtue. We need to ask practitioners to recognize that much of the best work they already do in the consulting room is to amplify strengths rather than repair the weaknesses of their clients."[10] Appreciating the "asset side" of workaday adolescent balance sheets is critical if we are to understand not only normal human development, but also the process of recovery when development has failed.

We imagine the sources of resilience as seeds. Adversity may bury them very deeply, but they remain present, dormant but still alive. They *may* germinate when the season and climate are right, giving rise to important processes by which human beings change and grow. That these seeds and processes may be obscured to the point of near invisibility, covered up by layer upon layer of dysfunctional thought and behavior, carries vital implications for parenting, teaching, helping, and studying—and for developing the policies we as a society direct toward adolescents. We must learn to look beyond the disruptiveness of teenage behavior if we are not to miss a great deal of future potential. This, we believe, is an incontrovertible conclusion.

Encouraging Agency and Relatedness

Our most successful subjects focused hopefully and persistently on mastering their social environments (in which they wisely included themselves). It is sobering indeed to look at how our society deals with children's sense of agency and their strivings for mastery. We require that even the best-adjusted of our children spend many hours each day in other-directed activities, and then look on with dismay as our teenagers' capacities for self-direction and self-motivation dissipate.[11] The autonomy of less successfully adapted children is further circumscribed by punishments, special school placements, and (when all else fails) the juvenile justice system. It is reasonable to want to protect kids from harm and society from disorder, but it is important to find ways of doing this that do not unduly restrict opportunities for constructive development and growth. Our own research suggests that excessive constraints on the autonomy of adolescents undermine not only their efforts at mastery, but also their capacity to reflect on their own thoughts and relate well to others.[12]

This is not to say that adolescents don't need limits. Of course they do—sometimes even the extreme limits of a locked hospital ward. But within the bounds of safety, they also need chances to try, to exercise, to experiment, *and to fail,* however disconcerting their efforts may temporarily be to custodial adults. It takes skill to harness teenagers' ferocious desires for independence and control without either driving them crazy or going mad oneself. But these are qualities on which resilience depends, and they require protection, especially in their early or archaic forms. Even when they are hard to appreciate, they shouldn't be stifled.

In the 1980s, we were evaluating community-based programs for high-risk adolescents. One of them in particular, the Youth Action Project in New York's East Harlem, caught our attention. YAP had had surprising success at recruiting gang members into the program and keeping them there. We asked the staff how they saw their task with these very troubled young folks. They were looking for kids with ridiculous, overblown, and unrealistic plans, they told us. Upon finding them, their goal was to discover every way they could to help make those plans come true. At the time we visited them, staff and kids were working together on a "clubhouse," the heart's desire of one of the local gangs. Kids and adults were practicing planning, carpentry, and responsibility skills as they renovated a building on their block. Their ultimate goal was to construct a youth center with rentable apartments above it.

Amazing and inspiring things can happen when teenagers' unlikelier strivings for mastery are harnessed instead of ignored or squelched. The Teen Outreach Program, started by Brenda Hostetler and developed by the Association of Junior Leagues,[13] engages young people in voluntary community service. In well-controlled studies, researchers have found that this program reduces rates of such (seemingly) unrelated behaviors as school dropout and even teenage pregnancy by up to 50 percent.[14]

The narratives of the resilient adolescents are compelling illustrations of the power of agency. They challenge us to create environments that can develop and harness this vital capacity. It is a formidable task for parents and teachers and lawmakers to remain firm yet engaged in the face of the insatiable adolescent thirst for autonomy and the challenges to authority that necessarily go with it.[15] Yet the havoc, the agonies, the sullenness are creative experiments in self-definition and in the skills that are needed to manage adult independence.

THE RESILIENT KIDS came to the conviction that relationships were worth figuring out, and they maintained this belief even in the context of the relational pathology in which they lived. They make a compelling case that children derive real benefits from remaining attentive and open to relationships, no matter what—yet this very openness leaves them terribly vulnerable to derailment when early relationships go awry.

So we must all attend carefully to children's interest in relationships, even when it manifests itself in repellent or infuriating behavior. Silence, withdrawal, rebuffs don't mean that connection is no longer desired, just as rebellion does not mean that containment is no longer needed. On the other hand, relationships that countenance only "good" feelings and behavior, like containment that leaves no room for experiment, foolishness, or failure, make the adolescent task of maturation much more difficult than it already is.

Rather than focusing preferentially on the destructive and angry responses of some adolescents to perceived insult, therefore, we might remind ourselves that those responses betray an essential interest in connection that has to be nurtured and developed. We may not yet know how to build—or plant—an interest in relationship where it doesn't exist, but we can at least limit the likelihood of destroying it inadvertently out of too shortsighted a view of the behavior in which it appears.

The Value of Reflection

Reflection is a quieter habit than agency and a more private one than relatedness, but neither of those other two desiderata can flourish to the full without it. And like them, it is fragile in its seedling phase. The resilient adolescents developed real skill in reflecting on themselves and on others with whom they related. They expanded their understanding; they rethought old judgments; they cultivated empathy. But Magda's enthusiastic youthful "psychoanalyzing" of her father faded slowly into utter indifference to his inner life and hers. What happened?

It is tempting, but too easy, to point to the ways children's lives are overscheduled and managed so as to crowd out almost any chance for reflective thought. The lives of the resilient teens are hardly the deep wells of silence and peace that are traditionally thought to support reflection. Yet we have to ask how our current structures for raising teens may be failing to foster their reflective capacities. Perhaps, like any other skill, this one needs the drive for mastery behind it if it is to prosper; perhaps to suppress the one is to suppress the other. Perhaps reflection cannot thrive without relational opportunities for testing out its fruits; perhaps here as well we clamp down too quickly on adolescent investigation of reflection, which often shows itself first in an unsettling combination of profound self-centeredness and laserlike focus on the shortcomings of a teacher or parent.

Reflection in adolescents is almost as widely distrusted in our society as autonomy—What *does* that kid do all alone in his room for hours, with the door closed? As well-intentioned but anxious parents strive to do right by their kids—and to reassure themselves—affluent teens may end up so busy with manufactured challenges that they barely have time to sleep, let alone think. Adolescents do some of their best reflecting hanging out with their peers—of whichever sex—but the feverish intensity of teenage affinities is unnerving too, and uneasy parents may welcome the distraction potential in homework and chores. Less privileged kids, in whom idleness is often perceived as the devil's workshop and a real threat, are frequently offered, or forced into, gratuitous activity in an attempt to keep them under control and away from crime or drugs or sex or whatever is worrying the authorities of the moment. Yet when the kids begin to manifest signs—anxiety, depression, boredom—suggesting the absence of a healthy reflective life, we often attribute this new malaise to idleness as well. We fall back on the same old solutions, hustling teenagers into activities, jobs, and "interests" more to keep them busy than because any real challenge is offered, and so we erode still further their chance to connect with themselves and discover their own needful pursuits.[16]

"Sweet are the uses of adversity," Shakespeare tells us. But adversity is a sword that cuts both ways. No one nowadays would argue that we should heap troubles upon our young people to build their resilience; life offers trouble aplenty without our help. It is true, however, that the value of a gifted teacher lies partly in the ability to find exercises that are "just right" to increase virtuosity while avoiding the ones that are too easy or too hard. This may be another benefit conferred by the "one good relationship." Positive psychology poses important questions about differentiating the challenging experiences that promote development from those that undermine it.[17] Ann Masten observes that "opportunities and choices at crucial junctures play an important role in the life course of resilient individuals who find mentors, enter the military, find new or deeper faith, marry healthy partners, leave deviant peer groups, or in other ways take action that has positive consequences for their life course."[18] We must make it easier for kids to do this—to find those healthier contexts, even at times when their behavior would seem to debar them from the very contexts they most need. The lives of the resilient High Valley kids certainly suggest that there may be value, perhaps even great value, in granting young people the time and place to find their own ways of experiencing life and reflecting upon its challenges.

The Dangers of Continuity

The High Valley narratives speak pointedly to the great plasticity of adolescence. However disturbed, this is above all a time of possibility. If kids of such troubled background and behavior as the four we have profiled in this book (and the others in our sample whom they represent) can go on to do so well, then we must reexamine the appropriateness of using a notoriously shifting and unstable developmental period to make irrevocable decisions about young people's futures.

All the High Valley patients were at risk of being pushed back by the forces of cumulative continuity toward lower levels of functioning. Some of these forces, such as the stigma of psychiatric hospitalization, were challenges that the resilient kids simply overcame. Others they were clearly lucky to avoid. Pete might have killed someone with his stolen gun. He could have wound up in jail for assault or worse, had one of his fights ended badly. Drugs might have seriously damaged Sandy, if her use of them had proceeded the way it often does in teenagers. That Pete and Sandy avoided the worst consequences of their risky behavior is attributable in part to their own skills and in part to good fortune. But some kids are always going to need more room than others to act on and test out their progressive stories, and society has to recognize that there may be important nascent strengths in such action even when its results are unacceptable. Not all kids who get into trouble are damned.

A study like this demonstrates clearly how important it is to challenge actively the forces of cumulative continuity. When we don't, we lose salvageable kids. Pete was one who might easily have been lost; the lawyer friend who insisted on getting him transferred to High Valley did him a real favor, however much Pete may at times have hated the place. Sandy's stepfather did her the same good turn when, instead of allying himself blindly with the "experts," he helped her find a school that would concentrate on her strengths instead of her weaknesses.

Drug abuse, theft, assault, truancy, and sexual promiscuity were widely practiced among the High Valley patients, including the ones who ultimately proved successful. The dire predictions commonly made on the basis of such behaviors would have been correct for some of our original patient population, *but not for all.* Luck was undoubtedly a factor to some degree. But that only adds strength to an unassailable conclusion: *in nine out of sixty-seven kids (13 percent), extremely poor functioning during the teenage years did* not *decline further into a lifetime of serious social and psychiatric troubles.* The stakes—these people's futures—are much too high for us not to reconsider, carefully and seriously, the endemic practice in this society of using adolescence as the great "tracking" and "sorting" period. Adolescents, however deviant they may be at any given moment, still retain the plasticity and potential of childhood; they should not be treated as we treat adults with long-solidified histories of antisocial behavior. It is always risky to try to predict the future on the basis of disturbed behavior, and adolescence is the worst possible time to choose as an indicator. Yet this practice is becoming increasingly common, routine, and implacable.

It is no longer unusual for juvenile criminals to be tried and sentenced "as adults" although they are demonstrably not. If one of Pete's fights had ended in the serious injury or death of an adversary, Pete and all of his future potential might have been imprisoned for life (or, until a very recent and very close Supreme Court decision, put to death under the laws of several states). More likely, and in some ways even more terrifying, a term in prison among career criminals would have initiated him into true criminality, justifying society's low expectations and preparing him only for periodic violent returns to the world that condemned him.

This is not to say that behavior like Pete's is not serious. Of course it is. That is one of the reasons that places like the Children's Center exist, and it is ultimately the answer to a question we raised earlier: With all their strengths, why were these young people at High Valley? They were there because they were dangerous to themselves or other people, and very strong measures were needed to contain that danger. Pete's behavior in particular was extremely alarming, should certainly have been addressed much earlier, and might easily have had far more dire consequences than it did. But to have treated him at fourteen as a hardened criminal on the basis of his early desperation would almost certainly have been not only a grievous error, but also a self-fulfilling prophecy.

The precipitousness of the criminal justice system is but one instance of an imprudent policy. Others are more subtle—the use of adolescent "performance" (a euphemism for high-school grades) as the major indicator of adult professional aptitude, for example. Performance-based measures have their place as a convenient shorthand, but it's irresponsible to use them that way unless we also remember to provide support and encouragement to those individuals whose backgrounds have not enabled them to perform well as adolescents. They may still have great potential to become fine and valuable adults.

These considerations apply to all kids—not just those who are disturbed. Adolescence is notorious for obnoxious behavior, yet it is also perhaps the most vulnerable time of life after early childhood. Parents live in intimate and uneasy association with this reality, and there is some comfort in the reminder that *teenagers change*. When we as parents and teachers lose track of this great truth, we forget to nurture the possibility for growth that still exists—indeed, is at its crest—in adolescents.

As professionals, we watch with concern the debate among our colleagues over whether some juvenile criminal offenders should be labeled "psychopaths,"[19] antisocial personalities—that is, whether it is possible or desirable to determine that certain young people (in some studies as young as twelve) are so fundamentally incorrigible as to require lifelong segregation from society. We are not arguing that such individuals don't exist. But we know how easy it would have been to have labeled some of the resilient High Valley kids that way on the basis of how they looked and talked at certain times in their teenage years. This is an appalling possibility. And if there is anything we *do* feel comfortable arguing, it is that kids like these should not be doomed to dysfunctional lives beyond society's pale on the basis of their early behavior. There's time enough to label and categorize, if we must do that, when the personality has settled into its adult lineaments. But when it comes to juveniles, the lesson of the High Valley narratives is clear: Wait. Be patient and wait.

Looking for the Light

There is much work yet to be done in resilience studies, a field in which little can be taken for granted. Our own findings will have to be tested rigorously and adventurously, then replicated, expanded to other populations, and tested again. In the meantime, though, there is hope in the possibility that even in seriously disturbed kids there may be constructive processes going on beneath the avoidance, self-destructiveness, and even violence. There is hope in the possibility that we may become able to hear these processes (if we are alert to them), recognize them for what they are, and encourage them. There may even be some relief to long-suffering adults in the possibility of an expanded context for their own teenagers' excursions into adolescent excess.

These constructive processes are not always visible in behavior, but we've tried to show what they sound like in stories. We've tried to show, too, that stories themselves are important. Just the fact that a kid can tell a good story is worthy of note. The telling, especially in contexts that encourage it, may provide practice in important life skills. And if nothing else, these narratives show how important it is for kids to be able to imagine themselves in process, in future contexts, beyond the present moment.

The storms of adolescence, the stubbornness, the faultfinding, the manipulations, the lies, are exercises in interpersonal psychology, in handling feelings, and in shaping environments. If all goes well, as those latter skills develop, the excesses settle down, and kids grow into the much more comfortable citizens we know as adults. To that end, whenever possible, the enterprise and the process must be valued even when the results cannot be. This isn't to say that a parent has to fall for a teenager's lies or manipulations. On the contrary. We adults have our own grasp of psychology, after all, and we're allowed—indeed, it's incumbent upon us—to offer some grownup storytelling in return. Kids learn from that kind of engagement, which encourages the awareness that beyond any personal story there's always another. That's another message of the High Valley narratives: when mistakes become stories, people can learn from them.

OUR AIM HAS BEEN to elucidate the internal experience of resilience, and the way it connects with the personal, relational, and social contexts in which resilience develops. In these narratives, concerned people—parents, teachers, judges, clinicians, researchers—can hear in detail what resilience feels like, and draw some preliminary conclusions about how to appreciate the characteristics that enable it. We have tried to show how these signs reveal themselves to the kids in their own narratives, encouraging them to act in accord with nascent resilient processes. And we have tried to portray how these processes can evolve over the years into forces strong enough to bring a resilient outcome to fruition in young adulthood.

Adolescence is a time rich with opportunities for growth, despite its turbulence and its problems. The stories of the resilient High Valley teenagers show how strengths temporarily buried under the wreckage of a brief life can began to grow again and push upward through the debris. We were reminded of

Suzanne Vega's observation: "Kids will grow like weeds on a fence / They look for the light, they try to make sense / They come up through the cracks / Like grass on the tracks."[20]

These kids demonstrate the deep, hidden, and surprising capacity of the human spirit to push past the barriers imposed upon it, to grow upward toward the sun, and to thrive.

Notes

1. The Puzzle of Resilience

1. Important overviews of this subject can be found in George E. Vaillant, *The Wisdom of the Ego* (Cambridge, Mass.: Harvard University Press, 1993); Suniya S. Luthar, ed., *Resilience and Vulnerability: Adaptation in the Context of Childhood Adversities* (Cambridge: Cambridge University Press, 2003); and Suniya S. Luthar, Dante Cicchetti, and Bronwyn Becker, "The Construct of Resilience: A Critical Evaluation and Guidelines for Future Work," *Child Development* 71 (2000): 543–562. A new comprehensive review is Suniya S. Luthar, "Resilience in Development: A Synthesis of Research across Five Decades," in Dante Cicchetti and Donald J. Cohen, eds., *Developmental Psychopathology: Risk, Disorder, and Adaptation, Volume 3*, 2nd ed. (New York: Wiley, 2006).

2. Jon E. Rolf, "Resilience: An Interview with Norman Garmezy," in Meyer D. Glantz and Jeanette L. Johnson, eds., *Resilience and Development: Positive Life Adaptation* (New York: Kluwer Academic / Plenum Publishers, 1999), 5.

3. Lois B. Murphy, *The Widening World of Childhood: Paths toward Mastery* (New York: Basic Books, 1962), 2.

4. Robert W. White, "Ego and Reality in Psychoanalytic Theory: A Proposal Regarding Independent Ego Energies," *Psychological Issues*, 11 (New York: International Universities Press, 1963), esp. 39.

5. Over the years, groups of resilience researchers have delineated in review papers the thinking of their times. See E. James Anthony, "Risk, Vulnerability and Resilience: An Overview," in E. James Anthony and Bertram J. Cohler, eds., *The Invulnerable Child* (New York: Guilford, 1987), 3–48; Norman Garmezy, "The Study of Stress and Competence in Children: A Building Block for Developmental Psychopathology," *Child Development* 55 (1984): 97–111; Michael Rutter, "Stress, Coping and Development: Some Issues and Some Questions," *Journal of Child Psychiatry and Psychology* 22 (1981): 323–356; and Michael Rutter, "Resilience Reconsidered: Conceptual Considerations, Empirical Findings, and Policy Implications," in Jack P. Shonkoff and Samuel J. Meisels, eds., *Handbook of Early Childhood Intervention*, 2nd ed. (Cambridge: Cambridge University Press, 2000).

6. Dante Cicchetti, "Against All Odds: Pathways to Resilient Adaptation in Maltreated Children—A Tribute to Donald J. Cohen," paper delivered at the Yale Child Study Center, June 19, 2002.

7. E. James Anthony, "The Syndrome of the Psychologically Invulnerable Child," in E. James Anthony and Cyrille Koupernik, eds., *The Child in His Family, Volume 3: Children at Psychiatric Risk* (New York: Wiley, 1974), 529–544; Carol Kauffman, Henry Grunebaum, Bertram Cohler, and Enid Gamer, "Superkids: Competent Children of Psychotic Mothers," *American Journal of Psychiatry* 136 (1979): 1398–1402; Norman Garmezy, "Vulnerability Research and the Issue of Primary Prevention," *American Journal of Orthopsychiatry* 41 (1971): 101–116.

8. Vaillant, *The Wisdom of the Ego*, 284.

9. Ann S. Masten and Jennifer L. Powell, "A Resilience Framework for Research, Policy, and Practice," in Luthar, *Resilience and Vulnerability*, 4 (emphasis added).

10. Ibid. (emphasis added).

11. A superb review of risk can be found in Rutter, "Resilience Reconsidered." On the comparison of risks, see Ann S. Masten, "Ordinary Magic: Resilience Processes in Development," *American Psychologist* 56 (2001): 228.

12. The literature on this subject is varied, and different protective factors in several categories have been described: gifts such as intelligence, physical and psychological attractiveness, or visible talent as in the arts or in athletics; personal resources such as responsive parents, socio-

economic advantage, availability of supportive adults; community resources such as good schools, after-school programs, helpful teachers
and coaches; attitudes such as hopefulness, self-understanding, and re-
ligious faith. Attractiveness to other people, especially adults, is often
cited as significant. Recent comprehensive reviews of "inventories" of
protective factors can be found in Rutter, "Resilience Reconsidered";
and Emmy E. Werner, "Protective Factors and Individual Resilience," in
Shonkoff and Meisels, *Handbook of Early Childhood Intervention,* 115–
132.

13. Masten, "Ordinary Magic," 234.

14. The critical overviews we have cited in this chapter also address
the compelling and complex challenge of the protective factors or
mechanisms. See Rutter, "Resilience Reconsidered"; Masten, "Ordinary
Magic"; and Werner, "Protective Factors and Individual Resilience." See
also Suniya S. Luthar and Laurel B. Zelazo, "Research on Resilience: An
Integrative Review," in Luthar, *Resilience and Vulnerability,* 510–549.

15. Masten, "Ordinary Magic," 227–238.

16. This view of narrative is discussed at length and in depth by psy-
choanalyst Roy Schafer in *Retelling a Life: Narration and Dialogue in
Psychoanalysis* (New York: Basic Books, 1992).

17. The Young Adult Development Project was launched in 1976 by
Stuart T. Hauser, Sally G. Powers, Gil G. Noam, and Alan M. Jacobson,
and was designed to investigate how family interactions contribute to,
and are shaped by, adolescent ego development. The researchers looked
at such questions as how teenagers with serious arrests in their
psychosocial development influenced the way their parents spoke with
them, and how family interactions contributed to precociously advanced ego development. The longitudinal study is presented in Stuart
T. Hauser with Sally I. Powers and Gil G. Noam, *Adolescents and Their
Families: Paths of Ego Development* (New York: Free Press, 1991); and in
Stuart T. Hauser, Sally Powers, Gil Noam, Alan M. Jacobson, Bedonna
R. Weiss, and Donna J. Follansbee, "Family Contexts of Adolescent Ego
Development," *Child Development* 55 (1984): 195–213. The resulting in-
vestigation of adolescent resilience was designed and pursued indepen-
dently of the original study by Stuart T. Hauser and Joseph P. Allen.
Other key contributors were project director Heidi Gralinski-Bakker
and research associates Karin Best, Rebecca Billings, Alison Brodhagen,

Andrea Cole, Ann Epstein, K. C. Haydon, Lynn Schultz, Cori Stott, Robert Waldinger, Niobe Way, and Lynn Walsh.

18. These were one- to two-hour individual sessions. The use of an interview guide ensured coverage of certain topics, but subjects were allowed to pursue these in their own ways and at their own pace, and opportunity was provided as well for spontaneous contributions. All of the interviews were recorded on audiotape and later transcribed.

19. Consent for participation in the original, follow-up, and resilience studies was obtained according to the protocols of the Massachusetts Mental Health Center Institutional Review Board and the Judge Baker Children's Center Human Research Review Committees, or HRRCs. (These institutions, like all affiliates of Harvard Medical School, handle such matters through autonomous committees of their own, following guidelines laid down by the National Institutes of Health.) Consent for inclusion in this book was obtained according to HRRC guidelines. All participants whose narratives have been used or quoted substantively here were approached individually by Stuart Hauser and invited to be included in the prospective book. He asked permission to use their own words to tell about their lives, and specified that identifying information—names, places, schools, occupations, genders of children, constellations of siblings, and so on—would be carefully disguised. Every participant was asked if he or she would consent to personal information being used in this way. They could refuse, consent after reviewing what had been written about them, or consent without further review. The participants included here all consented, with or without review.

20. The study and its methodology, with an inventory of these measures, are discussed in Hauser with Powers and Noam, *Adolescents and Their Families*, 236–243.

21. They carried diagnoses in three major categories: disruptive-behavior disorders, mood disorders, and personality disorders. Psychotic and mentally retarded patients were excluded from the study. So were people with evidence of organic or attention disorders and people with medical conditions that are associated with, mimic, or complicate psychiatric symptoms—seizure disorders, Tourette syndrome, adrenal insufficiency (Addison's disease), and hyper- or hypothyroidism, for example. No one was excluded, however, on the basis of behavior or of severity of symptoms.

22. The methodology of the High Valley Resilience Study, and the standardized measures and interviewing instruments used, are discussed in Joseph P. Allen, Stuart T. Hauser, and Emily Borman-Spurrell, "Attachment Theory as a Framework for Understanding Sequelae of Severe Adolescent Psychopathology: An Eleven-Year Follow-Up Study," *Journal of Consulting and Clinical Psychology* 64 (1996): 254–263; and in Stuart T. Hauser, "Understanding Resilient Outcomes: Adolescent Lives across Time and Generations," *Journal of Research on Adolescence* 9 (1999): 1–24.

23. Masten and Powell, "A Resilience Framework for Research, Policy, and Practice," 4.

24. Stuart T. Hauser, Eve Golden, and Joseph P. Allen discuss the developing use of narrative in the context of resilience in "Narration in the Study of Resilience," *Psychoanalytic Study of the Child* 61 (2006).

Psychiatrist Arthur Kleinman made an early contribution to the study of medical narrative in *The Illness Narratives: Suffering, Healing, and the Human Condition* (New York: Basic Books, 1988). Medical anthropologists Cheryl Mattingly and Linda Garro give a recent overview in *Narrative and the Clinical Construction of Illness and Healing* (Berkeley: University of California Press, 2000). Abraham Verghese explores storytelling in medicine in *My Own Country: A Doctor's Story* (New York: Simon and Schuster, 1994) and in "The Physician as Storyteller," *Annals of Internal Medicine* 135 (2001): 1012–1017. See also physician Rita Charon's essay "Narrative Medicine: A Model for Empathy, Reflection, Profession, and Trust," *Journal of the American Medical Association* 386 (2001): 1897–1902.

Family narratives are the focus of Barbara H. Fiese, Arnold J. Sameroff, Harold D. Grotevant, Frederick S. Wamboldt, Susan Dickstein, and Deborah Lewis Fravel in "The Stories That Families Tell: Narrative Coherence, Narrative Interaction, and Relationship Beliefs," *Monographs of the Society for Research in Child Development* 257 (1999): 1–162.

Anthropologist Gay Becker discusses narrative and disruption in *Disrupted Lives: How People Create Meaning in a Chaotic World* (Berkeley: University of California Press, 1997). A more general review is Clifford Geertz, "Learning with Bruner," *New York Review of Books*, April 10, 1997, 22–24. Other important contributions to this growing and multifaceted field include Jerome Bruner, *Acts of Mean-*

ing (Cambridge, Mass.: Harvard University Press, 1990); idem, *The Culture of Education* (Cambridge, Mass.: Harvard University Press, 1996); Elliot G. Mishler, "Models of Narrative Analysis: A Typology," *Journal of Narrative and Life History* 5 (1995): 87–123; idem, *Storylines: Craftartists' Narratives of Identity* (Cambridge, Mass.: Harvard University Press, 1999); Catherine Riessman, *Narrative Analysis* (Newbury Park, Calif.: Sage, 1993); and idem, "Analysis of Interview Research," in Jaber F. Gubrium and James A. Holstein, eds., *Handbook of Interview Research: Context and Method* (Thousand Oaks, Calif.: Sage, 2002), 695–710.

25. Riessman, "Analysis of Interview Research," 697. Riessman's approach shapes her book *Divorce Talk: Women and Men Make Sense of Their Relationships* (New Brunswick, N.J.: Rutgers University Press, 1990). Mishler's *Storylines* takes a narrative approach to a deft and intricate study of craft artists' lives and identities.

26. Bertram J. Cohler, "Adversity, Resilience, and the Study of Lives," in Anthony and Cohler, *The Invulnerable Child*, 363–424; Becker, *Disrupted Lives;* and Charon, "Narrative Medicine."

27. Mary Main and her colleagues, in their work on adult attachment representation, suggest that high narrative coherence in an interview about early attachment figures and separations reflects optimal attachment security. See Mary Main, Nancy Kaplan, and Jude Cassidy, "Security in Infancy, Childhood, and Adulthood: A Move to the Level of Representation," in Inge Bretherton and Everett Waters, eds., *Growing Points of Attachment: Theory and Research,* Monographs of the Society for Research in Child Development, 50, no. 209 (Chicago: University of Chicago Press, 1985), 66–104. Some attachment theorists argue, however, that narratives about secure attachment relationships may *underlie* successful coping in stressed individuals. Inge Bretherton suggests "at least two ways [in which] inner resources are linked to secure attachment relationships. First, the confident knowledge that an attachment figure is available for emotional support when needed tends to increase an individual's ability to consider alternative solutions when faced with difficult and stressful situations. . . . Second, a secure relationship with one or more attachment figures affects coping more indirectly through the impact of such relationships on the organization

and quality of an individual's representational system." Inge Bretherton, "Internal Working Models of Attachment Relationships as Related to Resilient Coping," in Gil G. Noam and Kurt W. Fischer, eds., *Development and Vulnerability in Close Relationships* (Mahaw, N.J.: Erlbaum, 1996), 3.

Jude Cassidy and Phillip R. Shaver, eds., *Handbook of Attachment: Theory, Research, and Clinical Applications* (New York: Guilford, 1999), is a fine collection of discussions of adult attachment. For more direct connections among attachment, narrative coherence, and resilience, see Glen I. Roisman, Elena Padron, L. Alan Sroufe, and Byron Egeland, "Earned Secure Attachment Status in Retrospect and Prospect," *Child Development* 73 (2002): 1204–1219.

28. Eric Hesse, "The Adult Attachment Interview: Historical and Clinical Perspectives," in Cassidy and Shaver, *Handbook of Attachment*, 395–443.

29. "Examining this list of potential protective factors suggests the operation of three broad categories of variables [in the phenomenon of resilience or stress-resistance]: (1) personality dispositions of the child; (2) a supportive family milieu; and (3) an external support system that encourages and reinforces a child's coping efforts and strengthens them by inculcating positive values." Norman Garmezy, "Stress-Resistant Children: The Search for Protective Factors," in James E. Stevenson, ed., *Recent Research in Developmental Psychopathology* (Oxford: Pergamon, 1985), pp. 213–233; quotation from p. 219. Over the years this triad has come to be described in terms of processes rather than as traits or situations. Luthar and colleagues comment that protective and vulnerability processes operate "at three broad levels. These include influences at the level of the community (e.g., neighborhoods and social supports), the family (e.g., parental warmth or maltreatment), and the child (e.g., traits such as intelligence or social skillfulness). This triarchic framework has served to organize much research on resilience." Luthar, Cicchetti, and Becker, "The Construct of Resilience," 552. See also Norman Garmezy, "Vulnerability and Resilience," in David C. Funder, Ross D. Parke, Carol Tomlinson-Keasey, and Keith Widaman, eds., *Studying Lives through Time* (Washington, D.C.: American Psychological Association), 377–398.

30. Arnold Sameroff, Leslie M. Gutman, and Stephen C. Peck, "Adaptation among Youth Facing Multiple Risks: Prospective Research Findings," in Luthar, *Resilience and Vulnerability,* 364–391.

31. "The accumulation of social risks across the family, peer group, school, and neighborhood . . . [has] a consistently negative effect." Sameroff, Gutman, and Peck, "Adaptation among Youth Facing Multiple Risks," 386.

32. Suniya S. Luthar, "The Culture of Affluence: Psychological Costs of Material Wealth," *Child Development* 74 (2003): 1581–1593.

33. We have modified descriptions as necessary to protect confidentiality, and edited the narratives for readability and for length. But we have not otherwise modified either the content or the process. It is in these that the value of this study lies.

2. High Valley

1. We want to emphasize, however, that the conclusions suggested by this study have nothing to do with High Valley at all; they have to do with the inner resources of resilient people. Hospitalization at High Valley constituted a definable and shared crisis in the lives of these young people, but it is of note only as a stimulus to their own internal processes.

3. Reading the Stories

1. These interviews are used by permission of the now-adult patients. Some details have been changed to protect privacy, but the stories are as true to life as we could responsibly make them. Comments inserted by the authors to call attention to important developments or to mark a passage for later discussion are distinguished from the source material by parentheses when there is any possibility of confusion. Text in quotation marks is exact quotation; omissions within exact quotes are noted with ellipses. Dialogue not in quotation marks has sometimes been paraphrased or pruned to highlight the actual rhythm and style of the conversation. To keep distraction to a minimum we've cleaned up some of the hemmings and hawings, the false starts, the "like"s and "you know"s. We have also tried to clarify the affective flow of the material when it isn't apparent from the text alone. Sometimes the interviewer and the respondent are getting on fine, playing off each other

and enhancing each other's visions of the picture they're drawing together. Sometimes they are at odds, and sometimes one or the other is absolutely clueless. We've tried to convey the vibes as well as the words.

2. Ann S. Masten, "Ordinary Magic: Resilience Processes in Development," *American Psychologist* 56 (2001): 234.

6. Sandy

1. *Diagnostic and Statistical Manual of Mental Disorders, Fourth Edition* (Washington, D.C.: American Psychiatric Association, 1994), 477.

8. Seeing in the Dark

1. Ann S. Masten, "Ordinary Magic: Resilience Process in Development," *American Psychologist* 56 (2001): 233.

2. David A. Armor and Shelley E. Taylor, "Situated Optimism: Specific Outcome Expectations and Self-Regulation," in Mark P. Zanna, ed., *Advances in Experimental Social Psychology* 30 (1998): 243–307.

3. Mary Main, "Metacognitive Knowledge, Metacognitive Monitoring, and Singular (Coherent) versus Multiple (Incoherent) Models of Attachment: Findings and Directions for Future Research," in Colin Murray Parkes, Joan Stevenson-Hinde, and Peter Marris, eds., *Attachment across the Life Cycle* (New York: Tavistock/Routledge, 1991), 127–159.

4. Rand D. Conger, Kim J. Conger, and Glen H. Elder, "Family Economic Hardship and Adolescent Adjustment: Mediating and Moderating Processes," in Greg J. Duncan and Jeanne Brooks-Gunn, eds., *Consequences of Growing Up Poor* (New York: Russell Sage Foundation, 1997), 288–310.

5. Bertram J. Cohler, Frances M. Stott, and Judith S. Musick, "Adversity, Vulnerability, and Resilience: Cultural and Developmental Perspectives," in Dante Cicchetti and Donald J. Cohen, eds., *Developmental Psychopathology, Volume 2: Risk, Disorder, and Adaptation* (New York: Wiley, 1995), 753–800; Kerry E. Bolger and Charlotte J. Patterson, "Sequelae of Child Maltreatment: Vulnerability and Resilience," in Suniya S. Luthar, ed., *Risk and Vulnerability: Adaptation in the Context of Childhood Adversities* (Cambridge: Cambridge University Press, 2003), 156–181; Ann Masten and Douglas Coatsworth, "The Development of Competence in Favorable and Unfavorable Environments: Lessons

from Research on Successful Children," *American Psychologist* 53 (1988): 205–220; and Emmy Werner and Ruth Smith, *Overcoming the Odds: High-Risk Children from Birth to Adulthood* (Ithaca: Cornell University Press, 1992).

6. Joan McCord, "The Cambridge-Somerville Study: A Pioneering Longitudinal-Experimental Study of Delinquency Prevention," in Joan McCord and Richard Tremblay, eds., *Preventing Antisocial Behavior: Interventions from Birth to Adolescence* (New York: Guilford, 1992), 196–209.

7. Masten, "Ordinary Magic," 233.

8. Elliot Mishler, "Missing Persons: Recovering Developmental Stories/Histories," in Richard Jessor, Anne Colby, and Richard A. Shweder, eds., *Ethnography and Human Development: Context and Meaning in Human Inquiry* (Chicago: University of Chicago Press, 1996), 75.

9. Avshalom Caspi, Daryl Bem, and Glen H. Elder, "Continuities and Consequences of Interactional Styles across the Life Course," *Journal of Personality* 57 (1989): 375–406.

10. Martin E. P. Seligman and Mihaly Csikszentmihalyi, "Positive Psychology: An Introduction," *American Psychologist* 55 (2000): 7–8.

11. Jacquelynne S. Eccles, Carol Midgley, Allan Wigfield, Christy M. Buchanan, David Reuman, Constance Flanagan, and Douglas MacIver, "Development during Adolescence: The Impact of Stage-Environment Fit on Young Adolescents' Experiences in Schools and Families," *American Psychologist* 48 (1993): 90–101.

12. Joseph P. Allen and Stuart T. Hauser, "Autonomy and Relatedness in Adolescent-Family Interactions as Predictors of Young Adults' States of Mind Regarding Attachment," *Development and Psychopathology* 8 (1996): 793–809; Joseph P. Allen, Stuart T. Hauser, Charlene Eickholt, Kathy L. Bell, and Thomas G. O'Connor, "Autonomy and Relatedness in Family Interactions as Predictors of Expressions of Negative Adolescent Affect," *Journal of Research on Adolescence* 4 (1994): 535–552; Joseph P. Allen, Penny Marsh, Christy McFarland, Kathleen B. McElhaney, Debbie Land, Katie M. Jodl, and Sheryl Peck, "Attachment and Autonomy as Predictors of the Development of Social Skills and Delinquency during Midadolescence," *Journal of Consulting and Clinical Psychology* 70 (2002): 56–66.

13. The Teen Outreach Program is now managed by the Cornerstone Consulting Group in Houston.

14. Joseph P. Allen, Gabriel Kuperminc, Susan Philliber, and Kathy Herre, "Programmatic Prevention of Adolescent Problem Behaviors: The Role of Autonomy, Relatedness, and Volunteer Service in the Teen Outreach Program," *American Journal of Community Psychology* 22 (1994): 617–638; Joseph P. Allen, Susan Philliber, Scott Herrling, and Gabriel Kuperminc, "Preventing Teen Pregnancy and Academic Failure: Experimental Evaluation of a Developmentally Based Approach," *Child Development* 68 (1997): 729–742.

15. Stuart T. Hauser with Sally I. Powers and Gil G. Noam, *Adolescents and Their Families: Paths of Ego Development* (New York: Free Press, 1991), 236–243.

16. Suniya S. Luthar, "The Culture of Affluence: Psychological Costs of Material Wealth," *Child Development* 74 (2003): 1581–1593.

17. Masten, "Ordinary Magic," 236.

18. Ibid., 233.

19. Daniel Seagrave and Thomas Grisso, "Adolescent Development and the Measurement of Juvenile Psychopathy," *Law and Human Behavior* 26 (2002): 219–239; Jennifer L. Skeem and Elizabeth Cauffman, "Views of the Downward Extension: Comparing the Youth Version of the Psychopathy Checklist with the Youth Psychopathic Traits Inventory," *Behavioral Sciences and the Law* 21 (2003): 737–770; Heather M. Gretton, Robert D. Hare, and Rosalind E. H. Catchpole, "Psychopathy and Offending from Adolescence to Adulthood: A Ten-Year Follow-Up," *Journal of Consulting and Clinical Psychology* 72 (2004): 636–645.

20. Suzanne Vega, *Standing* (Los Angeles: A&M Records, 1987); quotation is from the song "Ironbound."

References

Allen, Joseph P., and Stuart T. Hauser. 1996. "Autonomy and Related-ness in Adolescent-Family Interactions as Predictors of Young Adults' States of Mind Regarding Attachment." *Development and Psychopathology* 8: 793–809.

———— and Emily Borman-Spurrell. 1996. "Attachment Theory as a Framework for Understanding Sequelae of Severe Adolescent Psy-chopathology: An Eleven-Year Follow-up Study." *Journal of Con-sulting and Clinical Psychology* 64: 254–263.

Allen, Joseph P., Stuart T. Hauser, Charlene Eickholt, Kathy L. Bell, and Thomas G. O'Connor. 1994. "Autonomy and Relatedness in Family Interactions as Predictors of Expressions of Negative Adolescent Affect." *Journal of Research on Adolescence* 4: 535–552.

Allen, Joseph P., Gabriel Kuperminc, Susan Philliber, and Kathy Herre. 1994. "Programmatic Prevention of Adolescent Problem Behaviors: The Role of Autonomy, Relatedness, and Volunteer Service in the Teen Outreach Program." *American Journal of Community Psychol-ogy* 22: 617–638.

Allen, Joseph P., Penny Marsh, Christy McFarland, Kathleen B. McElhaney, Debbie Land, Katie M. Jodl, and Sheryl Peck. 2002. "Attachment and Autonomy as Predictors of the Development of Social Skills and Delinquency during Midadolescence." *Journal of Consulting and Clinical Psychology* 70: 56–66.

Allen, Joseph P., Susan Philliber, Scott Herrling, and Gabriel P. Kuperminc. 1997. "Preventing Teen Pregnancy and Academic Failure: Experimental Evaluation of a Developmentally Based Approach." *Child Development* 68: 729–742.

Anthony, E. James. 1974. "The Syndrome of the Psychologically Invulnerable Child." In E. James Anthony and Cyrille Koupernik, eds., *The Child in His Family, Volume 3: Children at Psychiatric Risk*, 529–544. New York: Wiley.

———— 1987. "Risk, Vulnerability and Resilience: An Overview." In E. James Anthony and Bertram J. Cohler, eds., *The Invulnerable Child*, 3–48. New York: Guilford.

Armor, David A., and Shelley E. Taylor. 1998. "Situated Optimism: Specific Outcome Expectations and Self-Regulation." In Mark P. Zanna, ed., *Advances in Experimental Social Psychology* 30: 243–307.

Becker, Gay. 1997. *Disrupted Lives: How People Create Meaning in a Chaotic World*. Berkeley: University of California Press.

Bolger, Kerry E., and Charlotte J. Patterson. 2003. "Sequelae of Child Maltreatment: Vulnerability and Resilience." In Suniya S. Luthar, ed., *Risk and Vulnerability: Adaptation in the Context of Childhood Adversities*, 156–181. Cambridge: Cambridge University Press.

Bretherton, Inge. 1996. "Internal Working Models of Attachment Relationships as Related to Resilient Coping." In Gil G. Noam and Kurt W. Fischer, eds., *Development and Vulnerability in Close Relationships*, 3–27. Mahaw, N.J.: Erlbaum.

Bruner, Jerome. 1990. *Acts of Meaning*. Cambridge, Mass.: Harvard University Press.

———— 1996. *The Culture of Education*. Cambridge, Mass.: Harvard University Press.

Caspi, Avshalom, Daryl Bem, and Glen H. Elder. 1989. "Continuities and Consequences of Interactional Styles across the Life Course." *Journal of Personality* 57: 375–406.

Cassidy, Jude, and Phillip R. Shaver, eds. 1999. *Handbook of Attachment: Theory, Research, and Clinical Applications*. New York: Guilford.

Charon, Rita. 2001. "Narrative Medicine: A Model for Empathy, Reflection, Profession, and Trust." *Journal of the American Medical Association* 286: 1897–1902.

Cicchetti, Dante. 2002. "Against All Odds: Pathways to Resilient Adaptation in Maltreated Children. A Tribute to Donald J. Cohen." Paper delivered at the Yale Child Study Center, June 19, 2002.

Cohler, Bertram J. 1987. "Adversity, Resilience, and the Study of Lives." In E. James Anthony and Bertram J. Cohler, eds., *The Invulnerable Child*, 363–424. New York: Guilford.

———— Frances M. Stott, and Judith S. Musick. 1995. "Adversity, Vulnerability, and Resilience: Cultural and Developmental Perspectives." In Dante Cicchetti and Donald J. Cohen, eds., *Developmental Psychopathology, Volume 2: Risk, Disorder, and Adaptation*, 753–800. New York: Wiley.

Conger, Rand D., Kim J. Conger, and Glen H. Elder. 1997. "Family Economic Hardship and Adolescent Adjustment: Mediating and Moderating Processes." In Greg J. Duncan and Jeanne Brooks-Gunn, eds., *Consequences of Growing Up Poor*, 288–310. New York: Russell Sage Foundation.

Diagnostic and Statistical Manual of Mental Disorders, Fourth Edition (DSM-IV). 1994. Washington, D.C.: American Psychiatric Association.

Eccles, Jacquelynne S., Carol Midgley, Allan Wigfield, Christy M. Buchanan, David Reuman, Constance Flanagan, and Douglas MacIver. 1993. "Development during Adolescence: The Impact of Stage-Environment Fit on Young Adolescents' Experiences in Schools and Families." *American Psychologist* 48: 90–101.

Fiese, Barbara H., Arnold J. Sameroff, Harold D. Grotevant, Frederick S. Wamboldt, Susan Dickstein, and Deborah Lewis Fravel. 1999. "The Stories That Families Tell: Narrative Coherence, Narrative Interaction, and Relationship Beliefs." *Monographs of the Society for Research in Child Development* 257: 1–162.

Garmezy, Norman. 1971. "Vulnerability Research and the Issue of Primary Prevention." *American Journal of Orthopsychiatry* 41: 101–116.

———— 1984. "The Study of Stress and Competence in Children: A Building Block for Developmental Psychopathology." *Child Development* 55: 97–111.

———— 1985. "Stress-Resistant Children: The Search for Protective Factors." In James E. Stevenson, ed., *Recent Research in Developmental Psychopathology*, 213–233. Oxford: Pergamon.

———— 1993. "Vulnerability and Resilience." In David C. Funder, Ross D. Parke, Carol Tomlinson-Keasey, and Keith Widaman, eds., *Studying Lives through Time*, 377–398. Washington, D.C.: American Psychological Association.

Geertz, Clifford. 1997. "Learning with Bruner." *New York Review of Books* (April 10), 22–24.

Gottesman, Irving I., and Daniel R. Hanson. 2005. "Human Development: Biological and Genetic Processes." In Susan T. Fiske, Alan E. Kazdin, and Daniel L. Schacter, eds., *Annual Review of Psychology* 56: 263–286.

Gretton, Heather M., Robert D. Hare, and Rosalind E. H. Catchpole. 2004. "Psychopathy and Offending from Adolescence to Adulthood: A Ten-Year Follow-Up." *Journal of Consulting and Clinical Psychology* 72: 636–645.

Hauser, Stuart T. 1999. "Understanding Resilient Outcomes: Adolescent Lives across Time and Generations." *Journal of Research on Adolescence* 9: 1–24.

———— with Sally I. Powers and Gil G. Noam. 1991. *Adolescents and Their Families: Paths of Ego Development*. New York: Free Press.

Hauser, Stuart T., Eve Golden, and Joseph P. Allen. 2006. "Narrative in the Study of Resilience." *Psychoanalytic Study of the Child* 61.

Hauser, Stuart T., Sally Powers, Gil Noam, Alan M. Jacobson, Bedonna R. Weiss, and Donna J. Follansbee. 1984. "Family Contexts of Adolescent Ego Development." *Child Development* 55: 195–213.

Hesse, Eric. 1999. "The Adult Attachment Interview: Historical and Clinical Perspectives." In Jude Cassidy and Phillip R. Shaver, eds., *Handbook of Attachment: Theory, Research, and Clinical Applications*, 395–443. New York: Guilford.

Kauffman, Carol, Henry Grunebaum, Bertram Cohler, and Enid Gamer. 1979. "Superkids: Competent Children of Psychotic Mothers." *American Journal of Psychiatry* 136: 1398–1402.

Kleinman, Arthur. 1988. *The Illness Narratives: Suffering, Healing, and the Human Condition*. New York: Basic Books.

Luthar, Suniya S. 2006. "Resilience in Development: A Synthesis of Research across Five Decades." In Dante Cicchetti and Donald J. Cohen, eds., *Developmental Psychopathology: Risk, Disorder, and Adaptation, Volume 3*, 2nd ed. New York: Wiley.

———— 2003a. "The Culture of Affluence: Psychological Costs of Material Wealth." *Child Development* 74: 1581–1593.

———— ed. 2003b. *Resilience and Vulnerability: Adaptation in the Context of Childhood Adversities.* Cambridge: Cambridge University Press.

Luthar, Suniya S., Dante Cicchetti, and Bronwyn Becker. 2000. "The Construct of Resilience: A Critical Evaluation and Guidelines for Future Work." *Child Development* 71: 543–562.

Luthar, Suniya S., and Laurel B. Zelazo. 2003. "Research on Resilience: An Integrative Review." In Suniya S. Luthar, ed., *Resilience and Vulnerability: Adaptation in the Context of Childhood Adversities,* 510–549. Cambridge: Cambridge University Press.

Main, Mary. 1991. "Metacognitive Knowledge, Metacognitive Monitoring, and Singular Coherent versus Multiple Incoherent Models of Attachment: Findings and Directions for Future Research." In Colin Murray Parkes, Joan Stevenson-Hinde, and Peter Marris, eds., *Attachment Across the Life Cycle,* 127–159. New York: Tavistock/Routledge.

Main, Mary, Nancy Kaplan, and Jude Cassidy. 1985. "Security in Infancy, Childhood, and Adulthood: A Move to the Level of Representation." In Inge Bretherton and Everett Waters, eds., *Growing Points of Attachment Theory and Research,* Monographs of the Society for Research in Child Development, 50, no. 209, 66–104. Chicago: University of Chicago Press.

Masten, Ann S. 2001. "Ordinary Magic: Resilience Processes in Development." *American Psychologist* 56: 227–238.

———— and Douglas Coatsworth. 1998. "The Development of Competence in Favorable and Unfavorable Environments: Lessons from Research on Successful Children." *American Psychologist* 53: 205–220.

Masten, Ann S., and Jennifer L. Powell. 2003. "A Resilience Framework for Research, Policy, and Practice." In Suniya S. Luthar, ed., *Resilience and Vulnerability: Adaptation in the Context of Childhood Adversities,* 1–25. Cambridge: Cambridge University Press.

Mattingly, Cheryl, and Linda Garro. 2000. *Narrative and the Clinical Construction of Illness and Healing.* Berkeley: University of California Press.

McCord, Joan. 1992. "The Cambridge-Somerville Study: A Pioneering Longitudinal-Experimental Study of Delinquency Prevention." In Joan McCord and Richard Tremblay, eds., *Preventing Antisocial Behavior: Interventions from Birth to Adolescence,* 196–209. New York: Guilford.

Mishler, Elliot G. 1995. "Models of Narrative Analysis: A Typology." *Journal of Narrative and Life History* 5: 87–123.

——— 1996. "Missing Persons: Recovering Developmental Stories / Histories." In Richard Jessor, Anne Colby, and Richard A. Shweder, eds., *Ethnography and Human Development: Context and Meaning in Human Inquiry,* 73–100. Chicago: University of Chicago Press.

——— 1999. *Storylines: Craftartists' Narratives of Identity.* Cambridge, Mass.: Harvard University Press.

Murphy, Lois B. 1962. *The Widening World of Childhood: Paths Toward Mastery.* New York: Basic Books.

Riessman, Catherine. 1990. *Divorce Talk: Women and Men Make Sense of Their Relationships.* New Brunswick, N.J.: Rutgers University Press.

——— 1993. *Narrative Analysis.* Newbury Park, Calif.: Sage.

——— 2002. "Analysis of Interview Research." In Jaber F. Gubrium and James A. Holstein, eds., *Handbook of Interview Research: Context and Method,* 695–710. Thousand Oaks, Calif.: Sage.

Roisman, Glen I., Elena Padron, L. Alan Sroufe, and Byron Egeland. 2002. "Earned Secure Attachment Status in Retrospect and Prospect." *Child Development* 73: 1204–1219.

Rolf, Jon E. 1999. "Resilience: An Interview with Norman Garmezy." In Meyer D. Glantz and Jeanette L. Johnson, eds., *Resilience and Development: Positive Life Adaptation,* 5–14. New York: Kluwer Academic / Plenum Publishers.

Rutter, Michael. 1981. "Stress, Coping and Development: Some Issues and Some Questions." *Journal of Child Psychiatry and Psychology* 22: 323–356.

——— 2000. "Resilience Reconsidered: Conceptual Considerations, Empirical Findings, and Policy Implications." In Jack P. Shonkoff and Samuel J. Meisels, eds., *Handbook of Early Childhood Intervention,* 2nd ed., 651–682. Cambridge: Cambridge University Press.

Sameroff, Arnold, Leslie M. Gutman, and Stephen C. Peck. 2003. "Adaptation among Youth Facing Multiple Risks: Prospective Research Findings." In Suniya S. Luthar, ed. *Resilience and Vulnerability: Adaptation in the Context of Childhood Adversities*, 364–391. Cambridge: Cambridge University Press.

Schafer, Roy. 1992. *Retelling a Life: Narration and Dialogue in Psychoanalysis*. New York: Basic Books.

Seagrave, Daniel, and Thomas Grisso. 2002. "Adolescent Development and the Measurement of Juvenile Psychopathy." *Law and Human Behavior* 26: 219–239.

Seligman, Martin E. P., and Mihaly Csikszentmihalyi. 2000. "Positive Psychology: An Introduction." *American Psychologist* 55: 5–14.

Skeem, Jennifer L., and Elizabeth Cauffman. 2003. "Views of the Downward Extension: Comparing the Youth Version of the Psychopathy Checklist with the Youth Psychopathic Traits Inventory." *Behavioral Sciences and the Law* 21: 737–770.

Vaillant, George E. 1993. *The Wisdom of the Ego: Sources of Resiliency in Adult Life*. Cambridge, Mass.: Harvard University Press.

Vega, Suzanne. 1987. *Standing*. Los Angeles: A&M Records.

Verghese, Abraham. 1994. *My Own Country: A Doctor's Story*. New York: Simon and Schuster.

——— 2001. "The Physician as Storyteller." *Annals of Internal Medicine* 135: 1012–1017.

Werner, Emmy E. 2000. "Protective Factors and Individual Resilience." In Jack P. Shonkoff and Samuel J. Meisels, eds. *Handbook of Early Childhood Intervention*, 115–132. Cambridge: Cambridge University Press.

——— and Ruth Smith. 1992. *Overcoming the Odds: High-Risk Children from Birth to Adulthood*. Ithaca: Cornell University Press.

White, Robert W. 1963. "Ego and Reality in Psychoanalytic Theory: A Proposal Regarding Independent Ego Energies." *Psychological Issues* 11: 1–210.

Index